SIGNIFICANT INCIDENT

Canada's Army, the Airborne,
and the Murder in Somalia

David Bercuson

M&S

Canadian Cataloguing in Publication Data

Bercuson, David Jay, 1945 –
   Significant incident: Canada's army, the Airborne, and the murder in Somalia

Includes bibliographical references and index.
ISBN 0-7710-1113-X

1. Canada – Armed Forces. 2. Canada. Canadian Armed Forces. Canadian Airborne Regiment Battle Group. 3. Somalia Affair, 1992 –   . I. Title.

UA600.B43 1996   355'.00971   C96-931373-X

The publishers acknowledge the support of the Canada Council and the Ontario Arts Council for their publishing program.

Typesetting by M&S, Toronto
Printed and bound in Canada

McClelland and Stewart Inc.
The Canadian Publishers
481 University Avenue
Toronto, Ontario
M5G 2E9

1 2 3 4 5 6   01 00 99 98 97 96

CONTENTS

To Col. Peter G. Kenward and Master Cpl. Bert Reed (ret'd), and to all the other *real* soldiers of the Canadian army.

PREFACE

July 6, 1995: I was sitting in a sparsely furnished room at Headquarters, Combat Training Centre, Canadian Forces Base Gagetown, New Brunswick. Seated around me were four senior non-commissioned officers (NCOs) who had served as proud members of the Canadian Airborne Regiment until it had been disbanded at the direction of the Minister of National Defence earlier in the year.

Each of these men had a different story to tell. The oldest of them had been in the army for thirty-four years; he had served in the Royal Canadian Regiment (RCR) before joining the Airborne. Another had served twenty-eight years, much of the time in the Royal 22e Régiment. The third had served with the RCR; he had twenty-two years in the army. The youngest, age thirty-five, had spent sixteen years in the army. He had been a member of the Princess Patricia's Canadian Light Infantry (PPCLI) before joining the Airborne.

These men had been deeply hurt when the Airborne had been disbanded (in disgrace, some of the press reported). They still carried their Airborne coin with them. The Airborne had been their family in the army. Now it was gone, and they felt homeless and misunderstood by their civilian masters.

These men were also deeply worried. Having spent all their adult lives being professional soldiers, helping to build an admittedly small but, they believed, highly professional army, they were vehement in their conviction that the army was on the verge of disaster. In their view, too many senior commanders were too worried about perks, advancement, career, to give a second thought to the welfare of the soldiers. Too many junior officers were bringing the self-centredness of the "me" generation into the Armed Forces. Not enough soldiers were dedicated to the ideals of duty, service, honour, nation, that the army of a democracy has to be built on. "I'm staying in in the hope that the top will be sorted out, sir," one said. "The army is still good, it's the top that's the problem," declared another.

These men were about as tough a group of soldiers as can be found anywhere, in any nation. I could easily picture them in helmets and battle fatigues, carrying their automatic rifles as they moved stealthily down a forest trail, leading their men into action. But they were also like other Canadian men of their age, concerned about families, mortgages, making ends meet. One had a fifteen-year-old-daughter. "I get pretty worried when she goes out," he admitted. "I remember what it is that all the guys want at that age." Were these men really murderers? Were these men capable of kicking and beating a Somali teenager to death while he was bound hand and foot? I didn't believe it then and I don't believe it now. But to read the newspapers and watch television in this country since the spring of 1993, virtually all Canadian soldiers have become suspect of foul deeds such as the one committed the night of March 16, 1993, when Shidane Abukar Arone was murdered in a Canadian Airborne Regiment encampment near Belet Huen, Somalia.

It's easy to blame a handful of unruly, even racist and murderous, soldiers for what ails the Canadian army today. But the problems underlying the murder in Somalia go far deeper, and are far more extensive and pervasive, than the governments of either Kim Campbell or Jean Chrétien can admit. If Ottawa was serious about fixing the Canadian army, it would have to begin with a thorough examination of how the military is being choked to death by successive budget cuts, how it has become bureaucratized by the National Defence Headquarters (NDHQ) structure, how that structure and other factors have generated rampant careerism and "cover your ass" attitudes among many in the officer corps, how and why the dedicated professional soldiers find it so difficult to come into important command positions, why so many good people leave the army while so many second-raters stay.

I believe a solid majority of the men and women serving in the Canadian army today joined, and stay, for the purest of motives. They believe in soldiering as a vocation, they want to hone their professionalism, they accept the "unlimited liability" of the soldier as inherent to the job, they want a well-ordered chain of command. They want to lead well, and they want to be well led. They also believe that the only people who ought to command an army are those, like themselves, who still remember that armies exist to fight wars, and that they are therefore very different from other types of human organizations.

These men and women, these professional soldiers, have become increasingly marginalized in the Canadian army by a country, government, and defence structure that no longer values real military virtues. Arone's murder was not a single isolated incident of misbehaviour in an organization that is sound, well led, and dedicated to high principles. The many outstanding soldiers in the Canadian army today – soldiers such as those men in that room at CFB Gagetown – try to do their duty, but they are outmanoeuvred time after time by a defence bureaucracy and a high command who, with some exceptions, extol "don't make waves" management and discourage traditional military leadership.

The Canadian army is in a state of crisis today, and the murder in Somalia is one sign of that crisis. The murder of Shidane Abukar Arone, and all the other incidents of unethical, marginally dishonest, or blatantly illegal behaviour by members of the Canadian Forces that preceded or followed that murder, and were connected to it, are rooted in that crisis. To understand what brought the Canadian army to this state of crisis, it is necessary to begin at the beginning.

INTRODUCTION

THE MURDER

March 16, 1993, at Canadian Airborne Regiment Battle Group (CARBG) headquarters, near Belet Huen, Somalia. Night falls quickly in the desert, and the relentless 50°C heat of the day begins to dissipate a bit. This day was much the same as the day before and the day before that. The hot sun broiled the sand, the rock, the scrub, and the main road into Belet Huen. It baked the hard mud and bricks of the town. There was no escape from the heat, or from the dust, the swarms of flies, and the stink of rot and excrement. After the short twilight, the air cooled from stifling to merely hot. It was still warm enough to raise a sweat on anyone who moved around much. In the army camp astride the road east of Belet Huen, the heat, the dirt, the frustrations of Somalia, the beer, and the biker-gang mentality of some members of No. 2 Commando, Canadian Airborne Regiment, would come together in an explosive combination. A Somali youth would be hideously tortured and murdered. The killing would be carried out by a man who didn't care much who his victim was. It would be aided, abetted, and tolerated by many others.

All the principals in this murderous drama fancied themselves soldiers. All wore the maple leaf of Canada on their uniforms. All forgot their sworn duty to uphold and protect the values of the democracy they represented. All were culpable in sparking the chain reaction of horror, scandal, and recrimination about to begin. All were part of a system that had itself already failed the very day these men arrived in Somalia.

Each night at about 7:30, the wind came up on the road to Belet Huen. It blew strongly from the direction of the town; it swirled the dust and dirt and sifted sand into everything. Men slept with T-shirts over their faces to keep the dust out of their noses and mouths. Tents flapped loudly and endlessly through the night. Those not anchored down with aircraft cargo straps, or water containers, or ammunition boxes, or anything heavy, blew away. The metal walls of the few temporary structures on the base were peppered with stones and grit.

After almost three months of this, it was easy for some of the men of the battle group to hate Somalia. They patrolled the town of Belet Huen and the outlying regions. They saw tonnes of humanitarian relief supplies sent to Somalia to feed starving people sold openly in the marketplace. They saw corruption, waste, and decay everywhere they looked. Day after day, Somali teenagers stole weapons, radio parts, personal effects, and army rations out of their vehicles; night after night, intruders squirmed through the camp perimeter wire and took anything of value they could carry. After almost three months, it was getting easy for some of the men to hate Somalis.

The 850-man battle group had come to Belet Huen in late December 1993 as part of a much larger American-led coalition force called UNITAF (Unified Task Force). The battle group consisted of the Canadian Airborne Regiment, A Squadron of the Royal Canadian Dragoons, and an engineer squadron. It had not come to Belet Huen to police a cease-fire between opposing sides, as Canadians had done for some two decades in Cyprus, nor to deliver humanitarian aid, as other Canadian soldiers were then doing in Bosnia. As the Canadian mission statement read: "The Canadian Joint Forces Somalia will provide, as part of the Unified Task Force, the secure environment necessary for the distribution of humanitarian supplies in Somalia."

The UNITAF mission – Operation Deliverance – had been authorized by UN Resolution 794 adopted on December 3, 1992. The mission aim was to intervene militarily in Somalia to impose peace on warring factions so that relief supplies might flow freely from the main Somali ports to the interior, where famine had been ravaging the land for months. There was no government in Somalia; the warlords vying for power there had gathered weapons, drafted militias, and were fighting it out in the towns and cities and across the countryside. They blocked the food convoys, or attacked them, or imposed heavy tolls on them that sometimes amounted to most of the food the relief trucks were carrying.

Operation Deliverance was sanctioned by the UN Security Council under Chapter VII of the UN Charter, which authorizes the dispatch of peace-enforcement troops rather than peacekeeping troops. It has been used only three times in the UN's history: to stop Communist aggression in Korea in 1950; to throw Iraq out of Kuwait in 1990; and to impose order in Somalia in 1992. Operation Deliverance was not a peacekeeping mission. The rival Somali factions were well armed. They favoured truck-mounted anti-aircraft guns that they called "technicals." Even in the hands of the rowdy and mostly untrained militiamen, these heavy-calibre, rapid-fire weapons were capable of inflicting great damage on people and structures alike. The troops of UNITAF were authorized to use deadly force if necessary to disarm these private armies; they were not to be taken lightly.

By mid-March 1993, the battle group had established a sizable and well-stocked base on the main road into Belet Huen. Two large compounds – one on the north side of the road, the other on the south side – housed the troops of the battle group, 427 Canadian Helicopter Squadron, a hospital, and the battle group headquarters and communications centre. Regular foot patrols were sent into Belet Huen by No. 2 Commando, while 1er and No. 3 Commandos and the Royal Canadian Dragoons patrolled large parts of the surrounding countryside aboard Canadian army vehicles. The base was a far cry from the crude facility the troops had scratched out of the desert floor near the primitive Belet Huen airstrip when they had first arrived just before New Year's Day. They and a detachment of American soldiers had quickly seized the airstrip, set up a defensive perimeter around it, and held it as the big Canadian Air Force Hercules transports shuttled in and out, bringing tents, food, ammunition, and all the other supplies necessary for a better-defended base.

For more than three weeks, the paratroopers slept in shallow slit trenches dug out of the sand and covered with ground sheets. There had been no electricity, almost no water, no fresh food, and no way to keep clean. Each day brought glaring sun, dust, dirt, filth, sickness, and isolation, as well as constant danger from the armed bands of Somali

irregulars. The Airborne suppressed and disarmed most of the militiamen in the vicinity of Belet Huen, and seized a large collection of
weapons and explosives including American- and Chinese-made automatic rifles, 120-mm mortars, medium and heavy machine guns, and
technicals. They even put one old American-built M-48 Patton tank
out of business.

The Canadians had been sent to Somalia with every expectation that
they would fight. They did some of that, but they also re-established the
local Somali police force, improved the roads in and around Belet Huen,
rebuilt a key bridge into town, and rebuilt and reopened the school.
Local relief agencies, such as the International Committee of the Red
Cross, resumed food distribution. At first the Somalis seemed pleased
with the restoration of order and resumed daily life much as before.
Then the Canadians closed the base at the airstrip and built a more
permanent facility east of Belet Huen. They set up a barbed-wire
perimeter, dug slit trenches, and built bunkers and watch-towers.
Electric generators were brought in to power lights, refrigerators, and
VCRs. The food got better. There was water for washing. There was beer
to lighten the boredom. There were satellite telephones to phone home.
And, as more equipment was brought in, illegal intrusions into the
camp, and the looting that went with those intrusions, increased by leaps
and bounds.

The young Somali men who slipped into and out of the camp made
looting into a science. Whenever an opening in the wire was left
unguarded, day or night, they'd sneak into camp, grab whatever they
could, and sneak out. But mostly they came at night. Stripping nearly
naked, they coated their bodies with cooking oil and squirmed through
the concertina wire. Some were caught by the guard detail, bound, and
kept in a bunker near the entrance to the No. 2 Commando compound.
Known as "the pit," the bunker had originally been built as a machine-
gun position. There was little to distinguish it from any other on the
base. The floor had been dug out of the ground and a frame built to hold
a corrugated iron roof. Sandbags formed the sides and protected the
roof, which stood about thirty centimetres above the sandbag walls.

The captured Somali intruders were not technically prisoners of war, but the battle group had been instructed to treat them as PoWs when in Canadian custody. Since No. 2 Commando had been assigned the job of local security – in Belet Huen as well as inside the base – it was No. 2 Commando's responsibility to hold the prisoners overnight, then release them in the morning. The Canadians had neither the supplies to feed them nor the facilities to hold them, and, again, they were not really prisoners of war. None was ever found to carry weapons, none ever mounted an attack against a Canadian soldier. Until the local police force was re-established, the intruders were handed over to their clan leaders; after, they were brought into Belet Huen by the first patrol of the day and given to the local police. The intruders were almost always released immediately and often returned to the camp for a second or a third try.

Canadian soldiers are taught how to treat prisoners of war. They are instructed in the rules of the Geneva Convention. They are supposed to know what they may, or may not, do to prisoners. Every Canadian soldier above the rank of master corporal learns that he or she is bound not to follow any order deemed to be illegal, including orders to mistreat prisoners. Every Canadian soldier who is entrusted with the power to command – to levy a charge under the Queen's Regulations and Orders – is taught the responsibilities that go with command. The system is designed to make sure that no Canadian soldier will ever attempt to justify murder, rape, torture, or any other war crime by claiming that he or she was "just following orders."

Canadian soldiers are also trained how to process prisoners of war. In combat, prisoners taken at the front invariably have important intelligence information. The fresher this information is, the better. So sections, platoons, and even companies are repeatedly told not to hold prisoners any longer than combat, or other local conditions, dictate. Prisoners are to be transported as quickly as possible to battalion headquarters, where they can be questioned by the battalion intelligence officer (10). The 10 has been trained to debrief prisoners, to interpret whatever snippets of information he or she can get from them, and to recognize when a piece of paper found in a pocket is a laundry list or an order of battle. It is, therefore, battalion personnel who receive the most training in the housing, feeding, and care of prisoners; company and

platoon soldiers are not supposed to have that responsibility. And yet at
Belet Huen there was no combat, and no need to burden battalion HQ
with an endless series of apprehended looters. When caught, they were
taken to the No. 2 Commando command post (CP), questioned briefly,
logged in, then brought to the holding bunker to be kept overnight. It
seemed the sensible thing to do.

Lt.-Col. Carol Mathieu had taken command of the Canadian Airborne
Regiment the previous October when the former commander, Lt.-Col.
Paul Morneault, had been removed for failing to adequately prepare the
regiment for its mission. As such, Mathieu was also the commander of
the battle group (in overall command of all the Canadian Forces in
Somalia was Col. Serge Labbé, based at Mogadishu). Tall, well built, and
ruggedly handsome, Mathieu looked every bit the paratroop commander. He had more than a quarter-century of army service under his belt,
having joined the Regular Officer Training Plan (ROTP) in 1966 and
served in Cyprus, at the Camp Gagetown Combat Training Centre, and
in Germany. He had been deputy commander of the Airborne from
1988 to 1991.

Mathieu had been concerned about camp security from the start. He
kept his men on high alert for the first few weeks, not knowing the extent
to which the local militias might resist the UNITAF troops. At night, a
near-total blackout was observed. On January 28, Mathieu gave his men
permission to shoot anyone infiltrating the compound. He later
explained, "This was more like the Gulf War than Cyprus or even
Yugoslavia. . . . Our task was to secure an area that was thirty thousand
square kilometres to make it safe for the distribution of relief supplies.
. . . We had put these [warlord] guys out of business."

Besides the security risk that infiltrators posed (were they there to
steal or to set explosives?), Mathieu was angry at the constant looting of
important supplies and equipment, some vital to his mission. By mid-
March, for example, the camp was down to its last helicopter refuelling
pump; the others had long since been stolen. If this pump disappeared,
Mathieu knew, the helicopters could not be refuelled. On March 4, one

Somali man was shot dead and another badly wounded in mysterious circumstances by members of No. 2 Commando patrolling outside the wire. The dead man was the second Somali killed by Canadians since the start of the operation (the first had been shot during a demonstration). But other UNITAF troops – Pakistanis, Italians, Americans – had killed dozens of Somalis by then.

On the morning of March 16, the commander of No. 2 Commando, Maj. Anthony Seward, formerly of the Princess Patricia's Canadian Light Infantry, held his regular O (orders) group at commando headquarters. This was the daily meeting at which the platoon commanders and their senior NCOs were filled in on events of the previous night, given a summary of what was happening elsewhere in the theatre, and issued their instructions for the day. Seward ordered Capt. Michael Sox's 4 Platoon to set up a snatch patrol to catch an intruder, then make an example of him. He told Sox not to use deadly force. Then he added, "Abuse [the intruders] if you have to, just make the capture."

What did Seward mean by that order? Commando Warrant Officer Brad Mills, who was present at the O group, later claimed that Seward told Sox, "He could abuse them [prisoners] if he had to during appre-hension." In other words, Seward did not order Sox to abuse prisoners after they had been captured, but it was all right for them to use physical force during the capture. No one who was present at that O group ever denied that the word "abuse" was used. Thus Seward's instructions were at worst illegal – if his intention was to have prisoners abused after capture – and at best loose, open to broad interpretation, and grossly irresponsible. As an infantry officer, Seward surely knew that his men would use whatever force was necessary to capture an intruder; they did not need to be instructed to do so. The key question is: If Seward had not intended his men to beat up prisoners after capture, why did he use the word "abuse" at all?

Captain Sox called his own O group later that day and assigned Sgt. Joseph Hillier's 2 Section to mount the ambush. Sgt. Mark Boland's 3 Section was to provide gate security until midnight, when it would be relieved by Sgt. Kevin Lloyd's 1 Section. Sgt. Anthony Skipton's 4 Section was assigned to late patrol duty. That gave Boland and Lloyd jurisdiction over the holding bunker and the responsibility for guarding any prisoners that Hillier's men might catch. Sox then told his platoon commanders, "We have the authority from two-niner to abuse prisoners" – "two-niner" was Major Seward's radio call-sign. When Boland asked Sox what he meant, Sox replied that they could "beat the shit out of the prisoners." Boland and Lloyd later claimed that they decided not to pass Sox's order on to their men because they felt "it was an illegal order." This may have been the case, but given the speed with which "the word" always circulates in any army camp, most of the men in No. 2 Commando were surely aware that any prisoner caught that night was going to have a rough time.

At about 8:00 P.M., Hillier's men took up their positions. Some waited outside an open gate in the perimeter fence that led into a now empty compound once used by U.S. Navy Seabees (engineers), just to the west of the No. 2 Commando compound. The others waited inside the empty compound. According to former Airborne Cpl. Matt McKay, the gate was deliberately opened by the men of 4 Platoon to lure in a Somali.

The camp settled into its night routine. Somalis walked by on the road yelling to one another and shouting to the Canadians behind the wire. Other Somalis, living in their small herder's huts in the desert close to the camp, yelled from one hut to another. Their babies cried, their children laughed, their donkeys brayed. Inside the camp, the soldiers talked, or laughed, or shouted at each other. Truck tailgates slammed, motors started up, vehicles drove out of and into the camp. In the tent lines, where the men slept, portable generators powered the radios and television sets that had to be played loudly to be heard over the other noise. Someone was watching a Clint Eastwood movie. In the north compound, two large semi-trailer generators, which powered the hospital and the battle group headquarters, roared constantly.

At about 8:45 P.M., Sergeant Hillier spotted sixteen-year-old Shidane Abukar Arone entering the compound and gave chase. Arone ran. He spotted a portable toilet and ducked in, Hillier fast on his heels. Hillier wrenched open the door, pulled out Arone, searched him, and bound his hands behind his back with self-tightening plastic handcuffs. Arone offered no resistance. Unlike those intruders who oiled their bodies to squirm through the concertina wire, Arone was fully dressed in a civilian shirt, gym shorts, sandals, and a skirt of the type worn by Somali men. He had not come to crawl through the wire.

Captain Sox came up quickly. He and another soldier jammed a riot baton between Arone's elbows and his body and hustled him over to the No. 2 Commando command post. Sox was angry and abusive and pushed Arone down as they made their way into the compound. They were joined by Cpl. Kyle Brown, who had just come off another patrol. Arone was logged in at the CP, and a message was sent to Major Seward that a prisoner had been taken. Then Sox told Brown to fetch Master Cpl. Clayton Matchee, who was on gate guard duty and who would have responsibility for the prisoner until his shift was up at 9:00 P.M. Finally, Sox, Sgt. Perry Gresty (on radio duty in the CP), and an interpreter brought Arone to the holding bunker for interrogation. Arone told them what clan he was from. He claimed he was sixteen and had entered the compound looking for a lost child. Arone's ankles were bound with plastic cuffs, and the baton behind his back was secured to a corner post of the bunker frame. Then he was left alone in the dark with Clayton Matchee.

Matchee was a full-blooded Cree Indian from Meadow Lake, Saskatchewan. He did not shave his head, as some of the paratroopers did, but wore his jet-black hair short. With his drooping moustache, his brooding good looks, and his dark sunglasses, he was the very archetype of the Hollywood bandito – and he acted the part. Matchee was a swaggerer and a bully. He was a "death from the skies" hell-raiser of a kind that had caused many disciplinary problems in the Airborne Regiment in recent years. He was bad news, and he wanted everyone to know it. To Matchee, and to those like him who had been allowed to join, and stay in, the Airborne Regiment, the maroon beret and parachute wings they wore were not badges testifying to superior military professionalism. They had become, instead, a warning that the man wearing them was ready to commit mayhem on anyone who got in his way.

Matchee was a master corporal and second-in-command of Sergeant

Boland's section. In the Canadian army, master corporal is a command rank. To become a master corporal (as opposed to a corporal, which is an automatic upgrade in rank that every private achieves after satisfactorily completing four years of service), a Canadian soldier has to impress his or her superiors that he or she has the capability to command a rifle section in the event of the section commander's absence. To qualify for master corporal, a soldier must pass a specific course of instruction teaching basic junior leader skills. Among the items taught are the laws of war and the responsibilities of command. Unlike a private or a corporal, a master corporal has the authority to lay charges under the Queen's Regulations and Orders. A master corporal in the Canadian army is a non-commissioned officer; according to the Canadian army, then, Clayton Matchee was good material.

Matchee watched Arone until about 8:55 P.M., when Boland showed up to relieve him. Sgt. Anthony Skipton and Warrant Officer Brad Mills accompanied Boland. Boland noticed that Arone's hand and ankle cuffs were too tight, but that he was otherwise in good shape. The plastic cuffs were cut off and metal handcuffs were substituted. Then everyone left, and Matchee and Boland were alone with Arone. Matchee suddenly pulled off Arone's T-shirt, tied it over his face, and poured water on it. Arone began to smother; Boland told Matchee to stop and Matchee did, lifting the shirt above Arone's mouth and nose but leaving him blindfolded. Then Matchee left and Boland began his shift.

At about 9:15 P.M., Mills was in the CP when he noticed a handful of men standing around the holding bunker. He went over to find out who they were and discovered they were members of 427 Helicopter Squadron who had come to look over the prisoner. Mills saw that Boland was there, so he did not enter the bunker to inspect Arone. There was, as yet, no sign that anything was amiss.

When Matchee left Boland, he was in a dangerous mood. He headed for the tent that Kyle Brown shared with Matt McKay. Described later in the *Calgary Sun* as someone who "marches to his own tune and doesn't give a damn," McKay is heavily tattooed with racist web designs and was once photographed giving a Nazi salute in front of a swastika.

Kyle Brown was a different sort. He was born and raised in Edmonton.

His mother died of an accidental drug overdose and his father committed suicide before Brown was fifteen. He came to the Canadian Airborne Regiment in 1992 after serving a stint with the Princess Patricia's Canadian Light Infantry. Brown is a contradiction. Most people who knew him remember him as a quiet and somewhat studious young man who was eager to ingratiate himself with the master corporals and sergeants who seemed to run the regiment from the bottom up. In effect, he was too eager. During pre-mission training, Sox and Platoon Warrant Officer Murphy had both concluded that neither Brown nor Matchee should go to Somalia. Sox recommended this to his superiors but was turned down.

The beer ration for the Canadian troops in Somalia was two cans per man per day, but it was an easy limit to get around. In the hour that Boland stood guard over Arone, Matchee drank beer after beer, getting drunker and meaner by the minute. Close to 10:00 P.M., he accompanied Brown over to the holding bunker to relieve Boland. Arone was still bound but was otherwise all right when Boland left. But Boland must have known what was about to happen because he told Brown and Matchee, "I don't care what you do, just don't kill the guy."

Matchee and Brown fell on Arone as soon as Boland left. Still bound and blindfolded, Arone was helpless. "I want to kill this fucker, I want to kill this guy," Matchee yelled as he repeatedly punched Arone in the ribs and kicked him in the face and legs. Brown also assaulted the prisoner, kicking him a number of times, but this seems to have been the only time in the night when he actually took part in the beatings. For the rest of the time, he was Matchee's accomplice. Since Brown was technically in charge of the prisoner, Matchee then left the bunker and went to McKay's tent to get more beer. Boland came into McKay's tent shortly after, was given a beer, then calmly sat on a barracks box facing McKay (who was lying on his bunk). Matchee told him that Brown had been beating the prisoner and declared that he was going to burn Arone's feet with a cigarette. Boland replied that Matchee's plan would leave too many marks. He suggested that Matchee put a telephone book on Arone's head and then beat him on the head with a riot stick. Boland later testified that he was only joking. Matchee couldn't find a telephone

book, so he grabbed a large ration pack and a wooden riot baton and
went to the bunker. He put the pack on Arone's head and pounded it with
the baton until the pack burst. Not long after, a member of 427 Squadron
looked into the bunker and saw Matchee kick Arone in the head at least
three times and stub out a cigarette on Arone's foot. He overheard Brown
saying, "You've got a good trophy there, sir."

Towards the end of the first hour of torture, Brown left the bunker,
fetched his camera, and borrowed some film. Then he and Matchee took
pictures of each other posing as hunters with their vanquished prey. In
one photo, Matchee holds a pistol to Arone's head. Outside the bunker,
Cpl. David Pusch, returning to his tent after making a telephone call
home, saw the light from the photo flash and looked in. Matchee told
him to watch, then struck Arone on the shins with an iron bar. The half-
dead youth screamed, "Canada, Canada." Matchee repeated the performance for another member of 427 Squadron several minutes later.

Sometime near 11:00 P.M., Pte. David Brocklebank showed up to
relieve Brown on guard duty, but Brown stayed around to watch the
show. With an iron bar, Matchee smashed Arone in the face, pounded
him in his ribs, and struck him on his feet. He kicked him repeatedly with
his heavy combat boots. Arone lapsed in and out of consciousness as the
blows rained down. Matchee used a lit cigar to burn Arone on the soles
of his feet. He cursed and swore that he would kill the Somali. Brown
seemed in a daze and wandered off around midnight. He would later tell
his court martial that since Matchee was apparently acting under orders,
he did not know what else he was supposed to do.

For more than two hours that night, Master Cpl. Clayton Matchee
punched, clubbed, kicked, and burned the life out of Shidane Abukar
Arone. During that whole time, at least six members of the Canadian
Airborne Regiment (excluding Brown) and two members of 427
Squadron witnessed this systematic destruction of a human being, but
did nothing to stop it or report it. Maj. Anthony Seward, whose fateful
words had been Arone's death warrant, was nowhere to be found. Nor

was Capt. Michael Sox, who had delivered the death warrant to the executioners. Sgt. Mark Boland would later claim that he was in his tent, sleeping, not knowing about the outcome of the beatings he knew were taking place. Not far away, Warrant Officer Brad Mills also slept, his stereo playing in his earphones, his T-shirt over his face. In the lighted CP less than twenty metres away from the holding bunker, Sgt. Perry Gresty dozed by the radio, his assistant ready to wake him in case of an emergency. In those fateful two hours, he was never awakened. He went off shift at midnight, claiming to have heard and seen nothing.

A number of men later told investigating military police that they had heard moans, and even screams, coming from the holding bunker. Maybe they had, or maybe they were trying to be helpful to the investigators. The noise of the wind and the sounds of the camp at night – the trucks going in and out, the generators, the radios, the television sets, the shouting of men going out or coming in from patrol, the yelling of the Somalis, and the braying of their donkeys – would have masked most of the sounds Arone uttered. But if they did hear anything, they mentioned it to no one at the time.

Not long after midnight, Sgt. Joseph Hillier returned from patrol and visited the bunker. He saw Arone bleeding profusely and heard his laborious breathing. He ordered Matchee to clean him up, then went over to the CP to file a patrol report. Sgt. Anthony Skipton entered the bunker a few minutes later, took off Arone's bonds, and checked for a pulse. There was none. He then hurried over to the CP to tell Hillier that Arone was probably dead and that they'd better tell Captain Sox. When Sox came over, he ordered Arone's battered body moved from the bunker to the hospital, where Capt. Neil Gibson gave it a cursory examination and placed the time of death at between midnight and 12:15 A.M.

Somali teenager Shidane Abukar Arone was dead, murdered by Clayton Matchee, aided by Kyle Brown, and with the connivance of many other Canadian soldiers. Within hours, the news of his death was radioed from Belet Huen to Headquarters, Canadian Joint Forces Somalia, in Mogadishu, and from there to National Defence Headquarters in the Pearkes Building in Ottawa. In army parlance, any death caused by a

Canadian soldier while on duty is a "significant incident" to be reported and handled in a special way. This particular significant incident would soon blow the lid off the Department of National Defence and the army, implicate a number of high-ranking officers, and create the deepest crisis of confidence in the history of the Canadian Armed Forces.

PART ONE

The Canadian Army

———————

Some two million Canadians served in two world wars and the Korean conflict in this century, and about one hundred thousand of them were killed in action. Yet Canadians tend to forget about their armed forces and their wars. And their politicians and media, in particular, have almost no understanding of things military, what they are, or what they do.

Armies are unique. They are state-sanctioned monopolies of deadly force. They have been around, in one form or another, for centuries. Today's armies are in a state of flux, especially in democracies like Canada. This is partly due to changing social values, the end of the Cold War, and the advance of democracy. But while armies must change in some ways to reflect the society around them, in other ways they must remain the same. They still exist to fight wars, and the essence of war is still to kill or be killed.

The fundamental challenge to Canada's army today is to make the necessary changes that will attract and hold good soldiers, while continuing to practise the age-old traits of successful military leadership. In the Canadian army hierarchy over the last two decades, there has been too much resistance to change and too weak a commitment to military professionalism.

1

ARMIES

A T Agincourt in 1415, an English army of about seven thousand men, including six thousand archers, famously and bloodily defeated a much larger French force consisting mainly of heavily armoured knights. After the battle, the English systematically killed their French prisoners and slaughtered their wounded enemies wherever they were found. Some they stuffed into cottages and incinerated *en masse* to save time. The battle and its aftermath were a horrifying bloodbath.

William Shakespeare's version of the battle, transcribed in his play *Henry V*, presents the actions of the English army in rosier terms than historians have used. The play, written a century and a half after the event, is mostly fiction. But *Henry V* contains some remarkable passages that accurately describe what good military leadership consists of, and others that convey with uncanny precision the viewpoint of the universal soldier. Shakespeare's observations are so good that some scholars believe either that he himself must have been a soldier at some point or that he witnessed battle firsthand.

As Shakespeare depicts him, the twenty-seven-year-old king is the epitome of a good commander. He is innovative, inspiring, decisive, and mindful of the welfare of the troops with whom he endures the physical hardships of the battlefield. Most important of all, Henry knows that although a variety of circumstances may bring a man to the battlefield, patriotism among them, only comradeship will sustain him when the fighting begins. "We would not die in that man's company that fears his fellowship to die with us, . . ." Shakespeare's king tells his men. "From this day to the ending of the world . . . we in it shall be remember'd; We few, we happy few, we band of brothers."

Shakespeare's ordinary soldiers are exactly the sort of men who have manned battle lines throughout history. "We see yonder the beginning of the day, but I think we shall never see the end of it," one man declares in the play. He and two of his comrades are then joined by the king, who is moving about the camp in disguise. They tell him they wish the king were somewhere else, and they with him. They claim to know little or nothing of the cause they are about to fight for. They do know "there are few die well that die in a battle."

Despite their fear, cynicism, and uncertainty, these men will fight when the dawn comes. They are English, and the French army awaits them. That is why they are there. They have chosen this course, the disguised king reminds them, because if they should survive, they will have seen their own greatness in the face of death. For the remainder of their days, they will be able to "teach others how they should prepare" for their deaths. They will be unique among men, members of a select group who have offered themselves in battle, killed the enemy, and, in so doing, passed one of the greatest tests that a human being can endure.

At the real Battle of Agincourt, Henry V's entire army was only a bit larger than a modern-day brigade group. If it can be said that he had a staff at all, it was a very small one. Henry was the chief strategist, tactician, and battle planner. He was responsible for the morale of his men. Although his army was divided into regiments headed by captains, it contained no specialized groups responsible for supplies, transportation, communication, civilian liaison, or internal policing. It most certainly had chaplains as well as a variety of camp followers – civilians peddling food, liquor, and sex. But the army itself was almost exclusively made up of fighters. It fed itself from what it seized along its line of march. Anyone who could not wield a sword, pull a longbow, or hold a pike was useless and not wanted. In modern parlance, Henry V's army would be described as virtually all "teeth" (fighting elements) with very little "tail" (support elements).

In today's armies, the size of the tail almost invariably approaches or even surpasses the size of the teeth. In the Second World War, the German *Wehrmacht* was, from this standpoint, among the best organized of the fighting forces on either side. A German mechanized (*panzergrenadier*) division contained almost 90 per cent fighting troops. By contrast, an American infantry division consisted of some 35 per cent administrative troops and 65 per cent combat personnel. Among the worst organized was the Canadian Army, which had the lowest ratio of fighting soldiers to administrative troops of the three western Allies. A Second World War Canadian infantry division contained 18,376 men. The largest group in the division was made up of the combat soldiers in the division's three brigades – 8,418 infantry-men (including mortarmen, machine gunners, anti-tank gunners, etc.). There were an additional 2,122 men in the attached field artillery. Most of the rest were medical personnel, signalmen, vehicle drivers, maintenance men, clerks, and other administrators.

Today's armies are too large to live off the land as they did in Henry V's day. Henry's soldiers fought with cutting and piercing weapons that they could easily carry. A Second World War infantry division, by contrast, expended literally tons of metal every day in the form of bullets, mortar and artillery shells, rockets, and mines. They could carry only a small portion of the ammunition they would need in the course of a campaign. The same was true of the gasoline, medicine, clothing, and all the other necessities that allowed them to fight. Thus a large and well-organized supply system was and is vitally necessary to sustain fighting troops. Even the Second World War *panzergrenadier* division mentioned above suffered constant supply shortages of everything from food to ammunition to reinforcements (replacements for soldiers wounded or killed).

Although today's armies are very different from those in the fifteenth century, all have had the same purpose – to fight wars. For as long as men and women have lived together in groups, their leaders have raised armies. The prime task of the men commanding those armies has been to bring soldiers to the field of battle. Once battle has been joined, those soldiers have been called upon to commit two unnatural acts: to kill other human beings who have done nothing personal to them; and to expose themselves to the risk of gruesome injury or painful death. The nature of violence doesn't change for those on the receiving end: a French pikeman disembowelled by sword thrusts at Agincourt was no less mutilated or dead (and his family suffered no less grievous a loss) than a Canadian infantryman disembowelled by a chunk of shrapnel in the Rhineland in 1945.

These things have remained constant. What has changed over time is the scale and duration of the violence that armies can inflict. As John Keegan pointed out in his book, *The Face of Battle*, what really changed from Agincourt to Waterloo (1815) to the Somme (1916) was scale. Governments consolidated and expanded the territory under their control while technology improved weaponry and communications. These developments produced armies that were generally much larger than those of ancient times. And as armies grew larger, so did battlefields and the number of casualties. In almost four years of war on the Eastern Front in the Second World War, between thirty million and fifty million soldiers and civilians are estimated to have died on both sides. That is more than the combined population of France and England in Henry's day.

Canada, too, has been shaped by war. War brought English and French together into one country when the British army and navy defeated the French army and navy in 1759. When the British army threw back invading American revolutionaries in 1775 and 1776, and defeated the forces of the fledgling United States in 1812-1814, Canada was given its separate destiny. The Civil War in the United States and the threat of a post-Civil War American invasion of Canada were the catalysts that brought Confederation about in 1865-1867. The defeat of Louis Riel's rebellion in 1885 cemented the west to Canada for all time. Canada gained its independence through war in 1914-1918 and secured its place in the world in 1939-1945. Whether for good or ill, war is woven into the fabric of this country, and Canada must continue to have its own armed forces no matter how peaceful the world may appear to its inhabitants. No one likes a slacker. If Canadians are to enjoy the benefits of membership in the western, market-oriented, democratic group of nations, they must help defend the interests of that group. If Canadians don't pay their dues, they may someday be kicked out of the club. They will most certainly be ignored when club members define the rules.

Of course, armies can perform many functions other than war fighting. In Canada, soldiers have fought floods and forest fires, kept the peace in city streets, and even picked peaches at harvest time when manpower was short during the Second World War. Most recently, the Canadian Forces have been heavily involved in peacekeeping missions, usually (but not always) under the auspices of the United Nations. Canada's own experience in two world wars and the Korean conflict shows, however, that whatever else armies may be called upon to do, they exist – first and foremost – to fight wars.

In the nineteenth century, Carl von Clausewitz – a Prussian officer who had seen action in the Napoleonic Wars and had been captured by the French – analysed the elements of warfare in his book *Vom Krieg* (*On War*). A controversial book because of Clausewitz's apparent advocacy of total war, *On War* was actually intended to do for war what Machiavelli had done for the exercise of political power: give guidance to those who would resort to war with respect to what war means and how it must be fought.

On War begins with a definition of war that sets the tone for everything that follows. War is an act of force to compel our enemy to do our will, Clausewitz declares. To succeed in war, the enemy must be rendered powerless. To render the enemy powerless – and to do so with as little damage as possible to one's own forces – war must be pursued with the maximum use of force. By this, Clausewitz did not mean that the wholesale slaughter of innocents was necessary or even sanctioned – his book says little about how non-combatants should be treated – but that the destruction of the enemy's ability to wage war must be the sole purpose of battle. Clausewitz took issue with those who believed war could be fought in a half-hearted fashion. "Kind-hearted people might, of course, think there was some ingenious way to disarm or defeat an enemy without too much bloodshed, and might imagine this is the true goal of

the art of war ... it is a fallacy that must be exposed: war is such a dangerous business that the mistakes which come from kindness are the very
worst. . . . To introduce the principle of moderation into the theory of
war itself would always lead to logical absurdity."[1]

Clausewitz's book is based on the idea that the destruction of the
enemy's ability to wage war, the total destruction or disbandment of his
armies, the killing, capture, or disarming of his soldiers, must be the
central aim of war. He has been proven correct time after time. Even
though *On War* is essentially a treatise on how nations or governments
should wage war on other nations or governments (it appeared long
before the development of so-called "peoples" wars), the essence of war
remains the same even in conflicts pitting guerillas against conventional
forces. The lightly armed guerilla in the jungle and the heavily armed
soldier of a tank division have the same objective: to force the enemy to
do something that the enemy is manifestly unwilling to do. What differs
are tactics and means.

Despite the life-and-death nature of war, or maybe because of it, a
complex set of "rules" has evolved as to how war should be fought.
Though dating back hundreds of years, those rules are, for the most part,
found in a series of international conventions laid down in the late nineteenth and early twentieth centuries. Popularly referred to as the Geneva
conventions (because most were agreed to in meetings at Geneva), they
fall into three broad categories: the treatment of captured enemy forces;
the treatment of non-combatants; and proscriptions on the use of
certain weapons such as poison gas. These rules are based primarily on
self-interest: nation A does not want nation B to use gas against its troops
or non-combatants and so signs an agreement with nation B that neither
will use gas. During war, the rules are adhered to primarily to avoid retal-
iation in kind.

The rules regarding treatment of non-combatants have evolved over
many centuries. They grew out of the practical problem of determining
the extent of a conquering army's responsibility for the civilian population that comes under its sway. In ancient times, for example, a besieged
city that did not surrender despite the hopelessness of its situation was
usually sacked and its inhabitants enslaved or put to the sword. That was

the conqueror's payback for having to keep his armies in the field even though he had obviously won the campaign. Since the custom was well established in many parts of the world, the inhabitants of a besieged city had a fair, if brutal, choice: give in and be spared or fight on and be killed or enslaved. From this tradition evolved the modern notion that if a country declares a city to be "open," it will not defend it, and the conqueror is therefore obliged not to destroy it.

The development of these rules of war paralleled the evolution of "laws" that establish the basic rituals by which war is declared, conducted, and ended. Virtually all such rules and laws are assumed to apply to those established nations or governments that declare in advance that they adhere to them. Guerrillas, terrorists, spies, or nations that refuse to adhere to the rules are held to be exempt. Sometimes adherence to the rules involves a fair bit of hair-splitting. During the Second World War, for example, a French man or woman who took up arms against the Nazis inside occupied France was subject to execution if caught. If the same man or woman left France, crossed the English Channel, and joined the Free French forces in England, he or she was held to be protected by the rules of war.

The idea that one's own soldiers are subject to a higher law when they are commanded to obey orders by a superior officer is relatively new. It stems from the Nuremberg and Tokyo war crimes trials held by the Allies at the end of the Second World War. Based loosely on the concept that the Axis powers had waged unlawful war on civilian populations – thus breaking established rules of war – the trials were precedent setting. According to Professor Martin van Creveld, the Nuremberg and Tokyo trials were aimed at patching up "the damage done to international society [by the totalitarian regimes] by defining the things which were and were not permissible."[2] This was done primarily by laying the blame for the war at the feet of a known group of accused war criminals. To make the charges stick, the concept of the "illegal" command was introduced: it was not good enough for a defendant to plead that he or she had just carried out orders and should, therefore, be exempt from punishment for evil deeds. Soldiers had to take some responsibility for their own actions.

The notion that a soldier must know how to distinguish between a legal and an illegal command, and be aware of his or her right to refuse the latter, is now part of the training of virtually all the armies of democratic countries. In Canada, for example, it is taught initially to those soldiers who aspire to the first rung of command – master corporal – and at practically every stage after. Soldiers are repeatedly instructed that they are to neither issue nor follow orders that are manifestly illegal. It is not always clear what an illegal order is, however, and the need to maintain order and discipline throughout the chain of command sometimes depends on blind obedience, especially when soldiers are under fire. Much, therefore, is of necessity left to the immediate discretion of the soldier and the commander, though both ought to be aware that their actions may later be judged by a court or a court martial.

In some ways, then, war is more refined today than it was a thousand years ago. There are rules of war, codes of conduct, rituals surrounding the making and concluding of war. There are even referees in the form of international bodies, such as the International Committee of the Red Cross – even the United Nations. In democracies, war is subject to the popular will: the people (through their elected representatives) decide when to make it, when to conclude it, who is to fight it, who is to pay for it. But at bottom the essence of war is unchanged. It remains the deliberate use of violence to achieve ends that cannot be achieved by peaceful means. Saddam Hussein was not talked out of Kuwait in 1991, he was blasted out. The Bosnian Serbs were not persuaded to come to the peace table in 1995, they were bombed to the peace table. Nations such as the United States, Britain, and France, whose own past holds the proof of the connection between war and liberty, know instinctively the role that violence plays in world affairs, in the maintenance of their independence, and the protection of their interests.

Throughout history, democracies have done a better job of war fighting than dictatorships. When a war is popular in the sense that it has widespread support (the Second World War, for example), the willingness of the majority of the citizens to fight and to organize their society for war seems irresistible. During peacetime, however, it has always been hard for citizens of democracies to acknowledge that armies are necessary and that the military way of life is, by definition, different. This reluctance to support things military varies from country to country, but it is almost always strong in nations like Canada, where people have a hard time understanding the connection between their personal well-being, national interests, and armed force. That lack of understanding may have serious consequences.

Governments have rarely had difficulty finding soldiers to fill their ranks, but they have gone about the job quite differently throughout history. In the seventeenth and eighteenth centuries, for example, the armies of western Europe were largely made up of men fighting for the chance to loot the battlefield after the battle. They were the dregs of society, men who could be kept in uniform and in line when the time came only by the harshest disciplinary methods, including the threat of execution. As late as 1831, the man who vanquished Napoleon at Waterloo – the Duke of Wellington – declared that the British army was composed of "the scum of the earth – the mere scum of the earth." Officers were distinguished from the men they led mainly by the accident of birth. They purchased their commissions and in most cases were no better qualified than the horses they rode into battle. It was assumed that members of the nobility were born with the martial spirit and the talent to lead and that no further training was required.

That changed almost completely by the end of the nineteenth century. The rise of nationalism and the emergence of the nation-state in Europe formed the backdrop for the concept of national military service. France under Napoleon led the way by drafting millions of men into the French army. Other nations followed suit. There were no major European wars on the scale of the Napoleonic conflict for the balance of the century after Waterloo, but Europe was the cockpit of new wars of national consolidation: Austria and Prussia versus Denmark (1864); Prussia versus Austria (1866); Prussia versus France (1870-1871); and the wars of Italian unification. Those responsible for the organization and maintenance of European armies tried to outdo one another in preparing for war. They created standard training regimes for the conscripted ranks, organized reserve units, built special schools and staff colleges for officers, and even devised theories as to how war should be fought. (Clausewitz was not alone in this.) At the same time, modern rifles, machine guns, and artillery were perfected, and there were significant developments with respect to communication (the telegraph) and the movement of troops and supplies (railways).

Canada has had almost no experience of conscription. The vast majority of Canadians who have served in the armed forces, even in the two world wars, have been volunteers. In the early 1960s, Great Britain abandoned "national service" (i.e., conscription) in favour of an all-volunteer force. The Americans did the same a decade later. Early in 1996, France also announced that it was converting its conscript army to an all-volunteer force. Although other European countries still resort to conscription to fill the ranks, the draft is a dying institution in the post-Cold War era. Armies increasingly exist not because governments create, mobilize, or call them into being but because apparently ordinary men (and rising numbers of women) choose to join them. In Canada today, for example, there are many more volunteers for the Canadian Forces than spaces available.

What is so attractive about armies and army life to those who would join? The answers are different in war and peace. In the Second World War, more than 1.2 million Canadians volunteered for service with the Canadian Army, Navy, or Air Force and with the forces of Allied nations, mainly the United Kingdom. Some joined out of a sense of patriotic duty. Others because they could not find satisfactory employment in an economy still feeling the aftershock of the Great Depression. Still others joined because friends, relatives, or classmates had signed up. Those who had served in the Depression-era militia often "went active" to stay with their comrades. Many recruits thought the war offered the chance of a lifetime to do something really extraordinary.

For the incentive of actual war (and it *is* an incentive to some), peace-time volunteers must find a substitute. The men and women who join the Canadian Forces in peacetime are most often motivated by practical considerations. They want to learn a trade or a profession; to advance themselves; to undertake challenging work; to have a responsible job.

Service to the nation is not high on their list of priorities. Perhaps the pertinent question is not why people join the armed forces (it is, after all, a reasonable post-high school career choice offering travel, training, and security) but why they stay beyond their initial term of service. Much of the answer has to do with the armed forces environment, particularly the social structure it provides.

Traditionally, military organizations are highly structured and ordered meritocracies. They are stable, conservative, and resistant to change. They operate under a special set of rules, have their own history and customs, and are governed by strict laws. Everyone knows his or her rank and place in the general scheme. On each soldier's uniform are the campaign and service ribbons that summarize his or her career. Status is transparent and palpable. At the same time, the military provides companionship and a built-in support system. A military organization is tough on individualists. It demands imaginative conformity. It rewards its members with a home for the duration of their service and an extended family that in many cases looks after them for life. In every society, the ready-made home and sense of family have proven to be a strong attraction to those who would be soldiers.

The army's unique structure is a direct result of the soldier's unusual vocation. J. Glenn Gray, a Second World War combat veteran of the U.S. army and later professor of philosophy, summarized it in his classic book *The Warriors*. "The professional soldier needs to reduce the capriciousness of his world as much as possible. He chooses to conceive an orderly universe with stable and traditional values, in which death must have its rank and time like everything else. In this attempted reduction of all things to the matter of fact and the predictable, the fatalistic soldier does not lose his subjective responses (i.e., fear), but they do become subordinated."[3] Armies throughout history have learned that the subordination of fear – which is vital if soldiers are to go deliberately into harm's way – can be achieved when soldiers stand in ordered ranks with others whose respect they value above everything, including life. Elmer Bendiner, a Second World War B-17 navigator, explained, "It is easier to walk to one's doom in company and in cadence than to step out of line to stand alone, exposed and naked."[4] An army (and navy and air force) must, therefore, provide the order, the structure, the ritual, and the belief systems that will provide its members with the spiritual support they may eventually need if called upon to offer up their lives. That order can be mightily attractive in its own right even to the clerks, the cooks, and the supply personnel who will likely never get close to battle because it removes major elements of chance that bedevil the lives of civilians.

There can be no doubt, however, that people also join armed forces, or stay in them, because they are in love with war. In mid-December 1862, Gen. Robert E. Lee stood on the heights above the Rappahannock River in northern Virginia and watched as the well-entrenched troops of his army drove back attack after attack from Union forces that had crossed the river intent on capturing Fredericksburg. Union losses were frightful: 1,284 killed, 9,600 wounded, and 1,769 missing. But time after time, the federals under Gen. Ambrose E. Burnside returned to the offensive. Lee marvelled at the sight. "It is well that war is terrible," he told his officers, "or we should grow too fond of it."

The theme is too strong to ignore. For some men, war is a "terrible beauty." "Millions of men in our day – like millions before us," Gray proclaimed in *The Warriors*, "have learned to live in war's strange element and have discovered in it a powerful fascination. The emotional environment of warfare has always been compelling; it has drawn most men under its spell." Though many men undoubtedly hate war, "yet many men both love and hate combat. They know why they hate it; it is harder to know and be articulate about why they love it."[5] Vietnam War veteran William Broyles, Jr., remarked, "I believe that most men who have been to war would have to admit, if they are honest, that somewhere inside themselves they loved it . . . loved it as much as anything that has happened to them before or since."[6]

Just what is it that some men love about war? It is the sensual experience of it. The seeing and hearing of sights and sounds that no one else will see or experience. It is the "lust of the eye," as the biblical phrase has it. It is the awful beauty of tracer fire at night, of a horizon lit by the gun flashes of a thousand field pieces, of a formation of hundreds of bombers droning through the sky despite bursts of anti-aircraft fire and the wanton attacks of enemy fighters. It is the experience of comradely love so strong as to cause men to sacrifice their lives without a moment's hesitation to save their fellows. The majority of American marines posthumously awarded the Congressional Medal of Honor in the Second World War died by throwing themselves on grenades to shield their buddies. It is also the licence that war gives to destroy, surely one of the deepest and most primordial impulses inside human beings. As Broyles sums it up:

> Part of the love of war stems from its being an experience of great intensity. . . . War stops time, intensifies experience to the point of a terrible ecstasy. It is the opposite of that moment of passion caught in "Ode on a Grecian Urn": "For ever warm and still to be enjoy'd/ For ever panting, and for ever young." War offers endless exotic experiences, enough "I couldn't fucking believe it!"'s to last a lifetime.[7]

Combat may well be the supreme test of a person's ability to face death and not flinch. Virtually all societies and all cultures have harboured people, usually men, who seek out death in order to defy it. Be it the young men who run before the bulls at Pamplona, Spain, or those men and women skydivers who leap from airplanes in flight, tempting one's ultimate fate is an age-old way of defeating it. Those who would join armies do so, in part, for the chance to discover how they will fare if they have the chance to face that supreme test. Unlike most men and women who, given the choice, avoid the terrors of combat, true soldiers seek it out because it gives their lives meaning even as it threatens to destroy them.

Because war is an activity based on the deliberate and organized destruction of human life, it is unlike anything else. Battle, too, is unlike anything else. Those who have never experienced it can never know its terrors, its tribulations, its wearing impact on the human soul, its debilitation of the human spirit. Nor can they know the jubilation that comes to some who fight battles: the freedom to engage in wanton destruction and to slip the bonds of civilized behaviour. Battle produces in soldiers a sublime love for those who share the same fate and a deep hatred for the nameless and usually faceless enemy who opposes them.

When Clausewitz characterized war as "the continuation of policy by other means" (possibly the most famous phrase of his entire life's work), he meant simply that war is the final means by which national leaders attempt to impose their will on other nations when diplomacy has failed. He was also warning those who would launch wars to ensure that they had a well-defined and achievable military objective. But that phrase may be the most misunderstood of all that Clausewitz wrote because it is often interpreted to mean that war is comparable to other competitive pursuits, such as politics, business, and sports.

War so seizes the imagination of many men (and some women) that they begin to think of themselves as soldiers going into combat when they battle the morning traffic. They describe what they do in war-related terms to such an extent that ordinary people can be forgiven for believing there is little difference between a day trading currency in front of a computer terminal and a day under mortar and artillery fire.

When the president of Hallmark Cards rallied his employees at the start of a major corporate reorganization in 1990, he declared, "We are going on a journey. And on this journey we will need to carry the wounded and shoot the stragglers." It was not true, of course. There would be no gunshot wounds in this battle, no bodies blown to smithereens, no triage at regimental aid stations to sort out those who could be treated from the hopeless cases. But it has become so fashionable to speak this way that legions of corporate executives now include the work of Chinese military philosopher Sun Tzu on their office bookshelves, not to mention Clausewitz. There is constant talk of "corporate wars" and "take-no-prisoners" marketing strategies. The language of war has become the language of commerce, sports, and virtually all other forms of modern competitive activity. It is easy, therefore, for businesspeople to delude themselves into thinking that they are like warriors and that the decisions they make sitting in the comfort of their offices are like those of a commander in battle. In reality, there is no comparison.

In November 1965, the U.S. army fought the North Vietnamese army at the Battle of the Ia Drang Valley. Lieut. Dennis Deal was a platoon leader in a company that had been surrounded and cut off. His account of the challenges he faced is all too typical of those a commander must deal with in battle:

> "Suddenly a lull occurred on the battlefield. During that lull one of the men in my platoon got up on his knees while the rest of us were flat on our stomachs. He was promptly shot in the upper body, ten feet from me, and I heard the bullet strike human flesh. It sounded exactly like when you take a canoe paddle and slap it into mud. . . . During the same lull, my radio operator's hip suddenly exploded . . . before the bleeding started I saw white, jagged bone sticking out."[8]

No oil company vice-president, advertising account executive, or securities trader has to make life-and-death decisions in these circumstances. It takes a special leadership quality not only to undergo battle but to overcome feelings of horror and fear in order to think clearly and make decisions affecting the outcome.

Battles are fought by soldiers who are in a constant state of fear. Even the hardest, most experienced soldiers endure it. James Jones, author of *From Here to Eternity*, was a line rifleman in the U.S. army in the Pacific theatre during the Second World War: "I went where I was told to go, and I did what I was told to do, but no more. I was scared shitless just about all the time." A U.S. Marine at Tarawa in 1943 described his fear no less eloquently: "Our lips were cracked with the dryness of fear and our voices sounded to us like the voices of complete strangers, voices we had never heard before. By the second day men's mouths were literally black with dryness from fear . . . all of them."[9] Elmer Lenox, a Canadian infantryman with the Calgary Highlanders in Normandy, recalled his first time under shellfire when he realized "somebody out there is intending a hell of a lot of harm to you . . . I said, 'Jesus, I'm scared' and meant it. And you stay that way, pretty well. If you don't stay scared, there is something wrong with you."[10]

There is no parallel between war and anything else that people do. Canadians, however, are inclined to forget what real war means. We haven't fought in a major war for half a century (Korea, 1950-1953). The only "total" wars we took part in – the two world wars – are even further in our past. So when sports figures, business leaders, politicians, journalists, and even religious and academic leaders use the terminology of war and the nomenclature of armies to describe what they do, it is a simple matter for the public to overlook the uniqueness and horror of war. It is also easy to forget that armies and soldiers *are* different, and must be, to carry out the tasks that society has charged them to do, tasks that set them well apart from the rest of us.

Although war is as old as civilization itself, the idea that war fighting requires a separate and specialized body of knowledge or theory is a relatively recent one. Prior to the eighteenth century, it was believed soldiers would acquire the know-how for battle primarily by being in it. The rank and file were trained in the basic skills they would need to shoulder arms and were drilled endlessly in the manoeuvres they would perform in the field. Once in the field, they would march in column, form lines, phalanxes, or boxes, wield their swords, and hold their shields, pikes, or muskets, as required by their commander. They didn't need to think, thinking was a distraction. They only needed to act. If they stood and fought, it was largely because the tightness of their ranks left them no room to run away. The only way out of danger was to eliminate its source – the enemy. So, although there were men who earned their livelihoods year in and year out by war fighting, and thus could be considered professional, their knowledge of war was entirely practical. It was not their brains but their living bodies that they hired out to their commanders.

Commanders, too, were usually untrained for war. Exceptional commanders such as Alexander the Great or Caesar emerged largely through an evolutionary process. Because they had courage and charisma, men followed them. Their instinct for battle – an eye for choosing favourable terrain, for example, or a sixth sense to anticipate what the enemy would do – made them victorious. For centuries, in fact, it was generally thought that the nobility were endowed with an ability to think in military terms and that to be well born was, in itself, sufficient qualification for command. That was the assumption underlying the system that allowed the purchase of commissions. Means and ability were thought to be one and the same.

That started to change in the late eighteenth century, as Martin van Creveld points out in his book *The Training of Officers*. Armies ceased to be largely temporary formations of men who gathered when necessary to fight for king or master and became standing armies instead. Over time, standing armies were increasingly organized by function: there were people to take care of weapons and uniforms, others to victual and to arrange bivouacs, and so on, which in turn required soldiers to acquire specialized knowledge. This specialization, and the growing realization among rulers that command in war had to be taught, led to the beginning of the officer training programs pioneered by Prussia's Frederick the Great.

In the last two centuries, the idea that there is a particular body of war-fighting theory has become almost universally accepted. The concept of the professional soldier flows naturally from this proposition. A soldier today is not simply a person who makes his or her living in the armed forces; he or she has mastered, or is in the process of mastering, the special skills and knowledge necessary for war fighting. Soldiering is no less a profession than practising before the bar or performing surgery. Like doctors or lawyers, men and women enter the military profession when they have mastered a body of knowledge. That knowledge is highly specialized and specific. The other members of the profession are responsible for gauging who has mastered that knowledge and who is thus eligible for membership. There are schools or academies in which the basic command skills are taught: West Point in the United States, for example, Sandhurst in the United Kingdom, and Royal Military College in Canada. There are also command, staff, and war colleges for imparting a higher order of knowledge to those in the senior ranks. Those below the commissioned ranks (in Canada, they are now termed NCMs or non-commissioned members) must also attend special courses and schools to advance up the ladder of command or to acquire the particular knowledge needed of combat engineers, or signallers, or the infantry.[11]

Armies prepare for their ultimate job – war fighting – by training. This is carried out in stages from a recruit's initial indoctrination into the army to training in fieldcraft, particular skills, and courses for junior and senior leaders. Basic training is primarily aimed at breaking down the recruit's individuality and instilling a sense of solidarity with other recruits in the training unit. In battle, soldiers fight and die for each other; in peace, they must be indoctrinated to see themselves as part of a larger organization that is ultimately more important than themselves. That is why the recruits are forced to dress and cut their hair in exactly the same fashion, and eat, sleep, and drill in unison. At all times, they are introduced to the notion of unit discipline and taught that such discipline is essential to survival in war.

Even in peacetime, and even in countries such as Canada where participation in war is unlikely, soldiers are, and must be, trained for war. This does not mean inculcating a "will to kill" or a "killer mentality" in the recruit. The "killer mentality," or hate for an enemy, will develop soon enough in soldiers under fire when their comrades are being killed and maimed beside them. But they will kill mostly because they know that the only way to be safe on a battlefield is to destroy those who are trying to destroy them. Soldiers are trained to advance *towards* the source of danger in order to eliminate it in defiance of everyone else's instinctive desire to run *away*. Training for war also means teaching the fieldcraft, the weaponry skills, and the individual tactics and tricks of battlefield survival that a soldier will need when under fire. If recruits don't learn these essential elements of soldiering, they will not be much good for anything else they may need to do, such as take part in UN peacekeeping operations.

Similarly, fighting units, from sections to platoons to brigades, must also be trained for war. Only when the soldiers in an infantry battalion have learned how to work together to achieve common goals under fire – to maintain, for example, the necessary order and discipline to wrest a well-defended position from a determined enemy – will they be able to handle any other task assigned them. A unit trained for combat must be disciplined, confident, well led, and ready to perform to the best of its ability under any circumstances.

Professional soldiers in virtually all armies share a number of characteristics. They have a strong allegiance to the profession of arms. Nowhere is this more evident than in the phenomenon of "old enemies, but enemies no more" demonstrated by celebrants of the fiftieth anniversary of the end of the Second World War. Former German fighter pilots raised a glass of beer with former Allied bomber crews. The bond shared by those who belong to the profession of war fighting is a strong one.

Another universal characteristic of the professional soldier is the acceptance that certain fundamental rules of his or her life must be adhered to if good order and discipline are to prevail. For example, virtually all armies observe a time-honoured separation between officers and non-commissioned officers (NCOs) in both work and social life. (Officers issue commands; non-commissioned officers see that the commands are carried out.) This separation of lives corresponds to another distinction: non-commissioned officers are considered to be "regimental." They can spend their entire professional career in one regiment, whereas officers typically move in and out of units as they climb the promotional ladder. The relationship is not unlike the upstairs-downstairs world of the upper-class Victorian home. The servants lived downstairs, did the jobs necessary to the running of the household, and were governed by a hierarchical structure headed by the butler. The master and his family lived upstairs, passed "commands" to the staff through the butler, expected the work to be performed satisfactorily, and provided the wages and the means of sustenance to those living downstairs. In today's armies, officers and NCOs have a finely developed sense of where their duties and responsibilities overlap, and where they do not.

A final characteristic shared by all professional soldiers is their need for ritual and a distinctive identity. In the British army, and in the armies of Commonwealth countries such as Canada that have borrowed heavily from British practice, this need is met most often by the regimental system. But even in Roman times, legions adopted special names, symbols, and rituals to help bind their men to one another and instil unit pride and cohesion.

All these attributes are tied to the fundamental reality that soldiers ultimately owe an unlimited liability to their leaders. They have joined an organization that may one day ask them to offer up their lives on the battlefield. That sets them apart even from police officers or firefighters. The latter work at jobs that may sometimes be dangerous. They may be killed or maimed on the job, and, like soldiers, they may be called upon to expose themselves to danger. But soldiers alone go to their work with the deliberate intention of destroying lives and property.

Because war, battle, armies, and soldiers are different from anything else, military leadership must also be different. The fighting units in an army invariably consist of young and spirited soldiers who would be in need of discipline in any institution they were part of. That situation calls for leaders who have the charisma and strength of character to ensure that their soldiers know what is demanded of them and what the limits of acceptable behaviour are. A good military leader almost never resorts to disciplinary measures; his soldiers trust and respect him, and adhere to the limits he sets for them, because they do not want to let him down. But when it is necessary, a military leader must be able to show that he is as decisive and incisive in his use of disciplinary measures as he is in fieldcraft, weaponry, and all the other skills demanded of him.

The conditions of battle demand much of a good military leader. Carl von Clausewitz believed that battlefield commanders had to have great courage. They had to maintain the ability to see the larger picture and keep it in focus, no matter how extreme the dangers around them. They had to be decisive and resolute and possess exceptional strength of character so as to impose their vision on their underlings. They had to have the mental agility to adapt their plans in the fluid conditions of battle. Clausewitz pointed out that even the simplest tasks were difficult when attempted under fire and that the "fog of war" (i.e., the confusion of battle) obscured every battlefield. The successful commander had to discharge his duties under immensely difficult conditions. Despite the sights, sounds, and smells of death and war around him, the commander had to "trust his judgment and stand like a rock on which the waves break in vain."

British Field Marshal Earl Wavell – supreme allied commander, southwest Pacific theatre, for a short time in 1942 and commander-in-chief, India, for most of 1943 – was also an author of some note. In his most famous book, *Soldiers and Soldiering*, Wavell laid out what he considered to be the most desirable attributes of a good military leader.

Wavell believed a successful commander had to be physically robust and capable of withstanding the rigours of the battlefield, where days without sleep, constant fear, adverse conditions, hunger, and the psychological shocks of battle were the rule. He had to have common sense and practical knowledge. He had to lead his men even when under great personal duress, and he had to make them feel that he cared for their welfare and their fate. He had to have the will to win, the instinct of a gambler, and the ability to make decisions under fire. At all times, he had to show that he was competent, that he knew what he was doing, and that he would either get his men through or ensure that their sacrifice was going to be worth something.

These characteristics are necessary, but in the armies of democratic nations even more is required. Leaders of such armies must also be prepared to do the bidding of a civilian leadership that often knows little or nothing of the profession of arms. Because armies in democratic countries are sanctioned to possess, train in, and, when necessary, use weapons of the deadliest kind, their leaders have a special responsibility to ensure that the soldiers in their charge conduct themselves in accordance with the rules, values, and customs of the democracy they are sworn to serve.

It is more difficult to train soldiers today than ever. This is partly because war is more technical and weapons more sophisticated than in the past, but it is also because battlefield conditions these days are likely to be so fluid that much depends upon the individual soldier's ability to react appropriately to suddenly changing conditions. Consequently, modern armies have learned that they must encourage their soldiers to think. This was not the case as recently as the Second World War, when American, British, and Canadian armies developed a variety of aptitude tests to direct the least-skilled, least-intelligent, and least-educated recruits to the infantry. The German army tended to do the opposite. The result was that the basic Allied infantry units (the section in the British and Canadian armies, the squad in the American) showed themselves to be less capable of adapting quickly to changing battlefield conditions than their German counterparts. German units consistently demonstrated a superior ability to fix the enemy with fire and destroy it through movement. This was not a function of courage but of resilience.

Armies today look for combat soldiers among those men and women who have demonstrated the intellectual capacity to think under fire. As Canadian military historian John English wrote, "Teaching a man how to think rather than what to think is a far better method of preparing him for the unexpectedness of war. A discipline of a kind that has nothing to do with common perceptions drills is therefore required. . . . The most effective soldier thus appears to be one who is mentally resourceful and capable of a certain amount of inventiveness or creativity."[12]

Extended peace poses the greatest challenge to both the discipline and the fighting ability of a modern army. It is difficult to prepare soldiers to be at the very peak of their mental and physical abilities when they know that their services may never be required. It is equally difficult to stop peacetime armies from bogging down in the minutiae of peacetime administration and to keep them focused on their prime purposes – fighting wars. Peace nurtures the leadership of soldier-bureaucrats while war demands the leadership of soldier-warriors.

In some ways, armies are easier to lead in war than they are in peace-time. Soldiers look on war as the ultimate test of their professional accomplishments; most want the chance to show what they can do. In peacetime, army life is a constant round of training, courses, and post-ings. These activities are enlivened by mess dinners, sports contests, and parades. But they are not war. Training exercises are as realistic as careful preparation and sophisticated technology can make them, but the possi-bility of imminent mass death is absent. Training may be gruelling. It may impose great physical hardship upon the soldiers in the field, but it is not war either, and everyone knows it.

It is in peacetime, therefore, that disciplinary problems can become most acute. Restless soldiers who are inadequately led may be involved in brawls with civilians, adopt unconventional articles of clothing, or in other ways undermine authority and the chain of command by their intemperate, undisciplined behaviour. The invention of bizarre rituals and initiation rites intended to test their mettle and manhood are not uncommon. In battle, there is no room for such artificial rites of passage. The only rite of passage that matters in war is that which a soldier endures when the enemy tries to kill him.

In an army at war, elitism among fighting men is usually more contrived and artificial than real because everyone fights and faces enemy fire. But this is not true of an army in peacetime. There is an almost universal perception in most western armies, for example, that airborne forces are elite units. The idea is based primarily on the fact that airborne training involves jumping out of airplanes, a task that is inherently dangerous and somewhat unnatural. Jumping out of airplanes is also real in a way that other, simulated military exercises are not. Leaving an aircraft in flight is as real as can be. Those who do it tend to scorn the "legs" or "groundpounders," whose activities are merely terrestrial. In war, the distinction means little because, again, combat itself divides those who have been under fire from those who haven't. In the Second World War, in fact, paratroopers usually saw far less action and for less sustained periods than did regular infantry outfits in all the Allied armies. The men who faced a storm of German fire when they hit the beaches on D-Day were every bit as much an "elite" as those who had been dropped from the air the night before.

It is harder to discern and remove poor leaders in peacetime than it is in war. In war, ineffective or incompetent commanders are either killed off or are quickly revealed and removed. Under fire, there is no room for failure. In August 1944, the Canadian Army fired a divisional commander during the Battle of Normandy. Many more brigadiers, battalion commanders, and company commanders were also fired as men who had led units in England were finally tested in combat. The best among them prevailed and eventually rose through the ranks. Those found wanting were replaced by better men.

Armies, then, are unique and so are the soldiers who form them. But although the way armies prepare for war – and fight it – is very different today than it was in the days of Henry V, the essential nature of war and the fundamental challenge to the individual soldier – to kill or be killed

– has not changed. That is why the essence of good military leadership is not much different today than it was in Shakespeare's time. The single biggest problem that the Canadian, American, and British armies have shared at different times since the end of the Second World War is remembering what good military leadership is.

2

THE "OLD" ARMY

THE British Royal Navy is known as the "senior service." The term denotes much more than mere age. From the days of Elizabeth I and the Spanish Armada, it was the navy that protected Britain from its enemies and gave it the power to build an overseas empire. The heroes of generations of young British males were apt to be the great naval commanders such as Sir Francis Drake, or Lord Horatio Nelson, whose traditions underpinned the modern Royal Navy. The Royal Navy was "senior," then, because of tradition, heritage, legacy, and the burdens and glories of history.

If Canada can be said to have a senior service, that service is the Canadian Army. Just as the Royal Navy shaped modern Britain with its victories at sea, the Canadian Army shaped modern Canada at Vimy Ridge in 1917 and on the beaches of Normandy in 1944. Until the late 1960s, the Canadian Army was largely a legacy of the two world wars. Its structure, traditions, values, and ethos embodied the army that had been tried by fire. It was an army designed to fight in Europe as part of a larger alliance. It was an army led in large measure by officers from the same Anglo-Saxon elite that dominated the rest of Canadian society. Its enlisted ranks were largely filled by men (and some women) with little formal education whose values reflected an older, more structured, less polyglot society.

As Canadian society changed in the 1960s, the army changed with it. That was both inevitable and proper. If an army does not reflect the values and composition of the larger society that nurtures it, it invariably loses the support and allegiance of that society. The challenge to the Canadian Army was to maintain the soldierly virtues that must lie at the heart of all armies, while adopting to new social realities. The crisis of leadership that emerged in the Canadian army in the early 1990s resulted in large measure from the failure of Canada's senior service to meet that dual challenge.

Canadians have always been reluctant to think about things military, except during times of major wars. Prior to Confederation, small colonial militias existed in Canada, New Brunswick, and Nova Scotia. They were social organizations as much as anything else. The core consisted of a handful of "active" militiamen who were actually equipped with rifles and uniforms and received rudimentary training. There were about five thousand of those in Upper and Lower Canada, many less in the Maritime colonies. In times of emergency, this small group was to be joined by the much larger "sedentary" militia, which was, in reality, just a list of males eligible for military service. Until 1860, there was little need for anything more. Britannia ruled the waves, and British regulars, garrisoned at places like Kingston, Quebec City, and Halifax, stiffened the colonists' military resolve.

That began to change with the outbreak of the American Civil War in 1861. Anxious to secure its sources of raw cotton, Britain backed the Confederacy, and relations between Britain and the United States deteriorated. The British built up their troop strength in Canada, but desperately sought to have the Canadians assume more of the burden of their own defence. The Canadians balked, dithered, and delayed until 1862, when Prime Minister John A. Macdonald reluctantly introduced a bill into the colonial legislature to expand the active militia to fifty thousand men and to provide adequate weapons and training for them. The bill was defeated, the Macdonald government resigned, and little was done to improve Canadian defences even when the British pulled their troops out of Canada after the American Civil War ended. By 1871, the British were gone except for a contingent left to guard the Royal Navy base at Halifax. Britain needed its army at home and believed that the burden of defending Canada should fall primarily on the Canadians.

Although the new government of the infant Dominion of Canada adopted a Militia Act in 1868, it did little more than its predecessors to see to Canadian defences. Macdonald believed that Canada could never mount a serious defence against the United States and that Canada's best security lay in good relations between Britain (and Canada) and the United States. Like many other Canadians, he believed that if the country was seriously threatened, its young men would rush to the colours in any case, and that no permanent, professional, fighting force could ever be as good as an aroused citizenry.

This attitude stemmed from the contempt in which most of Canadian society of the day held full-time soldiers. Macdonald and many others believed that these "regulars" were useful only for hunting, drinking, and chasing women, that they had no skills, and that they were soldiers because they were no good at anything else. Macdonald did not believe that soldiering was a true profession or that war fighting required specific skills that could only be learned in some formal fashion. The militia, on the other hand, was held to consist of hard-working farmers who were pure of motive and moral and who would fight with great spirit and daring when the time came to defend home and hearth. In part, these beliefs were rooted in the mistaken idea that the militia had saved Canada from the Yankee invaders in the War of 1812-14; in fact, British regulars had saved the day. But this "militia myth" was to dominate Canadian defence thinking until well into the twentieth century.

Since the heart of Canada's defence policy was to be the maintenance of an active militia, some provision was needed to train that militia. With the British army gone, the task would have to fall on Canadian shoulders. In October 1871, the first permanent Canadian military formation was inaugurated at Kingston, Ontario, to train the militia in the use of artillery. It was not until 1883, however, that a 750-man Permanent Force was set up, again primarily for training.

In the late nineteenth and early twentieth centuries, the growth of the Permanent Force was hindered by the prevalent attitude that soldiering was not a particularly difficult skill to acquire. That same attitude allowed successive Canadian governments to use the awarding of militia commissions as a form of patronage. When Canada went to war in 1914, many of its militia officers were incompetent political appointees who knew nothing about soldiering. Even so, Permanent Force officers were for the most part kept in Ottawa pushing paper while the militia officers were given the task of leading Canada's troops into battle.

When the First World War began in 1914, the Canadian Army consisted of a small Permanent Force and a larger but ill-trained and ill-equipped militia. By 1918, the army was able to field a four-division Canadian Corps with a strength of over one hundred thousand men. The Canadian Corps became one of the most proficient fighting formations on the Western Front. Its officers and men grew expert at the use of artillery and in preparing and carrying out mass infantry attacks with a minimum of casualties. The expertise did not come easily, but was acquired only after years of hard fighting in which the incompetent were weeded out and replaced by battle-hardened leaders who had learned the science of war fighting the hard way. By the end of the war, the Canadian Corps was commanded by a Canadian – Lt.-Gen. Sir Arthur Currie – who was considered one of the best tacticians on the Western Front. Virtually all the command and staff positions in the corps were also filled by Canadians. These officers, at one time untried and largely untrained Saturday-night soldiers, were counted among the best of the Allied professionals. That was not proof that the militia myth had any substance; it was proof of the very opposite. These militiamen learned the profession of arms the hard way, in action, and at considerable cost. By the end of the war, no one was more convinced of the importance of professional training and leadership than they were.

Learning came at a frightfully high cost in botched battles such as St-Éloi and Mont Sorrel in 1916. Currie, who rose rapidly from the rank of brigadier in the fall of 1915 to corps commander by mid-1917, had himself been a patronage appointment. But as he experienced battle and counted the cost, he grew determined to get rid of the incompetent officers in his command. Currie even refused to countenance the appointment of Garnet Hughes, son of Militia Minister Sir Sam Hughes, to command a division in France because he was convinced that Garnet Hughes could not do the job. Currie's argument with Hughes was indicative of a growing split between the fighting officers at the front and the staff officers running the Canadian Expeditionary Force in England about what constituted a qualified officer and who, therefore, should be promoted.

Canada's interwar governments did very little to ensure that the lessons learned on the Western Front would be sustained in the years that followed. True, a small number of Permanent Force regiments were kept in being with their primary mission to train the militia, but the militia myth was still very much alive. When Canada entered the Second World War in 1939, it did so with a Permanent Force of just over 4,000 men, of whom fewer than 450 were officers. Some of those regulars – and most of the militia officers – were simply unfit for command. They were too old, too lacking in modern military know-how, too devoid of charisma to lead men into battle. By mid-1941, largely at the behest of the British, the Canadian Army began to comb out the worst of the lot and send them home. Sometimes truly outstanding leaders took their place; more often the new commanders were merely competent. With substantial help from British Gen. Bernard Law Montgomery (later field marshal, but in 1941 still a corps commander), the Canadians began to learn how to take the measure of a war leader. In fact, however, much of the process of selecting the new group of battalion, brigade, and divisional commanders was little more than educated guesswork. No one really knew how a leader would perform under fire until he was under fire. Almost invariably, then, a second weeding out took place once a unit had been blooded.

By the end of the war, Canada had some 500,000 men in the army; in northwest Europe, there were five Canadian divisions and two independent armoured brigades. Those formations fought under the direct command of First Canadian Army – the only army headquarters Canada has ever fielded – and two corps. That army made a small but important contribution to the liberation of Europe, fighting in key battles such as Normandy, the Scheldt Estuary, and the Rhineland. It was able to do so only because, like the Canadian Corps of the First World War, it largely became a meritocracy under fire. By 1945, Canadian divisional commanders, brigadiers, and battalion commanders were second to none among the Allies. There is still debate as to the merits of Army Cmdr. H. D. G. Crerar and Corps Cmdr. Charles G. Foulkes (First Canadian Corps) and

G. G. "Guy" Simonds (Second Canadian Corps), but few argue about their basic ability to handle large formations in the field and in battle. Simonds is still considered by many scholars to have been one of the more imaginative Allied field commanders. He was the inventor of the armoured personnel carrier (APC) and the first to integrate APCs into mechanized forces in battle.

In both world wars, Canada's forces fought under the overall command of non-Canadians. Essentially, the Canadian government assumed responsibility for raising, paying, equipping, and, to a certain extent, training the Canadian Army, but then turned it over to others to use. Canadians commanded the field formations (from corps down in the First World War and from army down in the Second World War) and were responsible for supplies and administration. But the Canadian formations as a whole were part of larger coalition forces commanded in turn by the British and then the French in the First World War, and by the British and then the Anglo-American combined chiefs of staff in the Second World War. The precedent set in the two world wars has been followed ever since. In the Korean War, the Gulf War, and in every peacekeeping operation Canada has participated in, Canadian troops have ultimately been commanded by others. Even when a mission commander has been a Canadian (as in Rwanda), he acted on behalf of a non-Canadian agency (the UN). The primary function of the Canadian army today is no different than it was in 1914, 1939, or 1950 – raising and training formations to fight (or to peacekeep) under the operational control of others – the British, the Americans, NATO, NORAD, the UN, etc. In effect, Canada is a "lender" of forces, and the prime mission of National Defence Headquarters in Ottawa, and of the chief of the defence staff (CDS), is "force generation," not force command.

At the end of the Second World War, the Canadian government moved swiftly to chop its defence budget. The Liberals under Prime Minister William Lyon Mackenzie King had won the 1945 federal election by promising a smorgasbord of new welfare measures such as family allowances. But it also had amassed massive war debts that had to be paid off. The defence budget was the juiciest target for deep cuts. From almost 500,000 men, the army was reduced to slightly more than

15,000 in just two years. The postwar establishment consisted of three infantry battalions with one each from the Royal 22e Régiment (R22eR), the Royal Canadian Regiment (RCR), and the Princess Patricia's Canadian Light Infantry (PPCLI), two armoured regiments, one artillery regiment, and a number of other units such as combat engineers. Although the force paled in size to the wartime army, it was much larger than the Permanent Force had been in the interwar years. In the fall of 1946, Prime Minister King appointed Brooke Claxton as the minister of national defence with a mandate to cut even further. Claxton did what he could, but was more interested in creating a smaller and more efficiently administered military than he was in just slashing budgets.

From 1947 to 1950, Claxton eliminated needless duplication among the three services while giving them a well-defined, multi-role, postwar mission. In a highly symbolic first step, Claxton ordered the three service chiefs and their immediate staffs to move into a single headquarters building on Cartier Square in Ottawa. He dubbed it National Defence Headquarters and ordered that a Canadian flag be flown in front of it instead of the Union Jack. He then set about defining the mission and role that the three services were to play. The army was to have three goals: keep up-to-date in equipment and training; provide a nucleus for any future expeditionary force that might be called upon to fight a coalition war; help defend Canada. The militia was to be given adequate resources and training to be able to mobilize enough battalions in time of emergency to give the whole army a viable force. To accomplish these objectives on his limited budget, Claxton consolidated the Department of National Defence (DND) under one minister (there had been three during wartime), unified sixteen different service functions such as medical services and recruitment, and charged his deputy minister (C. M. "Bud" Drury, a former brigadier) with working directly with the three services in formulating the department's budget.

Claxton was, without doubt, the best postwar minister of national defence Canada has had. He was tireless, driven, intelligent, and vitally interested in getting the best out of his department. A battery sergeant major in the First World War, he had been decorated for bravery under fire. Although his wartime experiences in the ranks produced in him a healthy scepticism of the brass, he had a solid grasp of military values and traditions. When necessary, he was not afraid to kick a strong personality like Guy Simonds (who became chief of the general staff in 1951) into line. But although the three service chiefs had virtually unimpeded access to him, or maybe because of it, he wanted an independent and trusted source of military advice.

In early 1951, Claxton created the position of chairman, Chiefs of Staff Committee (CCOS), to act as his military adviser. He appointed Charles Foulkes to the position. Foulkes's job was to preside over CCOS meetings and attend meetings of the Cabinet Defence Committee and the Defence Council (the last was largely concerned with administrative matters). Wherever possible, he was to create consensus among the service chiefs. That was important because Claxton believed that interservice rivalries impeded good military, as well as good budgetary, planning. At the same time, however, Foulkes commanded nothing, while the service chiefs continued to enjoy the right to place their views directly before the minister. Thus Foulkes was supposed to provide Claxton with the type of advice on military matters that Drury gave on civilian issues. The big and crucial difference was that Drury actually ran the large civilian establishment at the Defence Department, while Foulkes ran only his small office. That was not a particular problem as long as an active, interested, and strong minister such as Claxton (who retired in 1954) ran the whole show.

Claxton's ideal of a small but highly trained, highly professional, and up-to-date army rested on outstanding leadership at all ranks. That would only be possible if the Canadian officers received the best education and the best training possible. Thus, Claxton reopened Royal Military College (RMC), which had been in existence since 1876 but had been closed for the duration of the war, with a modernized curriculum. In keeping with Claxton's program of consolidation, RMC was henceforth to be a tri-service officers' academy. Some years later, Claxton established Collège militaire royal de St-Jean, Quebec, to entice francophone officers into the army. It, and Royal Roads in Victoria, provided the first two years of the RMC curriculum; officer cadets then went to Kingston to complete their education. Claxton also established the National Defence College at

Kingston and placed the head of the Defence Research Board, O. M. Solandt, on the Chiefs of Staff Committee.

Claxton was careful to ensure that the reforms he introduced did not alter or interfere with the established chain of command. He knew that a well-ordered chain of command, unhindered by civilian interference in strictly military areas of decision-making, was essential to allow the best military leadership to emerge. His aims were better integration within the forces and greater consensus within the high command, but preservation of the practices, traditions, and values that made each service, and each unit in the services, unique. He implicitly accepted that the business of soldiers was soldiering, not managing military bureaucracies.

From the late 1940s to the late 1950s, the operational heart of the postwar Canadian Army was the Mobile Striking Force (MSF). The MSF was originally designed to be a reinforced battalion of air-droppable troops that could be flown to a remote location in the vast tracts of northern Canada to counter an enemy lodgement. Later the MSF was enlarged to the size of a brigade. The MSF concept was based on the knowledge that the U.S.S.R.'s long-range bomber force, consisting of TU-4 copies of the American B-29 that had bombed Hiroshima and Nagasaki, did not have sufficient range to bomb American targets and return to the U.S.S.R. Thus one scenario in the event of a war with the U.S.S.R. was that Soviet paratroopers might seize an airstrip somewhere in Canada so that a fleet of Soviet bombers could land there, refuel, and then continue on their mission. It was the MSF's job to be flown to the vicinity of the lodgement, drop nearby, destroy the Soviet bombers, and make short work of the Soviet paratroopers.

Canada did not have nearly enough resources for an army large enough to defend the Canadian landmass. The MSF was designed, in effect, to provide point defence until reinforcements could be mustered from elsewhere. Since Canada did not have the budget to provide for its own defence, it would provide the defence that fit its budget. The MSF was a way of "making do," something the Canadian armed forces have been doing since Macdonald's day. But although all of Canada's three standing postwar infantry battalions were trained to be jump-capable, the MSF remained largely a concept rather than an operational reality. For one thing, it never had quite enough aircraft of the right type to carry out its full mission.

In June 1950, Communist North Korea crossed the 38th parallel that separated North and South Korea in a full-scale invasion. The United States considered the invasion a challenge to the Free World and used its then-dominant position at the UN to declare North Korea an aggressor and organize a UN military force under American Gen. Douglas MacArthur to counter the invasion. At first, the North Koreans drove the South Koreans and their allies into a small perimeter around the southern port city of Pusan. Then, in September, MacArthur's troops pulled off a daring landing at Inchon, near Seoul (the South Korean capital), and drove the North Koreans back over the border towards the Yalu River and China beyond. In November, the Chinese responded and threw almost a half-million "volunteers" into the fray. The UN forces were driven back south of the 38th parallel. A UN counter-offensive early in 1951 pushed the Chinese back to the vicinity of the 38th parallel. From the summer of 1951 to the end of the war in August 1953, the front remained at about the same place though fighting continued in a vicious war of attrition.

In August 1950, the Canadian government acceded to pressure from Washington, London, and its Commonwealth allies and promised a brigade group to fight under UN command in Korea. The immediate problem was that there were no troops to send, short of dispatching the MSF contingents and leaving Canada totally defenceless. The solution was to recruit a special force solely for Korea service and to fill the ranks of this force largely with Second World War veterans already familiar with army life. The contingent was dubbed the Canadian Army Special Force (later designated the 25th Canadian Infantry Brigade) and trained at Fort Lewis, Washington. It was initially composed of newly created 2nd Battalions of the three regular force regiments with artillery, armour, and other supporting contingents added. 2 PPCLI, the first Canadian troops to arrive in Korea, landed there at the end of 1950; the rest of the brigade followed in May 1951. In June 1951, it joined the other

Commonwealth contingents as part of 1st Commonwealth Division. The Canadian battalions were rotated home every twelve months and replaced with fresh battalions from each of the three regiments; eventually some twenty-two thousand Canadian soldiers served in the Korean conflict.

The Canadian Army was completely unready for the Korean War. At Claxton's order, the first contingent was recruited with great haste, and many of the basic tests of mental and physical competence usually applied to new recruits were done away with. That allowed many misfits into the first contingent. Some of the men were totally unfit for battle – too old, too lame, too physically or mentally unfit. The brigade suffered constant serious disciplinary problems in its first months in the field. A number of Korean civilians were murdered by Canadian soldiers. The Canadian troops had the highest crime rates of the Commonwealth forces, the highest VD rates, and the highest desertion rates. The disciplinary problems began to recede to more normal levels as the misfits were sent home; when the second and third contingents arrived in 1951 and 1952, discipline problems and desertions dropped back to levels comparable to the Second World War and to those of the other Commonwealth units.

Much of the equipment used by Canadian troops in Korea was dangerously outmoded. Their Sten submachine guns were almost useless and were left behind most of the time when troops went out on patrol. Their bolt-action, First World War-era rifles had too slow a rate of fire for the type of short, sharp, hilltop fighting that took place along the Korean ridges. The Canadian Army's winter clothing was substandard. Their helmets were totally obsolete and rarely worn. Unlike the American troops, they did not receive newly developed armoured flak vests in anything like sufficient numbers until near the end of the campaign.

But in action, the Canadians were superb. Even the first contingent distinguished itself. At Kap'yong in April 1951, for example, the PPCLI held a key hilltop position in an all-night battle against a Chinese force at least five times its size. The Canadians suffered heavy casualties. At one time during the night, a Patricia company commander ordered artillery fire down on his own positions to kill a Chinese force that was penetrating the perimeter. But the Canadians slaughtered hundreds of Chinese soldiers and helped block a major Chinese offensive aimed at outflanking UN positions near Seoul. Their stand that night earned them a United States Presidential Unit Citation – the only Canadian military unit ever so honoured.

Why did the first group of Canadians acquit themselves so well on the battlefield despite all the problems of discipline and morale that arose behind the lines? Because the men who led them in the bunkers, slit trenches, and firing pits were first-class. All three brigade commanders – John Rockingham, M. P. Bogert, and Jean-Victor Allard – had compiled outstanding records leading brigades during the Second World War and most of their staff officers were similarly experienced. A reservist at the time the war broke out, Rockingham was hand-picked by Claxton to head the first contingent. He, in turn, personally chose his battalion commanders, all three of whom were also reservists with distinguished wartime leadership records. To lead 2 R22eR, for example, Rockingham wanted Jacques Dextraze, who had commanded Les Fusiliers Mont-Royal in the Second World War. Dextraze agreed, provided he could choose his own officers. As he later recalled, "All majors would be selected from captains who had wartime experience. Captains would be selected from senior lieutenants with wartime experience, and the subalterns (lieutenants) could be green as grass. I would then train my officers *my* way."[1] Thus virtually all the battalion commanders, their battle adjutants (the battalion staff captain), and the company commanders were either regulars with Second World War experience who had stayed in the army or experienced reservists specially called back for service in Korea. The great majority of the senior NCOs fell into the same category. The quality of these senior leaders was such that the largely untried platoon leaders who filled out the officer ranks learned quickly. That all these officers and senior NCOs were initially saddled with a larger than usual number of misfits is a fact; that those misfits were quickly weeded out is also a fact. When judged by its performance in combat, the Canadian Army in Korea did a masterful job.

Korea was a temporary aberration for the Canadian Army; the real action was to be focused on Europe. In 1949, Canada joined the North Atlantic Treaty Organization (NATO); in the fall of 1950, with the Korean War raging in Southeast Asia, Ottawa acceded to NATO pressure to offer a permanent contribution to the defence of Europe. A new brigade was raised and trained, recruited primarily from militia units, and designated the 27th Canadian Infantry Brigade. It was sent to Europe in the fall of 1951 and initially stationed near Hanover under command of the British army of the Rhine.

The raising of the Canadian NATO brigade took place at a time of great crisis among the western countries. Convinced that the Communist invasion of South Korea was, in reality, a test of the new Atlantic Alliance, the western allies were thrown into a virtual panic in late 1950 when the Chinese intervention seemed to presage UN defeat. In December 1950, Claxton and Minister of External Affairs Lester B. Pearson told their cabinet colleagues that "the period of greatest danger" had begun and that a Communist victory in Korea would greatly increase the chances of other Communist assaults in Europe and Asia.[2] Claxton and Pearson urged a rapid expansion of the Canadian armed forces; their colleagues agreed.

From 1950 to 1953, the Canadian defence budget increased from 3.1 per cent of the nation's gross national product to 8.8 per cent. That increase fuelled the largest peacetime mobilization in Canadian history. Although a larger percentage of the spending increase was directed to the Royal Canadian Air Force than to the other services, the Canadian Army almost tripled in size within half a decade. From three regiments with one battalion each in the field in 1950, the infantry corps increased to six regiments, each fielding two battalions. The armoured corps added two regular regiments to the two already in existence. The other corps – engineers, medical corps, service corps, etc. – grew proportionately. New camps were opened. New training facilities were established. The intake of officers was greatly increased. Some serious problems developed because of this rapid expansion. The Army Works Service was caught in a scandal when thefts and misuse of property was discovered at Camp Petawawa, Ontario. Some senior officers were implicated. Subsequent investigation showed that the scandal was as much the result of careless bookkeeping as it was malfeasance. The problems that initially plagued the 27th Brigade in Germany were much more serious.

The organizational structure of the 27th Brigade was somewhat peculiar. Like the 25th Brigade, it had to be built from scratch and in the least possible time. The scheme that Simonds and Claxton came up with was to recruit men from a number of different militia formations and place them in three new composite battalions. There was almost no unit cohesion in these battalions and much internal bickering and rivalry. To make matters worse, the men could not bring their families over from Canada. That was not so of the British or Americans; for the Belgians and the Dutch, distance was not a factor. The Canadian soldiers were thus alone, well paid (compared to the Germans), young, and bent on getting as much sex and booze as they could. Discipline and good order suffered badly. There were numerous instances of clashes with the locals, and the press at home soon got wind of the situation. Simonds would not brook such newfangled notions as appointing officers with special responsibility to raise and maintain morale. The problems eventually disappeared after the brigade moved to permanent quarters at Soest (later at Lahr) and the men were allowed to bring their families over. Lack of unit cohesion was dealt with by disbanding the composite battalions and replacing them with regular units. At the same time, the brigade's designation was changed to 4th Canadian Infantry Brigade, even as it took on the mechanized role (a mechanized unit is one in which the infantry are carried into battle on tracked armoured personnel carriers, usually in accompaniment with tanks).

Canada's land force contribution to NATO was never more than token. It was politically important for Ottawa to be seen doing its part to defend its European allies; it was also important to the Europeans and the Americans that a second North American country have a military presence in Europe. But a single brigade group was not much use to NATO, especially when the other Allies were contributing at least an army corps of two or more divisions. In the event of war, Canada was supposed to augment the brigade with two others from home, forming a division, but unless and until that happened, the Canadian brigade in Germany was part of a British division until 1967. Thereafter, it became an independent brigade first under British then American command. As such, it was too small to be easily administered, commanded, or supplied. But at the same time, it was a national contingent and could not simply be taken under the wing of the larger formations of the other NATO countries. Once again, Canada was "lending" troops to others, apparently unconcerned about how they were to be used. As one defence analyst recently wrote, "The military credibility of the Canadian Army's Brigade Group in Germany was always in question, even in the 1950s and 1960s."[3]

The Canadian Army's mechanized brigade group in Germany was not very important to the Allies as a military formation, but it was very important to the officers and men of the Canadian Army. Germany and NATO were the "big time." The North German Plain was where the heavy Soviet armoured and motorized rifle divisions were going to make their dash to the Pyrenees if the Third World War ever broke out. This was the place where Allied and Communist forces would decide the fate of Europe, and maybe the world, in massive battles pitting hundreds of tank, infantry, and mechanized and motorized divisions against each other. This was where heavy artillery and tactical air power would turn the battlefield into a charnel house. Always within reach were the tactical nuclear weapons and the chemical and biological weapons that would be used if either side were in danger of defeat.

After the fighting in Korea ended, the Canadian Army's focus reverted to maintaining the Canadian brigade in Europe. As historian Sean Maloney has observed, "The NATO role in Central Europe formed the focus of [Canadian] Army doctrinal development and structure."[4] In Europe, the Canadian Army prepared for its main mission – full-scale war. Beginning in 1954, the armoured regiments were equipped with new British-built Centurion main battle tanks (MBTs). Other heavy equipment was also acquired – 155-mm self-propelled guns and two batteries of Honest John nuclear-tipped battlefield missiles. In 1957 and 1958, the army's armoured capacity doubled when the Fort Garry Horse and the 8th Canadian Hussars were activated. For a time, the Canadian brigade was as well equipped as any unit of comparable size in NATO. The maintenance of up-to-date heavy armoured units is the most important measure of a modern army's intention to play a major role in modern war. This does not come cheap. But at the height of the Cold War in the early to mid-1950s, when Soviet invasion of western Europe seemed a distinct possibility, Canada was prepared to pay up. Canada was even prepared to pay in the late 1970s when the Centurions became obsolete; in 1979, they were replaced by a much smaller number of German-built Leopard 1 tanks. Canada was prepared to stay in the armoured business for a while longer.

Service with the 4th Brigade formed a focal point for the old army. For officers, a tour of duty in Germany was a chance to grapple with major tactical problems, learn how to handle sizable formations of armoured and mechanized forces, and train on the ground where the next real war was going to be fought in conjunction with Canada's much larger NATO allies. For the ranks, Germany was a chance to drive the tanks and shoot the big guns that had attracted many of them into the army in the first place. Officers and men brought their families to Germany and made Soest, Lahr, and other smaller bases into a small piece of Canada. Before too many German farm fields were chewed into mud, and too many roads and bridges damaged by tanks and other heavy vehicles, the NATO troops were universally welcomed as defenders and as people spending lots of money in the local economy.

Unlike a peacekeeping stint, duty in Germany was pleasant, fun, even exotic. A tour usually lasted for at least two years. There was plenty of time to settle in, soak up the local culture, buy duty-free goods at the Canex, and gawk at the sights of Paris, Rome, London, even Berlin. Don Barry of the Lord Strathcona's Horse armoured regiment spent several years at Lahr in the late 1970s and early 1980s. He remembers Germany with great fondness. "My tour in Germany was the best in all my career. I enjoyed myself the most. I didn't want to leave Germany." Barry married a German woman and returned to Canada with her in 1983. Germany was an especially good place to be when the Canadian dollar was still strong against the German mark, as Steve Bellingham, another Strathcona trooper, remembers, "We did a fair bit of travelling and a lot of partying because Germany at that time, well, the whole of Europe, was open to us. We were making very good money considering the value of the mark. We travelled and we drank an awful lot . . . it was a very good time. We lived on the economy quite cheaply."

But duty in Germany also had its drawbacks. The wide-open attitude towards drinking made the army's already serious alcohol problem even worse. One soldier who did a tour there in the 1970s ran into serious difficulties. "In Germany . . . drinking was very, very prevalent. We even had beer in the fridge in the Quartermaster's office. At coffee break in the morning, we would sit down if we wanted to and not have a coffee, we would have a beer. It was totally acceptable over there. So I would." This soldier, like many others, continued to drink to excess after returning to Canada and was forced to seek treatment at an army alcohol rehabilitation centre.

For the most part, however, service in Germany was a prime goal – the only long-service overseas placement for a Canadian soldier that offered a real chance to exercise one's military skills and compare one's soldierly abilities with the soldiers of the other NATO countries. Most soldiers and their spouses who served there still remember Germany fondly and with more than a touch of nostalgia. In 1994, the Canadian base at Lahr was closed. The Cold War was over, and Ottawa decided it was too expensive and not much use maintaining a Canadian contingent in Europe. The Leopard tanks were brought home. Some were placed in storage, others used for training. They will probably not be replaced. The closing of Lahr and the virtual withdrawal of the Canadian army from armoured warfare training was undoubtedly the right move in an economy-minded era and after the collapse of the U.S.S.R. But for the soldiers who never got to Germany, or for those who had and wanted to return, the world of the Canadian army suddenly became much smaller than it once was.

Successive Canadian governments have found that a place among the great western powers can be purchased with a little military muscle and a lot of pious cant about being an honest broker in an evil world. From the launching of the first peacekeeping mission to the present, the temptation has existed to withdraw from the nasty business of killing people to the caring and sharing rituals now associated with keeping people alive. This has been a great convenience to politicians and, perhaps, to people disinclined to take risks or responsibility, who find in peacekeeping missions a kind of moral crutch. It started in Egypt.

In late November 1956, some three hundred Canadian Army administrative personnel arrived in Egypt to spearhead Canada's contribution to the newly created United Nations Emergency Force (UNEF). Eventually, close to ten thousand Canadian soldiers would serve in UNEF, as many as one thousand at a time. UNEF was the brainchild of Canadian Minister of External Affairs Lester B. Pearson, who suggested the force at the height of the 1956 Sinai–Suez War that pitted Britain, France, and Israel against Egypt. Pearson proposed UNEF to the UN General Assembly (and eventually won a Nobel Peace Prize for his idea) to replace British, French, and Israeli forces that had invaded Egypt and occupied virtually all of the Sinai Peninsula and the Suez Canal Zone. Since UNEF was a Canadian idea, Canada was called upon to participate. Canadian Maj.-Gen. E. L. M. Burns, a Second World War corps commander, was named to command UNEF from its inception until 1959. Canadian soldiers had served in a variety of UN missions prior to UNEF, but those had primarily been truce-observer operations and had used the services of only a few hundred men in total.

UNEF was the start of Canada's entry into the peacekeeping business, a business that has ostensibly become a Canadian specialty. As of this writing, some one hundred thousand Canadian troops have participated in more than thirty UN and non-UN peacekeeping operations in virtually all the world's trouble spots since 1956. UNEF (now known as UNEF I since a second UNEF was set up after the 1973 Arab–Israeli War) was the first; UNPROFOR, the UN mission to Bosnia and Croatia, took the largest number of Canadian soldiers at a single time – twenty-four hundred. UNFICYP, the peacekeeping operation on Cyprus, was the longest, from 1964 to 1993. Most of the operations consisted of patrolling neutral zones between antagonists who had agreed to have a third party between them. Others were missions to observe elections, monitor cease-fires, clear mines, feed refugees. The theory behind classical peacekeeping is simple:

a neutral group or organization provides lightly armed soldiers to stand between antagonists who have decided to stop killing each other but don't trust each other. The peacekeeping troops are lightly armed to defend themselves if directly threatened, but that is all. They are, in effect, hostages to fortune. They are there not to be shot at. Their purpose is to help the antagonists keep the battlefield quiet so that truce talks, peace talks, or armistice talks can move the conflict from the battlefield to the bargaining table. Sometimes both antagonists refuse to move to the peacetable; they find it convenient to hide behind the peace-keepers. Cyprus was the classic example of that. The rules of engagement of these peacekeeping missions are well defined under Chapter VI of the UN Charter; they are *not* peace enforcement operations such as the UN campaign in Korea.

Soldiers cannot do peacekeeping well if they are not well trained. It takes iron nerves and excellent discipline to stand between two enemies, who are sometimes firing at each other, and not give up the ground. Canadian soldier Don Barry was one of many who did a tour of duty in Cyprus. "There were two threats," he recalled. "Number one, we were on the green line between the Turks and the Greeks. You had threats of sniper fire, or if they were shooting at each other, you'd get the brunt of it. The other was demonstrations, because the families on the Greek side wanted to get their houses back, which were on the Turkish side." Once, when delivering travel documents to men of a unit about to go on leave, Barry ran into such a demonstration. "As I turned the corner in my van, I was surrounded by about 250 demonstrators who proceeded to rock me back and forth. The demonstrators were mostly students." Barry escaped without injury; other Canadian peacekeepers were not so lucky. More than one hundred have been killed on peacekeeping operations.

Although Canada has become well known as a peacekeeper, neither the Canadian government nor the Canadian military was at first enthu-siastic about peacekeeping. Peacekeeping was a diversion from the larger show – Germany and NATO – and a drain on scarce resources. From the very beginning, the Canadian Army took the point of view that good peacekeepers can only be fashioned from soldiers who have been well trained to fight wars. Canada's soldiers rightly believe that troops who know how to defend themselves, who are trained in fieldcraft, weaponry, small-unit tactics under fire, and who have had a good sense of field discipline instilled in them can be taught the art of peacekeeping as an add-on. But troops who have been taught primarily to be peacekeepers will have neither the weapons skills, the discipline, nor the instinct for the battlefield that they will need if they become endangered.

Peacekeeping has become so integral to what the Canadian army does that Canadians tend to forget that all armies, including their own, exist first and foremost to fight wars. That mass amnesia was never so apparent as in the months leading up to Operation Desert Storm, the UN-sanctioned, U.S.-led military operation to push Iraq out of Kuwait. While most of Canada's NATO partners joined the coalition forces, Canada dithered while Canadians debated the merits of involvement. The most frequent argument heard against Canadian participation was that Canada was traditionally a peaceloving nation dedicated to peacekeeping and that participating in an actual shooting war would run completely counter to everything Canadians believed in. That argument could only have been credible to citizens of a nation that had utterly forsaken its own history. One-and-three-quarter million Canadians fought in two world wars and in the Korean conflict in this century and one hundred thousand of them never came back. This was a price Canadians paid to ensure their sovereignty and acceptance as an equal by the other nations that have been their partners and allies.

Peacekeeping missions and tours of duty in Germany provided operational experience for large numbers of Canadian soldiers in the late 1950s and early 1960s, but most of the time the army, and army life, centred on the barracks, the base, and the home unit. The old army was a more or less stable organization whose members were certain of their place in the military scheme of things and whose values and traditions closely resembled those of an old boys' club. During the raucous 1960s, the youth culture, the self-indulgence of a newly prosperous middle class, and the sexual revolution and feminism began to produce radical changes in Canadian society and politics. But armies have always been rather conservative organizations, and it was some time before the changes that were starting to take place outside the barracks began to find their way inside.

In the old army, a recruit's service life began in the regimental depot, where he received his basic training and was indoctrinated into his regiment. The process generally took six months and was about equally divided into training and indoctrination. In the words of Col. Ian Fraser, who commanded the Canadian Airborne Regiment in the mid-1970s, "It was really a form of brainwashing. The new soldiers memorized battle honours and the names of regimental heroes. They learned about regimental history, ceremonies, customs and traditions, music, bugle calls, order of dress, special drill movements, and all the other trappings that made each regiment in the Canadian Army unique. When they left the depot ... the soldiers weren't prepared to admit that any other regiments even existed, much less discuss them with anything other than scorn."[5]

After regimental depot training, the soldiers took a year of advanced training with their battalions or regiments (battalion in the infantry, regiment in the armour or artillery). Every summer, they took part in exercises at Camp Wainwright in Alberta or Camp Gagetown in New Brunswick. Their home was usually an army camp built in the Second World War and designed to accommodate a single battalion or regiment. Spread across Canada, many of these camps were located near small towns. They were almost self-contained: there were barracks for the single men, officers' quarters for both single and married officers, messes, drill halls, canteens, kitchens, eating facilities, gyms, chapels, a library, a guard room, a small hospital, even a dental clinic. Very few of the troops were married. The single men lived in barracks under the watchful eye of the corporals. The corporals were responsible for discipline in their sections and often knew their men better than anyone else in the army. They answered directly to the platoon sergeants.

Discipline was usually strict. Men were regularly put on charges for all sorts of minor offences; those who committed repeated minor offences were likely to be "counselled" by their NCOs behind the barracks. Collective punishment was the order of the day. It was believed to instil unit cohesion. Since few soldiers owned cars or left the base regularly, drinking and driving was not a serious problem; the drinking was done on the base. Alcohol was an integral part of the culture of the old army. Officers and men were expected to drink regularly and heavily in the messes after work, during "happy hours" and at special functions. The liquor was cheap. Alcoholism was rife and the army maintained alcohol treatment centres in Germany and across Canada. Those who refused to treat themselves and whose drinking contributed to violence, disobedience, or inability to perform basic tasks were eventually drummed out of the army, but hardly ever quickly.

There was no place for women in the old army. Army wives were an institutional inconvenience. They lived on base. They generally did not work. They were supposed to go where their husbands were posted without complaint – to Germany if they were lucky, to Gagetown, or Shilo, or Wainwright if they were not. The army's attitude was simple; soldiers were married to the army first, to wives and families a distant second. Most soldiers thought that was right and expected their wives to go along. The wives sat at home Friday nights while their husbands drank to excess in the messes or during equally sodden mess dinners. There were very few women actually in uniform and certainly none performing what were thought to be "men's" trades, which were everything associated with the combat arms and its support and supply units.

A soldier's life centred on the regiment, but his daily living was done inside his own unit – his company in the infantry, his battery in the artillery, his squadron in the armour. In an infantry battalion of roughly nine hundred men, there were four rifle companies, a support company, and a headquarters company. A rifle company was commanded by a major and divided into company headquarters and three rifle platoons, each led by a lieutenant aided by a platoon sergeant. The lieutenants were usually younger and less experienced than the platoon sergeants, who actually administered the platoons.

The NCOs had an organizational structure that paralleled that of the officers. The senior NCO in the battalion was the regimental sergeant major (RSM), who linked the battalion commander to the NCOs. He answered only to the battalion commander and yet was subordinate to every officer in the battalion, even the youngest subaltern. He kept a grip on the other NCOs and a close watch on the ranks. He gave advice to the young officers, monitored discipline and morale, and worked with the adjutant to keep things on an even keel. A good RSM became a legend in his regiment. He was the keeper of the regimental tradition and the guardian of the regimental memory. Unlike the commanding officer or the company commanders who served their time and then went on to other things, the RSM could spend his entire army career in the same regiment.

In each company, the company sergeant major (CSM) answered only to the company commander and was a link to the platoon sergeants and the section leaders. These last – the lance-corporals – led the nine-man infantry sections that made up a platoon. The section was (and still is) the smallest fighting element in the army and the most important. In combat, the sections and the section leaders bore the brunt of the action. Corporals were the only men in the entire army who actually commanded troops; everybody else commanded another leader or commander all the way to the top.

Virtually everything that was important in the regiment was in some fashion controlled by the regiment and administered by the battalion commander and his staff in the camp. That included the administration of a large part of the Queen's Regulations and Orders, the basic military code of justice, and the responsibility for keeping the books, maintaining the stores, and overseeing the daily training regimen. All the military police, administrative personnel, drivers, medical and intelligence personnel, the regimental band, and even the chaplains worked out of battalion headquarters. According to Colonel Fraser, "If a battalion was efficient and happy, it had a good commanding officer, adjutant, and RSM. If it was sloppy and sullen, it had a poor commanding officer, adjutant, and RSM. It was really that simple."[6] Good leadership was as important a factor in camp during peacetime as it was on the front line during war.

In the old army, there was little interaction between the soldiers in the camps and the civilians in the towns and cities nearby. In fact, there wasn't much interaction between the soldiers and most of the larger civilian society. The camp was the focus of both military and social life for the soldiers, and although officers and men mingled with civilians from time to time, such interaction was rare. That made the fence around the camp as much a barrier to understanding as it was a physical obstacle. Soldiers did things their way, it was not the civilian way, and they didn't have to explain or apologize for what they did.

The Canadian Army of the 1960s was quite different from Canadian society in its ethnic and social composition. Men of British heritage or origin were over-represented compared to the rest of Canadian society, while francophones and other ethnic groups were under-represented. This was especially true of officers, some 73 per cent of whom could trace their roots to the British Isles, compared to only 44 per cent of Canadian society as a whole. Francophones were not only under-represented in the army but they were especially under-represented among the officer ranks.[7]

The Canadian Army was also unbalanced in regional origin. There were proportionately fewer Quebeckers and more Westerners and Atlantic Canadians than in the population as a whole. Westerners were especially over-represented among the higher ranks; although Westerners made up 21.1 per cent of the population of the country, they were 31.5 per cent of the officers in the army. Atlantic Canadians made up just over 11 per cent of the population as a whole and 13 per cent of the army officers. This phenomenon was not unlike that found in the United States, where Southerners were long over-represented largely because of the presence of so many military bases in that section of the nation.

The old Canadian Army was predominantly urban. More than 80 per cent of the officer corps were Protestant; more than 43 per cent of the ranks were Roman Catholic. There were significant class divisions in the old army; more than 53 per cent of the men were working class in origin, but less than 30 per cent of the officers, whose fathers usually came from managerial or professional and technical occupations, had working-class backgrounds. Only 11.4 per cent of the officers had followed their fathers into the military; 5.3 per cent of the enlisted ranks had. The old army was not well educated. As a group, the general officers and colonels had about 14.5 years of formal education while junior officers had 13.4 years. In the ranks, the median number of years of formal education was less than ten. Slightly more than 35 per cent of Canadian Army officers were university graduates compared to 57 per cent of officers in the U.S. army. Sociologist Pierre Coulombe, of the Canadian Forces Personnel Applied Research Unit (CFPARU), concluded that in the 1960s "the educational attainment of Canadian military personnel [was] substantially lower than in the United States."[8]

There are still soldiers in the Canadian army who remember the old army with great nostalgia. In the words of one currently serving RSM who joined in the mid-1960s, "The old army was based on discipline. You have to have discipline to make an army. Today people don't want to hear about that. In the old army, we took it for granted." Perhaps that is true. The officers and NCOs in the old army did not have to cope with the Charter of Rights and Freedoms, which no doubt restricts the range of choices they have to impose discipline. But the new army differs from the old army in many other ways as well, ways that stem not from the Charter but from the changing attitudes and values of the people of Canada.

In the late 1960s, when Canadian society entered what has possibly been the most dramatic period of change in its history, it was inevitable that the army, too, would have to change. That was not a bad thing. To the contrary, it was both positive and necessary. An army that holds fast to outmoded social values will be looked upon as an anachronism by society, as no longer relevant, maybe even as not worth having anymore. But when armies do change to fit the evolution of social values, it is important that they not change their basic approach to war and the preparation for war. That is because war does not change in its essence. This was the challenge that the Canadian army faced in the decades of the 1970s and 1980s. It had to preserve its essential ability to identify, nurture, encourage, sustain, and reward good military leadership and good soldierly qualities. But at the same time it had to ensure that those anachronistic values it still nurtured were properly laid to rest.

3

THE "OLD" ARMY PASSES AWAY

THE Second World War was the great watershed of Canadian history; almost everything changed in Canada because of it. More than a million veterans returned home to raise families and spend the money they and their wives and sweethearts and parents had been putting into war-savings schemes since 1940. They went to school, started businesses, bought houses and cars, washing machines and radios. When their kids started to grow up, they needed new schools and health clinics, parks and playgrounds. The men and women who had stayed home to work in the war plants made good money and saved it – there had not been a whole lot to spend it on during the war. For the first time since the Great Depression began in 1929, Canadians looked to the future with confidence. The small prewar middle class had grown into the nation's most important social group. The so-called working class was better off than at any time in Canadian history. It was a time when a man on a loading dock could buy a home, pay a mortgage (especially if he was a war veteran), and dream of sending his kids to university.

The government of the day knew that the postwar Canadian dream could not be sustained on Canada's rather small population of some twelve million people, so, in 1948, it threw open the gates to the country. In the next decade, hundreds of thousands of immigrants entered, mostly from central and southern Europe, many of them war refugees. Although immigration quotas rose and fell in the decades that followed, an important principle had been established – Canada needed new blood. When the flow of immigrants slowed from Europe, Canada began to welcome large numbers of people from East and South Asia, Vietnam, Hong Kong, Taiwan, Africa, the Caribbean and Latin America.

The main difference between the Canada of 1945 and today is that there are far fewer Canadians who think of themselves as either British or French. According to the latest census, some 30 per cent of Canadians cannot trace their origins to one or another of the antagonists who fought at the Plains of Abraham in 1759. Canada, today, is a plural society.

It was largely the growth of Canadian pluralism that led to the demand by increasing numbers of Canadians in the 1960s and 1970s for a written charter of rights entrenched in the Canadian constitution. Prime Minister Pierre Elliott Trudeau did not foist the Charter on an unwilling nation. Canadians, by the end of the 1970s, wanted it. Pluralism had naturally given rise to the notion that in a democracy people had a right to expect to be treated as equals before the law.

Demand for the Charter did not spring from immigration alone; far from it. Many other changes prepared the ground for the Charter and drastically affected the environment in which the Canadian military operated. Canadians were becoming better educated. They were more aware of what was going on in the world. This was happening not just through the formal education system but also, and progressively, because of the increasing reach of television, cable TV, and video.

As the war babies grew up, they learned more about the world through the TV screen. They witnessed the struggle for civil rights for blacks in the United States, the drawn-out debacle of the Vietnam War, the impact of the sexual revolution, and other developments – including the celebration of violence and the spread of the drug culture – associated with an increasingly permissive society. Their parents could afford those TV sets and the cable and the VCRs because of the new postwar affluence that eventually put cars in every driveway and colour TVs in every home. Whatever ideas percolated on the TV screen soon spilled freely through society. The communications revolution was a major portent of the Charter.

With the development of "the pill," women were free to choose if and when they would become mothers. They were free to apply their brains and talent to anything they wanted, but they also quickly discovered that age-old barriers and biases would not simply disappear. Feminism, which had been around since the nineteenth century at least, had a new cause to fight for – equality for women in society and in the workplace. Part of that fight was conducted in traditional political ways, but a large part was also waged through demands for written provincial human rights acts or bills of rights.

All these factors, then – postwar prosperity, immigration, education, upward mobility, the feminist revolution – changed Canada forever. They laid the foundations for the Charter of Rights and Freedoms. They set the stage for the Canadian welfare state – the Canada Pension Plan, medicare, and other measures. They contributed to the new – and false – image Canadians developed of themselves as a uniquely caring and sharing people. They also made it absolutely certain that the men – and the increasing numbers of women – who entered the Canadian Army would be a different breed than those who had gone before. Not only did the officers and "men" bring different ideas and values into the army but also the structural changes that occurred in the army itself in the 1960s and 1970s opened it completely to the ebb and flow of ideas in the society around it.

In some ways, the structural changes were inevitable. Armies are the products of the societies that sustain them and to a certain extent reflect the socio-economic changes in those societies. In Canada, however, the changes that took place in the Canadian Forces were also due to the deliberate action of government. When Lester Pearson became prime minister in 1963, the notion took hold in Ottawa that the government had a specific duty to re-engineer Canadian society. The old monarchist, conservative, straight-laced, male-controlled, dual Anglo-Saxon / French-dominated Canada was passing away, a new one would be created by Ottawa to take its place. The new Canada would be rights-driven. It would be bilingual. It would "understand" Quebec. It would be multicultural. It would be a "peaceable kingdom." And the Canadian forces would lead the way. The forces, after all, were directly under Ottawa's control. They were a perfect testing ground for the social experiments that Pearson, Pierre Trudeau, and a generation of bureaucrats hoped would point the way to a better Canada. Their aims were, in some ways, commendable. The problem was that armed forces are intended first and foremost to fight wars, not to lead the way to social change.

The old army began to pass away in 1963 when the Glassco Royal Commission into federal government waste and inefficiency issued its report after three years of study and analysis. The commission had been mandated to look into all manner of government operations and was highly critical of the Department of National Defence and the three Canadian services. It found hundreds of areas of overlap and duplication and gross administrative waste. At a time when defence budgets were shrinking from their historic peacetime highs of the mid-1950s, the Glassco message was clear: save dollars wasted by bureaucratic inefficiency and put them to better use.

Glassco was certainly correct about overlap and inefficiency. Brooke Claxton's reforms of the late 1940s and early 1950s had barely scratched the surface before the Korean War broke out and the rapid Cold War mobilization of the Canadian military went into overdrive. There was another major problem that needed to be resolved as well. The organization of the high command and the relationship of the service chiefs to one another and to the minister of national defence led to constant wrangling over priorities, planning, and appropriations within the forces. What was needed was for the military to proffer a single stream of advice to its political masters so that the government could plan, budget, and make defence decisions in a way that was both wiser and more financially prudent.

Paul Hellyer was sworn in as minister of national defence in April 1963. He had served briefly as associate minister of national defence in the late 1950s before being swept into the political wilderness by the Diefenbaker landslide of 1958. Hellyer was determined to introduce major changes to his department. He wanted to save money, he wanted a much more efficient decision-making structure. He wanted to ensure that Canadian defence policy was being made by the government and then passed down to the military, not the other way around. His initial solution, introduced in 1964, was to establish the position of chief of the defence staff (CDS), abolish the service chiefs and the Chiefs of Staff Committee, and replace the old command structure with six functional commands. On July 7, 1965, the service chiefs disappeared and were replaced by the commanders of Air Defence Command, Air Transport Command, Mobile Command, Maritime Command, Training Command, and Material Command. Communications Command was added later. Air, army, and naval camps and bases became Canadian Forces bases, a single basic-training system was established for the three services, and a single pay scale was instituted.

The new head of the armed forces was the chief of the defence staff, appointed by the prime minister to serve as the chief military adviser to the government. The CDS was the commander of the Canadian military in that he was the only person who could issue a valid order to the armed forces. He had a wide variety of other functions and memberships on various committees but, at bottom, he was the operational link between the armed forces and the elected government. His position was analogous to that of the governor of the Bank of Canada. He was ultimately responsible to the government in a general way, and he was free to make whatever decisions he needed to run the armed forces without ministerial interference. He could be directly ordered to carry out some task even if he did not wish to do so, but such an order would be unusual, indicating a breakdown of trust; and he could be dismissed. To aid him in his job of running the military, a unified armed forces command was hammered together. Dubbed Canadian Forces Headquarters (CFHQ), it was supposed to tackle the administrative problems that Glassco had identified and to achieve the bureaucratic and political goals that Hellyer desired. CFHQ worked well over the course of its brief life, but never had a chance to achieve long-lasting reforms.

The establishment of the position of CDS did not alter the basic and long-standing function of Canada's political and military hierarchy to raise forces and to "lend" them to others. The CDS is not a field commander. When Canadian forces are sent abroad to carry out UN peacekeeping operations, for example, they are placed under the authority of the mission commander who reports directly to UN headquarters in New

York on all operational matters. That commander may even be a Canadian soldier, but he still reports to New York, not to Ottawa. The CDS is responsible for force generation, not force command.

Hellyer moved on from National Defence in September 1967, but not before piloting the Canadian Forces Reorganization Act through Parliament. It was proclaimed into law in early 1968. At one fell swoop, Hellyer purported to create a single Canadian Forces, with one uniform, one rank system, and one command structure. The already unified base, training system, and pay structures were maintained, as were the functional commands. It was a bold move, one that none of Canada's allies has yet replicated.

By the mid-1970s, Maritime Command, Air Command, and Mobile Command had emerged as the three key elements of the Armed Forces (Maritime Command was based at Halifax, Mobile Command at St-Hubert, Quebec, and Air Command in Winnipeg) and the force commanders were given the right to sit at the table with the CDS and the deputy minister. In the mid-1980s, the Mulroney Tories restored distinctive service uniforms. Today, military personnel and government defence officials routinely refer to "the army," "the navy," and the "air force" when discussing the functional units of the Canadian military. As of this writing, the Chrétien government has announced plans to move the three force commands to Ottawa.

Canada elected a new prime minister in late June 1968. A former law professor, Pierre Elliott Trudeau carried most of the intellectual class's biases against the military into his new position. Despite the opposition of his first minister of national defence, Léo Cadieux, Trudeau executed a major reduction of Canada's international defence commitments in the summer of 1969. The Brigade Group in Europe was cut in half and shifted to the American sector in the south. The overall size of the Forces was cut from 110,000 to between 80,000 and 85,000. The army had five regular regiments chopped from the active list.

Contrary to popular belief, Trudeau did not make deep cuts in the defence budget soon after he won the 1968 election. Defence spending was reduced in 1968 and 1969, but increased in 1970 and in subsequent years. The figures distort the true picture, however. As inflation began to erode the purchasing power of the Canadian dollar, large budget increases were the order of the day for virtually all federal government departments except National Defence. Defence expenditures as a percentage of the federal budget actually fell dramatically from around 17 per cent in fiscal year 1968-69 to about 8.5 per cent ten years later. All areas of defence expenditure were affected. In addition to the personnel reductions mentioned above, the effect of declining expenditures was that outmoded equipment was not replaced, and that new, more advanced equipment was not procured. The Canadian army, always expert at "making do" during peacetime, would be patching and wiring its equipment together for years to come.

The last major administrative change of the Trudeau era was the establishment of a new National Defence Headquarters (NDHQ) in 1972. Unlike Claxton's NDHQ of 1947, the new NDHQ brought the civil and military functions under the minister of national defence into one organization. NDHQ became a dyarchy: the civilian deputy minister (DM) and the military CDS were to share authority. Over the years, the power and influence of the DM have increased while those of the CDS have declined. That was probably inevitable given that the CDS normally holds office for a three-year term, while a deputy minister can, and usually does, serve for much longer periods. Many army officers today believe that the CDS now works for the DM.

When the new NDHQ was put in place, O. M. Solandt, head of the Defence Research Board, called the move "an act of mayhem committed in the name of administrative madness."[1] That may have been extreme, but there can be little doubt that administrative efficiency and bureaucratic control of the military were unification's chief aims. The creation of a truly effective fighting force did not figure in the government's agenda. Unification did not create a single military culture in Canada, nor did it enhance the quality of advice flowing from the military to the government. Instead, it brought civilian bureaucrats into the process of military decision-making. The effects have been to confuse the chain of command and to place administrative acumen above military insight on the list of qualities required of Canadian Forces officers.

In his recent history of the office of the CDS, defence analyst and

former tank officer Doug Bland has examined NDHQ's impact on the
Armed Forces. The planning process has moved into civilian hands.
Civilian bureaucrats use their control of funding to govern how officers
in subordinate headquarters (area HQs, bases, etc.) spend those funds.
The CDS has become a captive of the process of consensus building
within NDHQ. Consequently, the office of CDS is looked upon by the
soldiers as the patsy of the NDHQ bureaucracy. This is a key point: people
working in the same institution tend naturally to want to get along with
the people they have to work with. In the case of NDHQ, the desire to
reduce friction "overcame the more important notion that meeting the
letter and the spirit of their admittedly conflicting and shared responsibilities for national defence is the first order of business, while seeking
harmony is a distant second-order consideration."[2] For all these reasons,
the soldiers in NDHQ are unable to give the government their considered
and unfettered advice as military professionals.

Even if they had the means, however, it isn't clear that they would give
that advice if it was seen to go against what the government wants to
hear. All promotions above the rank of colonel must be approved by the
minister of national defence upon recommendation of the CDS. It would
be naive in the extreme to believe that an officer who did not please the
deputy minister would find promotion easy. As one former high-ranking
officer who served at NDHQ observed, the deputy minister has immense
power to influence the career paths of the high command. Officers are
undoubtedly aware that their prospects in the military – and after it –
may well depend on their compliance in acceding to the wishes of the
bureaucrats at NDHQ.

The whole idea behind NDHQ is that the military's senior commanders
should become functionally indistinguishable from their civilian counterparts. In the years that followed the reorganization, this "bureaucratization" of the high command set the pattern for further bureaucratization
of the senior and middle ranks. One study revealed that many officers were
confused about their proper role. Running an army, they concluded, was
not unlike running any large corporation. A "significant minority" of
those studied reported that they were "reluctant" to enter combat.[3] The
man who conducted the study, Maj. Charles A. Cotton, laid the blame for

the growth of this managerial frame of mind at the door of unification. In his opinion, unification had increased the importance and relative number of the "administrative-technical support segment" in the Canadian Forces, thereby decreasing the proportion of officers who had joined to fight wars. The domination of the army by fighting soldiers was being challenged by the rise of military technocrats.[4]

The merging of military and civilian advisers at NDHQ has been disastrous. The civil service exists to carry out the will of Parliament. Senior bureaucrats take direction from the cabinet, tender advice, then act on the instructions given. They execute policy decisions. They have no right to oppose government policy once it has been decided. They are, in fact, as well as name, civil *servants*, obliged to serve their democratically elected bosses.

Unlike their civilian counterparts, military commanders have a responsibility to the Forces under their command that is independent of their responsibility to Parliament. They exist – or should exist – to maintain an effective fighting force. Their lives are governed by the military ethos – a way of behaving and thinking that is different from that of civilians. Civilian bureaucrats are not required to lay down their lives, but soldiers sometimes are. A soldier's liability is unlimited. Military commanders should not be temporizing their professional advice to please their political masters. More to the point, their views should be based purely on military considerations and nothing else. It is up to others in government to add the social, political, and economic factors into the defence and military-policy equation. Under no circumstances should the deputy minister stand between the military and the minister or attempt to "blend" his views with those of the CDS. Doug Bland minces no words about NDHQ. In his view, the system has "failed irrevocably" and "needs to be rebuilt on a sound legal base."[5]

The NDHQ system has civilianized the high command's way of making decisions, hindered the military's ability to give professional advice, and adulterated the evaluations that the military does offer. It has done this by giving civilians the authority to make military decisions at the highest level and by fostering docility among the high command and those aspiring to it. None of this was necessary to foster civilian control of the military, which everyone acknowledges is a touchstone of democracy. Parliament and, more specifically, the governor-in-council (i.e., the cabinet) have always controlled the military in Canada, and the changes made in the early 1970s altered nothing in that regard. Those changes were designed solely to ensure that the military did the bidding of the bureaucracy.

Unification changed the old army in other ways. Across Canada, the small, self-contained regimental garrisons were closed and army units moved to the newly consolidated Canadian Forces bases. The process worked like this: in a location where the CFB was, by function, primarily navy – such as at Esquimalt – army and air force personnel and units were moved to that base and placed within the naval administrative structure that existed there. The navy's training base at Cornwallis, Nova Scotia, for example, was converted to CFB Cornwallis, which subsequently became the location for basic recruit training for all the commands. The assumption was that basic training ought to be the same for all recruits no matter what command they would later enter or which specialty they would choose.

On the consolidated bases, former army, navy, and air force personnel worked together. On a base that housed only army units, for example, the medical personnel might be primarily navy, the police and Judge Advocate General people might be air force. The arrangement was doubtless cost effective, but it had its drawbacks. Specialists who cross over are not always familiar with the specific requirements of the service they are tasked to work with. The 1980 report of the Task Force on Review of Unification of the Canadian Forces summed up the problem, "When unification was introduced it was not the intent to convert servicemen to 'jacks-of-all-trades.' However, in the support services this has happened with the result that support to the operational forces is inadequate."

The CFBs are like small cities centrally administered by special base personnel. The days when the regiment existed in an isolated and self-contained facility are over. Regimental officers lost responsibility for much of the administration of their units. The context for army life became larger and more impersonal. Base and brigade commanders were increasingly required to administer their charges on a cost-efficient, book-balancing basis. Battalions, brigades, and higher formations were expected to plan, budget, and spend like a business. Comparable changes in Britain, according to journalist and former British army officer Anthony Beevor, have undermined the military ethos there. "An army, to mix a paraphrase, does not march on its pay scales alone. 'If you turn us into a monetary organization,' said a major from the Parachute Regiment, 'you get a monetary mentality.'"6

Canadian officers share this view. "Fundamentally, I don't think we operate a business," observed one base administrative officer. "Fundamentally, what we are doing, or should be doing, is training for war. . . . You won't be successful at war if you operate as a business, always concerned about the bottom line and the dollar sign." Cost effectiveness and operational efficiency are not necessarily the same thing.

One of the most important post-unification changes instituted in the early 1970s was the ending of free room and board for military personnel. The change was partly an economy measure, partly to place military personnel on a par with civil servants, and partly to avoid large-scale construction of new barracks and living quarters on the consolidated bases. It had a profound impact on army life. Although new members must live in barracks when they join their unit, no one else has to. Where a soldier and his or her family lives depends on factors such as price and convenience.

Base quarters – married quarters are referred to as PMQs (the P is for post) – give military families a number of advantages. They are close to work. They are located within the relatively safe confines of the base. When the soldier spouse is off on a tasking, the husband or (more likely) wife has several built-in support systems. But PMQ rents are no longer a bargain. The quarters can be small, cramped, and run-down. They can also be hard to get. At CFB Calgary, for example, about half of the twenty-eight-hundred-member garrison live in PMQs or barracks; the rest live "on the economy" and rent or buy living quarters off base.

As a result, Canadian Forces bases are hives of activity by day but largely empty at night. If a tank commander (a master corporal) lives off base, for example, he will leave his home for work in the morning just as his neighbour does. His neighbour may spend the day at a grocery store or in an office while the tank commander practises armoured/infantry advances to contact. At about 5:00 P.M., both go home for dinner. The soldier has become a nine-to-five worker, just like his neighbour. He may never eat in a base dining room or drink at the junior ranks mess, especially if he is married and his wife insists on his being home Friday nights. Because he chooses to live off base, he probably has a car, giving him mobility and causing him to spend still more time in a civilian milieu. He is probably married. In all-volunteer forces such as those of Canada, Britain, and the United States, the majority of soldiers have a spouse. If he has kids, too, they probably attend the public school. And he and his wife buy the groceries in the local mall, not on the base.

Living off base is not altogether a bad thing. Soldiers and their families have more choices, are less insular, take part in more community activities, and play an important part in the local economy. But the trend poses major challenges to the army. The regimental garrison had formed the centre of a soldier's life. Because the base provided virtually everything they needed, soldiers were content to spend most of their time there. The difference between soldiers and civilians was obvious. The closeness and familiarity of life on base helped to build unit cohesion and made it easier to impose discipline. Now, because soldiers no longer automatically live, sleep, drink, and play together, unit cohesion and discipline are less easily maintained.

In the old army, soldiers were promoted on the basis of seniority, examinations, and annual assessments by their superior officers. It was far from being a perfect system. Rife with cronyism, it sometimes failed to promote the best, particularly among the ranks of the NCOs. That system passed away in the late 1960s when the government introduced centralized civilian-management techniques to the military. According to a later study, "The tendency in the late 1960s was to view military organization as a management problem, and to this end a centralized career management system was developed which emphasized skills, occupations, and military positions as administrative tools rather than the loci of commitment and cohesion."7 The soldiers call it the "PER System," and some think it unfair, arbitrary, and a boon for careerists. In a confidential memo on morale in the army, one colonel wrote, "The PER system is a source of near *universal* upset, and the fact that it isn't changed in spite of near universal complaint serves as one more cause for the loss of confidence and feelings of helplessness over an increasingly *impotent military leadership and uncaring system.*"8

Under the PER system, all military members are subject to an annual review by their immediate superior. Each member is given a score on a scale of ten and a written evaluation, and the result is recorded on a PER (personal evaluation report). The scores of all members (both written evaluation and a numerical score) are then collated, and a rank-ordered merit list is produced to decide who is eligible for promotion. A quota system is used to ensure that scores are "fairly" distributed within units – a unit is allowed no more than X number of PERs of this or that score. That has created immense problems for some units. If a unit has only six sergeants, for example, and all are outstanding, only one or two will receive the rating he or she deserves because the total number of people in that category in the unit is too small to warrant the award of more than one such evaluation. For non-commissioned officers, a unit is told how many points it may distribute in total, which means that if Sergeant Jones gets a high score, Sergeant Smith must get a lower score to even things out. Changes may be made soon. Greater flexibility is being introduced. But the system still generates confusion, injustice, and resentment.

Merit lists are the basis of a complex consultation procedure carried out by merit boards that vary in composition. They are usually regimental in the case of NCOs; rank-wide in the case of officers. Membership on merit boards varies, but invariably include officers or senior NCOs with knowledge of the rank requirements, the regiments, and the pool of members under consideration. Career managers, who are NDHQ officers, oversee promotions and postings and try to strike a balance between the best interests of both the member and the military. Each of the officer ranks has one career manager; NCO career managers divide their responsibilities by corps. So all colonels have one career manager, as do all brigadier-generals, but there are no career managers for sergeants or master corporals whose career files are pooled with other soldiers in the same branch of the service – armoured corps, engineers, infantry, etc. Postings are almost as important as promotions, because advancement through the ranks is heavily dependent on what courses and postings a member has had. If a member cannot get posted to the course that is required for sergeants, for example, she cannot become a sergeant.

The many grievances, complaints, and criticisms levelled by both officers and NCOs regarding the PER system boil down to this: they believe it is too impersonal and that it encourages careerism – meaning a concern for personal advancement that gets in the way of getting the job done. There is a widely held belief that those who do not rock the boat are favoured over those who do, and that officers who create waves by sorting out wayward units, for example, are less likely to be promoted than those who sweep problems under the rug. It is difficult to judge to what extent these grievances are accurate. Those who fail to achieve promotion in any system often blame others for their own shortcomings. But when the PER system is viewed within the context of another relatively recent innovation in the army – the two-year standardized posting for officers – the potential for abuse is obvious. Why would any officer on a twenty-four-month posting, knowing that the PER system rewards loyalty to one's superiors and keeping one's unit on an even keel, risk unit stability by trying to root out troublemakers? The PER system may not be an impediment to good leadership, but it offers little encouragement for it either.

When unification went into effect, the Trudeau government tied military ranks and pay directly to the civil-service pay structure. To bring the pay rates of the lower ranks into line with those of the lowest classifications of the civil service, a large number of privates were elevated to the rank of corporal. Until this time, the rank of corporal consisted of two gradations: lance-corporal, the lower of the two, and corporal. The lance-corporal in the old army was the lowest but, in some ways, the most important command rank. A soldier was promoted to lance-corporal after mastering the appropriate junior leader skills. The lance-corporal was both leader and disciplinarian. In an infantry unit, he was the section leader. He commanded the eight or nine or ten men who formed the basic manoeuvring unit of an infantry battalion in combat. To the men in his section, the lance-corporal's leadership skills, tactical expertise, and experience under fire were a matter of life and death. The lance-corporal was also responsible for his section in barracks. He lived with them, kept tabs on them, helped them with their problems, and, when necessary, disciplined them.

When many of the privates became corporals in the late 1960s, the position of lance-corporal disappeared and the bottom of the rank structure was reorganized. Henceforth, privates became corporals automatically after four years of satisfactory service. But the rank of corporal ceased to be a command rank and became merely a pay classification. The former corporals were promoted to the rank of sergeant and, as sergeants, were the new section leaders. A new primary command rank entitled "master corporal" was created, which, like the old lance-corporal, could only be achieved through promotion. But although a master corporal had the power to lay charges and thus mete out discipline, and lived in the barracks with the other men, he was not section commander but second-in-command of the section. The sergeant was the person with the command authority in the section, but he lived apart from the men and could easily fall out of touch with them. There were many things that needed changing in the old army, but this was not one of them. At bottom, the maintenance of order and discipline rests on a commander's knowledge of his troops. That knowledge is crucial to his assessment of a disciplinary problem, in gauging, for example, whether harsh or moderate action is called for or whether advice and counselling will suffice. The introduction of the "Hellyer corporal," as the new, non-promotion corporal rank was dubbed, broke the chain of intimacy between a section leader and his men and made it more difficult to keep tabs on what was going on in the barracks.

In the early 1970s, inflation became a major problem for the Canadian army. As the rapidly rising cost of living chewed up the military's salaries, the government granted significant pay increases to the public service; military pay lagged far behind. Then, in October 1972, Ottawa gave the Armed Forces a major raise in pay. The immediate result was positive. Service personnel received increases averaging more than 11 per cent, and the exodus of skilled military technicians (including mechanics, computer programmers, paramedical personnel) to the private sector stopped. But because pay and rank were (and are) tied together, the long-term result was rank inflation.

Analysing the Canadian rank structure in the mid-1970s, British writer Patrick Esmonde-White declared that the Canadian military was "vastly overstaffed with officers. . . ."[9] That is even more true today. At the end of the 1960s, about 15 per cent of the military personnel in the Canadian Forces were officers; in 1995, that number had risen to 20 per cent. There are even more members in the higher ranks today than was the case a quarter-century ago.

RANKS AS A PERCENTAGE OF THE TOTAL ESTABLISHMENT

	c. 1970		*1995*
Col. & above	0.4		0.6
Lt.-Col.	1.0		1.7
Maj.	3.3		5.4
Capt.	6.4		8.9
Lieut.	3.9		3.5
CWO	1.0		1.2
MWO	3.0		3.3
WO	5.4		6.8
Sgt.	11.7		13.4
Cpl.[a]	20.0		
Pte. 1st Class[b]	22.6	Master Cpl.	15.7
Pte.[c]	21.3	Pte. & Cpl.	40.0

[a] The corporal of 1970 is the equivalent of the rank of sergeant in 1995.
[b] The private first class of 1970 is the equivalent of a master corporal in 1995.
[c] The private of 1970 is the equivalent of a private or a corporal in 1995.

In the Second World War, the Canadian Army in northwest Europe fielded some 240,000 officers and men. Commanding that force were a full general, two lieutenant-generals, and six major-generals. In 1995, Land Force Command (formerly Mobile Command) had one full general (the CDS), one lieutenant-general, and six major-generals to command a force less than one-tenth the size of the wartime complement. To some extent, the imbalance is deliberate: the current army is supposed to be the nucleus of a much expanded army in the event of national mobilization. And, in part, it is due to the government's insistence that the CDS be a full general, equivalent to an American four-star general, so that he will meet his counterparts in NATO and elsewhere on an equal basis. This rank-consciousness doesn't seem to bother our other allies, however. The Israel Defence Forces (which is a unified force of army, navy, and air force) numbers more than half a million soldiers and is headed by a chief of staff who holds the rank of lieutenant-general.

Two Canadian army officers writing in 1980 decried the growing tendency of government to treat the military as just another government organization and to apply to the military personnel policies developed for the civil service. "Our [personnel] policies must be directed toward eliminating the general idea that somehow our military forces are directly comparable to civilian counterparts in other sectors of our society."[10] That warning is still echoed in the ranks of the army today because it has not been heeded.

Of all the institutional changes that have taken place in the Canadian army over the last two or three decades, the impact of the Charter of Rights and Freedoms may well be the most controversial. Depending on the individual soldier's viewpoint, the Charter is either blamed or praised for just about all the non-institutional changes that the army has had to accept. In late 1992, for example, the Federal Court of Canada declared that those policies of the Canadian Forces that discriminate against homosexuals were contrary to the Charter and, therefore, illegal. The *Canadian Forces Personnel Newsletter* stated the matter succinctly, "While this decision may be difficult for some members to accept, the

CDS has clearly stated that revocation of the policy on homosexuality has his full support . . . attitudes and legislation have changed." The Canadian Forces now take the approach that any sort of inappropriate sexual activity between serving members, heterosexual or homosexual, is out of bounds. That is surely fair, even though it is unpopular with most members.

Another consequence of the Charter has been the movement of women into trades and specialties that were once the preserve of men. When the barriers to female participation in the combat arms were lifted in 1989, many traditionally minded soldiers complained vehemently that women would ruin unit cohesion and undermine *esprit de corps*. They argued that with women in the trenches, men's attention would be diverted from the task of killing the enemy to that of saving the lives – and honour – of female trenchmates. There is a great deal of grumbling and much snide comment from both NCOs and officers about women in the army, but the fact is that their presence in the combat arms is negligible. The standards for entrance to the battle school at CFB Gagetown were lowered when the "women in combat" policy was adopted, presumably to give female applicants a chance to get in the door. But, while numbers of women have applied for combat training, most have failed. Few women possess the physical capabilities needed for the combat trades; 83 per cent of the women who tried out for combat positions in 1993 were turned away. In all of Land Force Western Area in the summer of 1993, there were only 195 female soldiers, six of whom were in combat units. The Charter aims for equality of opportunity; it does not guarantee equality of output. So, women are entering navy and air force ranks in much larger numbers than before, but the army remains a male bastion by virtue of the nature of combat itself, a fact that is unlikely to change much in the years ahead.

To many long-serving soldiers, the Charter's most important – and most negative – impact on the army has been that soldiers are subject to the provisions protecting citizens from arbitrary policing measures such as illegal searches. Long-serving NCOs maintain that the Charter has undermined their ability to keep order in the ranks and that this is the root cause of the problem that emerged so dramatically in Somalia. A soldier's barracks box is inviolate now, runs the common complaint. A search warrant is required to open it just as one is needed to look inside a soldier's home. How can those responsible for discipline possibly operate under these constraints? How can a senior NCO know whether a soldier is hiding drugs, alcohol, or racist literature?

Another gripe heard often among senior NCOs and some junior officers is that NCOs or company commanders must have solid evidence and follow proper Charter procedures before laying a charge. This is true even in preparing for a summary trial – a trial on a minor charge that takes place in front of the accused's CO. In the pre-Charter days, summary trials were often a sham. The old joke is that a summary trial commenced when the CO's aide bellowed out, "Bring the guilty bastard in." That is no longer the case. The Charter does not allow charges to be laid in the absence of evidence that would hold up in court. Older soldiers claim that these changes make it easier for miscreants to avoid punishment and that discipline has suffered accordingly.

Not so, declares Maj. Anthony Thomas, who represents the Judge Advocate General at CFB Calgary. In his view, that's the argument made by "people who don't want to do things by the rules." He likens army complaints about the Charter to the complaints still heard from some police officers. But, says Thomas, "They [the police] are not in the business to get convictions, that is not how our criminal justice system works." In his view, the Charter "hasn't made any more difference in military justice than it has in justice downtown, in the criminal justice system as we know it." Thomas points out that the Charter would be worthless if it did not guarantee fundamental rights for all Canadians, in uniform or out.[11]

All Canadians are governed by one Constitution, one Charter of Rights, and one set of laws. But because the military is unique in form and function, the government in Canada (and in most countries) gives it the power to enforce additional laws and regulations for its members and to do so in a military way. The military justice system is, accordingly, a special body of regulations, procedures, and punishments that applies only to military personnel. It neither supplants nor exists in parallel with the Canadian criminal justice system. It adds additional constraints to it that are necessary for military life. Failing to show up for work, for example, may get a civilian employee fired from his job, but it is not a criminal offence. A soldier who fails to "show up for work," however, may endanger the lives of his or her trenchmates. Under certain circumstances, that can be considered desertion in the face of the enemy, which is, according to the Queen's Regulations and Orders, a serious criminal offence.

Because every aspect of Canadian criminal law applies also to the military, the Charter has not changed the basic application of military justice any more than it has justice in a civilian court. In fact, the courts do not question the need for a special system of justice operated by the military according to its own rules. For example, the convention by which a majority vote may be sufficient for a finding of guilty in a military court martial, rather than the unanimous vote that is required in a civil criminal proceeding, is not considered a Charter violation. No less an authority than the Supreme Court of Canada decided in 1992 that "recourse to the ordinary criminal courts would, as a general rule, be inadequate to serve the particular disciplinary needs of the military. There is thus a need for separate tribunals to enforce disciplinary standards in the military."

No doubt the Charter makes the imposition of punishment more difficult in the military now than it was before. It is also quite true that punishment is the ultimate means of enforcing military discipline. But experienced soldiers know that the threat, let alone the use, of punishment is always a last resort. They know that the constant recourse to punishment probably points as much to a failure of leadership as to an ingrained disciplinary problem. "There are no bad soldiers, there are only bad officers" is a commonly heard military adage. And this was as true in the old army as it is in the new. The former (now retired) commander of Mobile Command, Lt.-Gen. Kent Foster, believes that laying the blame for bad discipline at the door of the Charter "is a mind-set." Foster's approach as commander was that "if you tell me you can't do something [because of the Charter], you've got my attention."[12]

To what extent is discipline the key factor in the maintenance of good order and morale? Does the harshness of discipline determine an army's performance in combat, let alone in the barracks? Those old army men who argue that the Charter has eroded discipline by making it more difficult to mete out punishment ought to consider this: In the Second World War, the German soldier fought with great skill and tenacity. At the same time, discipline in the German army was brutal. More than forty thousand German soldiers were executed for desertion or for alleged cowardice in the face of the enemy. As far as the *Wehrmacht* was concerned, Frederick the Great of Prussia (1712-1786) had it right when he declared that soldiers ought to fear their officers more than they fear the enemy. On the other hand, the Israeli soldier has also fought with great skill and tenacity in more than four conventional wars since 1948. No Israeli soldier has ever been executed for desertion or cowardice in the face of the enemy.

Soldiers fight well, and deport themselves well in peacetime, under a variety of disciplinary regimes. The Israeli soldier lives in a democracy and fights to protect his family and his society, who are, quite literally, not far behind the front lines. The *Wehrmacht* soldier was far from home (most of the time) and was quite aware of the brutality of the regime he fought for and the harshness of its discipline. It is, therefore, much too simple to blame disciplinary problems in the Canadian army on the Charter of Rights and Freedoms. In a democracy with an all-volunteer force such as Canada, and with better-educated, healthier, more affluent, and more aware recruits entering the army, how can the somewhat harder, though certainly more arbitrary, discipline of a bygone era possibly be revived? Why should it be?

Canada is not the only country whose army has had to cope with major social and political change in the last quarter-century. Other armies have faced (and are facing) similar challenges. In his book *Inside the British Army*, Anthony Beevor analysed and explained the major societal changes that have impacted on one of the world's oldest and most tradition-bound fighting forces. In the British army, values, practices, rituals, and beliefs that are centuries old are being undermined by television, by affluence, by new attitudes of individualism and personal liberty. The British army is adapting in some ways – more openness to women in the military, more recognition of the importance of not making a soldier choose between the army and his family – but not in others. There are still major changes to come not just because of post-Cold War budget cuts but because the new recruit is better educated, more world-wise, more affluent, and less enamoured of his elders than earlier British recruits have been.[13] Australia is also witnessing important changes in its military culture. That nation's growing pluralism, its feminist revolution, the greater recognition of human rights in Australian society (which has no formal charter or bill of rights), and the increased sophistication of the nation's occupational structure have all helped drive change in the military. At heart, Australia is becoming a "rights-driven society like the United States and Canada, and the military must follow suit."[14]

Even in Israel, the army faces different social attitudes than in the past and is being forced to rethink and restructure many concepts it once held inviolate. Two decades of runaway inflation in the 1970s and 1980s forced Israeli governments to make drastic budget cuts – the once sacrosanct defence budget has been chopped and chopped again. As former Israeli chief of staff Lt.-Gen. Ehud said, "What does not shoot must be cut." Cutting a defence budget in Israel, however, is not simply an economic measure, it constitutes a near-ideological revolution and, indeed, there has been a major change in the public's attitude towards the Israeli army and military service. More young men are less willing to serve, the army is increasingly looked upon as just another branch of government, even the most gentle army meddling in Israeli politics is now deeply resented. In the words of Israeli defence analyst Stuart A. Cohen, the Israeli army is now "operating in a significantly less sympathetic domestic environment" and is "beginning to forge a new persona" more in tune with the times.[15]

There is a widely held view inside the Canadian army, and among soldiers who have recently served and some military analysts, that the changes that have marked the transition from old to new army have been mostly bad, especially those stemming from the Charter. The common theme of their complaint is that a nation like Canada that extols human rights ought to, at least in part, exempt the military from having to live up to the same norms that govern everyone else. Why? So that the military can continue to expect and enforce that degree of discipline they claim is necessary for its unique job.

Put another way, men and women in civilian society have jobs; men and women in the military have a vocation that may ultimately demand of them that they be killed. In the words of the Reverend Arthur E. Gans, a retired major and former Canadian Forces chaplain, "If the military is . . . a vocation, a calling, then, I believe, it is fair to say that those who join must live at a higher standard than that expected by the outside society. They may even have to give up certain 'rights' which the civilian society enjoys."[16] Nick Stethem, a Canadian military and international affairs analyst, has similar views. "Effective combat forces and the forces of political correctness may be able to coexist as they have in the past. But there is no way on earth that they can actually live together."[17]

Maj.-Gen. Thomas de Faye is one senior Canadian army officer who doesn't agree with these views. De Faye has had experience in both command and staff positions and is a past commandant of the Canadian Land Force Staff College in Kingston, Ontario. In 1993, he was named to head up the board of inquiry into the conduct of the Canadian Airborne Regiment Battle Group in Somalia. De Faye sees no contradiction between good order and discipline in a modern army and civil rights. In his view, it is a question of good leadership. "We are dealing with people who have decided to join the army," he says. "Our job is to instil self-discipline in them. We do need to use minor punishment, but the ideal state is to get the soldiers to follow the rules because they believe in them." Once the army has succeeded in instilling self-discipline in a recruit, de Faye believes, collective discipline follows automatically.[18]

"I support the changes that have taken place," one NDHQ staff officer recently declared. "They are making for a better, more representative, more intelligent army." Possibly so, but that is not the point. Whether or not he supports change, change has happened, and it isn't over yet. The old army is gone forever. Whether the army likes it or not, Canada is now a rights-driven society, and Canadian youth are both better educated and more aware of their rights, and more aware of the world around them. If the leaders of the Canadian army are in tune with the changing times, Canadian soldiers will continue to be able to perform their various missions with the same degree of effectiveness in the future as they have in the past. That is the biggest obstacle that the leaders of the new Canadian army face. As de Faye says, "This is the most difficult era to exercise military leadership than any in the past . . . the challenge to the Canadian army is to institutionally, collectively, recognize and deal with that."[19]

De Faye is right, of course, but there is more. The challenge facing the Canadian army is to meet the new social and economic realities of Canadian society today, while maintaining tried and true soldierly virtues that have sustained effective fighting forces throughout history.

PART TWO

CANADA'S SOLDIERS NOW

In wartime, armies and soldiers have a well-defined role, and there is little need to ponder the nature of good soldiering or effective military leadership. The answers usually become evident when battle is joined. It is much more difficult to lead, and be part of, a peacetime army, especially in a democracy and particularly in a country like Canada, where ignorance of military affairs is pervasive.

It is not easy to maintain an effective all-volunteer army in peacetime. There is no single cause to motivate volunteers. To attract and keep good soldiers, Canada's army must provide the mental and physical challenges that aspiring soldiers look for while providing them with an acceptable standard of living in a supportive environment for their families.

The best soldiers in the world cannot make an efficient, confident, proficient army without effective leadership. But what is effective leadership in a peacetime army? The officer corps in the Canadian army is today torn between those who think of themselves primarily as personnel managers and those who strongly believe that their ultimate responsibility is to prepare soldiers for war.

In Bosnia, Canada's soldiers proved their mettle, but they were all but ignored back home. Canada's soldiers are not failing their army or their nation; their nation and their army is failing them.

4

THE CANADIAN ARMY

THE end of the Cold War marked the beginning of yet another period of transformation. Since the early 1950s, Canada's military planning had been focused on northern Europe. The Canadian army had been structured, equipped, trained, and located to fight a major all-arms battle alongside Canada's NATO allies against the Soviet army. The army's other activities, from peacekeeping in Cyprus or the Middle East to patrolling the streets of Montreal during the FLQ kidnappings of 1970, had been, relatively speaking, minor assignments. Virtually overnight the possibility of a war in Europe – as remote as it was – disappeared. In the first half of this decade, therefore, the government, the Canadian Forces, and the army have been forced to rethink, reformulate, and restructure the army's basic mission and role. The job has been made more difficult by the need to institute deep government spending cuts to halt runaway deficits; as usual, the Canadian Forces have been front and centre for the chop. Now, more than at any time since Korea, the army needs the best possible leadership at all ranks. It has not been getting it.

At the end of 1995, Land Force Command consisted of some 21,533 regular force troops and an additional 21,556 primary reserves, i.e., militia. The regular and reserve forces are supposed to complement each other in such a way that they can be combined into a "total force" when necessary. As former commander of Land Force Command, Lt.-Gen. J. C. Gervais said in 1992, "Sufficient resources do not exist to meet the number and scope of current and potential defence commitments with regular troops only; reservists are also needed and have a vital role to play." Consequently, reserve and regular force structures are integrated, and regular units sent abroad on operations now frequently contain reservists. The men and women of the militia, whose normal training consists mainly of weekend drills and summer exercises, are given about three months of additional training before they are attached to the regular units. Once brought up to standard, however, they have proven the equal of their regular force counterparts. In Canada, reservists cannot be "called up" (as reservists in the United States may be) when needed for operations. They must volunteer of their own accord and make their own arrangements for time off from jobs or school.

Land Force Command is located at St-Hubert, near Montreal, but due to be moved to Ottawa (along with the other commands) as a cost-saving measure in the summer of 1996. It is responsible for four Area Commands and 1 Canadian Division Headquarters. The Area Commands – Western, Central (Ontario), Quebec, and Atlantic – are the regional command centres for all the regular and militia land force units in their areas, including training establishments. 1 Canadian Division HQ, located at Kingston, Ontario, is a tactical headquarters-in-waiting; in the event that Canada's regular force combat units are mobilized together, they will operate under its command.

The core of the army today is the regular force combat units of the infantry, armour, artillery, and combat engineers, together with supporting units such as the military police, service battalions, and medical units. On paper, they appear to be a reasonable force for a nation of this size. The infantry component consists of the 1st, 2nd, and 3rd Battalions of the Royal 22e Régiment, the Royal Canadian Regiment, and the Princess Patricia's Canadian Light Infantry. The regular force armoured units are the Lord Strathcona's Horse (Royal Canadians), the Royal Canadian Dragoons, and the 12e Régiment blindé du Canada. There are three artillery regiments: the 1st and 2nd Regiments of the Royal Canadian Horse Artillery and the 5e Régiment d'artillerie légère du Canada. These elements, plus combat engineers and other units, are organized into 1st and 2nd Canadian Mechanized Brigade Groups, and 5e Brigade mécanise du Canada. The other major concentration of regular force troops is the Combat Training Centre located at CFB Gagetown, New Brunswick. Until Canada's withdrawal from Europe, there was also a 4th

Canadian Mechanized Brigade Group, with headquarters at Lahr, Germany. That has been disbanded.

The ending of Canada's on-the-ground commitment to NATO coincided with a reduction of Land Force Command strength from 23,500 at the start of the 1990s to its current strength as well as the depletion of a number of regular force units. The regular force was supposed to be reduced further to some 20,500, but in the 1994 Defence white paper, the government announced its intention of increasing the regular force by 3,000 and paying for that expansion largely out of savings realized from the closure of bases across Canada.

Although Canada no longer has troops based in Europe, it remains a member of NATO and is committed to "flying over" a brigade group in the event of an emergency. The other two brigade groups are supposed to operate with American forces in defence of North America as part of the Canada–United States Basic Security Plan. In addition to these commitments, three reinforced battalions (battalion groups) are tasked as additional standing commitments to NATO, to the Canada–U.S. Basic Security Plan, and to the UN.

The army's hardware is mostly obsolete or on the verge of obsolescence. The 114 Leopard C-1 tanks are approaching the end of their service lives. Even upgraded as they have been, they are at least one generation behind the latest main battle tanks built and operated by the United States, Germany, Britain, France, Russia, and even Israel. They will probably not be replaced; when they are retired, the Canadian army's current armoured regiments will become something else. The army also has some sixteen hundred light armoured vehicles, reconnaissance vehicles, and tracked and wheeled armoured personnel carriers (APC). The largest contingent is the 1960s-era M-113. This vehicle has been upgraded considerably and has proved useful in operations in the former Yugoslavia, but even if further refurbished with strengthened armour (as the government recently announced it will do with several hundred), the M-113 is very old kit. Towards the end of 1995, the government announced that it would purchase 240 new APCs with options on another 291. The new APC, to be supplied by the diesel division of General Motors, is a wheeled vehicle and was the least expensive of the off-the-shelf models under consideration. The army's artillery capability consists of some 460 tubes varying from pack howitzers to the M-109, a self-propelled 155-mm howitzer. One recent army memo described these weapons as "on the down side of the curve." In addition, the army has a variety of anti-tank and anti-aircraft defence weapons systems; some are relatively up-to-date.

Canadian soldiers are somewhat better equipped when it comes to small arms. The Canadian-built C-7A1 assault rifle, equipped with a three-power optical sight, is a much improved version of the American M-16. It is as good as any rifle in the world. So, too, is the C-9 light machine gun, a Belgian-built weapon. The C-6 general-purpose machine gun is old, but reliable and very accurate. The Second World War-era Browning .5-calibre heavy machine gun is still in use, but there are only sixteen hundred in the entire Canadian army. Shortages are the rule of thumb for crucial items such as night-imaging equipment, flak jackets, and Kevlar helmets (currently in use on operations only).

The Canadian army does not have a single major piece of equipment that is first line, first generation, or completely up-to-date. Nor is it likely to get any. In a memo written after his take-over of Land Force Command in 1993, Lt.-Gen. G. M. Reay told high-ranking officers, "My projects, which are not deemed to be sexy, always seem to provoke debate and delay. Put another way, we never seem to argue if we should have fighters or frigates, we argue only over the type to acquire. Yet I find myself more often than I should defending the very notion that the Land Force should have infantry and armoured fighting vehicles."[1]

Canadian soldiers have been "making do" with old and obsolete equipment for a long time now; keeping the old stuff running has become a source of pride. Despite its outdated equipment and scarce personnel, the Canadian army took part in, and excelled at, a large number of peacekeeping operations in the first half of the 1990s, sometimes under very difficult and dangerous conditions. Contrary to popular belief, Canadian troops did a generally superb job under trying conditions in Somalia. But when Canada was called upon by its allies to participate in a real war, obsolescence and undermanning forced Ottawa to relegate the army to the sidelines.

In the fall of 1990, Britain, and then the United States, sounded out the Canadian government about contributing a mechanized brigade group to Saudi Arabia to take part in Operation Desert Shield (and the subsequent Desert Storm). NDHQ and Land Force Command began to plan for the possibility of sending the 4th Canadian Mechanized Brigade from Germany, augmented by troops from Canada, to be attached as a reserve to the American 1st Armoured Division. Canada's tanks and troop carriers were too old to take part in the initial assault on Iraq, but were thought to be acceptable as a mop-up force. After some months of cogitating, the government turned down the request. Canadian military historian Sean Maloney believes that the failure to send troops "highlighted some of the structural weaknesses that have existed in the Canadian army since 1970." He points particularly to the virtual disappearance of the militia in the 1960s, the failure to maintain Canada's brigade groups at full strength, and the undermanning of Canada's infantry battalions as the basic cause. Lack of sufficient manpower reserves virtually ensured there would be too few reinforcements in the event the Canadian brigade sustained heavy casualties.[2] Considering that the army has about the same number of regular force troops today as it did in the fall of 1990, it is difficult to see how a similar request from Canada's allies could be met in a different way now. CDS Gen. Jean Boyle said as much in early 1996 when he declared that the Canadian army is just not battle-ready.

Some Canadians no doubt would just as soon keep their military forces as far from a real battlefield as possible. They ignore the hard reality that all international relations, including trade, rest on a foundation of military power. Canada does not have now, never has had, and probably never will have the capacity to fight wars on its own. But Canada gained its independence from Britain, its membership in the UN and other international organizations, and its entrée into innumerable foreign markets because of its participation in coalition wars and its troop commitments to NATO, the UN, etc. If Canada stops paying its dues, it won't be allowed into the clubs it must belong to. No one respects a freeloader.

In early 1994, Reay issued a summary of the army's capabilities, intentions, and requirements as it headed towards the next century. The trend was away from Europe, towards force generation (rather than the maintenance of standing forces), and towards a more efficient total force structure. The army would be able to "undertake a wide range of tasks in support of national interests," Reay observed, but "the flexibility it offers to Government is constrained by its level of personnel resources, by the growing obsolescence of several core equipment capabilities and by the impact of fiscal restraint on its ability to train."[3]

Reay's warning may have had some impact on the government's defence policy. Against a background of growing operational commitments, the Department of National Defence issued a new white paper in 1994, laying out the government's plans for the Canadian Forces for the next half-decade or so. The department is going to attempt to reduce the "tooth-to-tail" ratio in the Canadian army by eliminating overlap and duplication in command structures and by increasing the combat arms by three thousand regular force soldiers. In April 1995, Reay announced his intention to use these new troops to bring existing infantry, armoured corps, and artillery regiments up to previously authorized strength levels.

This increase will barely restore the army's fighting forces to where they were before the pull-out from Germany. When asked to make a contribution to NATO's peace implementation force in Bosnia (IFOR), Canada could raise only one thousand troops. Evan Potter, editor of *Canadian Foreign Policy Magazine*, told the press in January 1996 that "because of reduced budgets, we haven't been able to maintain even a minimal level of preparedness." He thinks the government is turning Canada's military into a glorified constabulary.

Who joins Canada's army and why? Cpl. Tracy Meisner Coulter, a member of the anti-tank (TOW) troop of the Lord Strathcona's Horse (Royal Canadians) is from Nova Scotia. Her older sister was driving a truck for the army when her younger sister decided to join too. So Meisner Coulter went to Halifax to help her sister enlist. She had no plans to go to college and had not yet decided what she wanted to do, so she also joined.[4] Jacques Painchaud, former regimental commander of the Canadian Airborne Regiment, was born in Quebec City in 1935. He loved the idea of soldiering, especially with Quebec's Van Doos. In fact, his allegiance is primarily to the regiment. "When I joined the army, I joined the Van Doos," he says. He relished the personal challenge of the army and hoped he'd have a chance to prove himself in combat.[5] Jim Cox, former commander of 1st Canadian Mechanized Brigade Group, had a friend in the militia when he was a teenager. One evening when young Jim and his dad were heading to a baseball game, he saw his friend in full regalia. Shortly after, Cox joined the cadets. He considers himself lucky to have discovered his calling right away.[6] Master Warrant Officer Don Thomas of the Combat Engineers was born in New Brunswick to a military family. As a child, he heard stories about the exploits of the family's young men in the two world wars. "The Maritimes looks at the military more as a home thing," he says. It was natural to join.[7]

In peacetime, people join the army as a career, for adventure, and out of a sense of service. A recent survey of Canadian recruits by the Canadian Forces Personnel Applied Research Unit (CFPARU) found that applicants listed "challenging work" as the most important motivating factor. Career advancement was second, and the opportunity to learn a trade was third. Also listed were the chance to hold down a responsible job, opportunities for fellowship and job security, and a chance to serve their country. Applicants for the Canadian Forces today are usually between seventeen and twenty-four years of age and still mainly of British or French stock, as they were twenty years ago. Other ethnic groups are vastly under-represented. More applicants are bilingual than is the bilingual proportion of the population.

The lack of non-British or French-origin soldiers in the Canadian army has been a constant in recruiting for some time. The Canadian Forces regular force does not reflect the Canadian cultural mosaic. Italians, Chinese, blacks, and migrants from southern Asia are especially under-represented.[8] This is an undoubted problem. Ethnic, racial, and religious bias emerges much more quickly and openly in a homogeneous group than in one that contains a cross-section of the population. Even so, the Canadian Forces did not see the need to take any special measures to combat racism in its ranks until after the Somalia incidents of 1993. The army believed that existing sections of the National Defence Act and the Queen's Regulations and Orders would deal with any problems. They didn't.

"New" Canadians are a growing political force in Canada, especially as the large number of immigrants admitted into Canada in the late 1980s and early 1990s take up citizenship. To most of these people, the Canadian military is an unknown, if not an alien, force. Many come from non-democratic societies where the military either runs the local dictatorship or supports it. How can the Canadian Forces hope to find a sympathetic constituency, for example, among Chilean refugees whose family members may have been tortured or murdered by the Chilean army in the 1970s, unless it makes a special effort to do so?

The Canadian Forces are receiving more female applicants than ever before. Some 20 per cent of all applicants are women, but women have not been particularly successful in surviving the initial stages of the recruitment process. Most applicants, male or female, are either in school or unemployed, which is not surprising considering the age at which they approach the recruiting office. They are overwhelmingly urban. On the whole, they are much better educated than they used to be, but they are still not on a par with the equivalent age group within the general population. One recent Canadian Forces study concluded, "The socio-demographic composition of the CF applicant pool tends to be relatively narrow, representing primarily young, urbanized, secondary school educated males with British or French ethnic backgrounds."9 Some 60 per cent of the applicants who survive initial screening to become recruits either come from military families or have had some military experience (as cadets or in the militia), or both.

A transformation of sorts has taken place in Canadian military culture; it is no longer considered seemly for a soldier to be overweight or sedentary. Today's Canadian soldiers are generally fitter and healthier than those of a generation ago. They are smoking and drinking far less, and they are getting more exercise. Virtually everyone tries to stay trim; physical conditioning has become a measure of a soldier's commitment to the military vocation. Drinking in the mess after duty is increasingly rare. So is non-medical use of drugs. A recent survey by the Surgeon

General Branch reported that "most behaviours have changed for the better since 1989." This is due largely to changing societal trends, a better-educated soldier, and the increasing effectiveness of new Canadian Forces health and fitness programs. Today, because the Canadian Forces are less willing to tolerate it, alcohol counselling is no longer as widely available as it once was, and continuing alcohol abuse is likely to lead to dismissal after only one or two warnings. Even so, alcohol remains a problem.[10]

Why do soldiers leave the Canadian Forces? Younger soldiers leave to return to school, to earn more money, to seek a different type of job, or because they feel themselves "undervalued in society."[11] But the most common reason given by both younger and older soldiers is the lack of a stable family life. Soldiers feel that they are away from home too much and that they miss the opportunity to put down roots in a single community. It isn't surprising that they feel this way; the few soldiers in the Canadian army who are actually combat-capable shoulder a disproportionate burden of what Ottawa thinks the military should be doing. Put simply, there are too few men and women in the front lines, and their family life is suffering as never before in peacetime.

Our soldiers too frequently find themselves returning from a six-month posting overseas only to be sent across the country to take or teach a course, or for any of a dozen different reasons, with scarcely an interval in which to unpack their bags. In recent years, such "over-tasking" has emerged as a major factor undermining morale. Over-tasking exacerbates the continuing conflict between family obligations and a military career, a conflict that was largely ignored in times past because a soldier was thought to be "married" to the army. But no more. Today, reconciling family and army is, without doubt, the largest social problem the Canadian army faces.

It may strike many people as just common sense that worries about spouse and family back home are likely to affect a corporal's steadiness when defusing mines in Bosnia, but it has taken military establishments all over the world, including the Canadian Forces, some time to figure it out. The CF now recognize that a soldier's physical and emotional well-being have an important bearing on his or her ability to do the job. The

Canadian soldier and his or her family can now call on a wide range of counselling services aimed at alleviating stress caused by marital discord, excessive drinking, separations due to service taskings, financial difficulties, and parent-child conflicts. But while these services are more than ever in demand, there are still many soldiers who refuse to use them. The higher in rank a soldier is, the less likely he or she will seek assistance. Many unit commanders still perceive psychological problems as a weakness that might be discovered by subordinates, undermining authority. But the major obstacle to the use of these services is the widespread belief among soldiers that any "blemish" on their record will result in their dismissal. The fear is understandable when "downsizing" has become the norm; who better to downsize than someone who has problems? In a recent confidential report, one army colonel wrote, "Our people are now hiding personal, family, administrative and health problems that could even remotely lead to their release." More soldiers are going off base to civilian doctors so that any "problems" will not be recorded in their personnel records.[12]

Problems with family life, difficulties with career management systems, complaints about poor equipment, and gripes about officers and NCOs (and gripes from officers and NCOs about the ranks) are a normal part of army life. When soldiers believe that their leaders, both governmental and military, care about them and appreciate their sacrifices, the complaints mean little. But that is not the case in the Canadian Forces today. A recent survey showed that fewer than 15 per cent of the civilian employees of the Department of National Defence and just 17 per cent of the soldiers are confident that the senior officers and politicians have what it takes to bring the Canadian Forces through the current crises of budget and confidence. That is a bad sign; if the soldiers do not believe in the integrity or ability of their commanders, the morale of the entire force will be undermined and its effectiveness destroyed.

The process started with the fusion of civilian and military functions in NDHQ and continued through a generation of budget cuts and force reductions. As the army shrank, opportunities to command larger units such as brigades, and to advance to the highest ranks through the combat arms, also shrank. Getting ahead increasingly meant honing bureaucratic and administrative skills instead of command abilities. The process has been made worse by Canada's withdrawal of troops from Europe. There, at least, Canadian army officers got a chance to work at NATO divisional and corps headquarters and to gain higher command experience. Today the army is over-managed and over-administered. With a few exceptions, soldiers who want to get ahead had better learn how to fit in with the military bureaucracy or resign themselves to staying at the field-grade rank forever.

It is hardly surprising, in these circumstances, that both the civilian and military members of the Department of National Defence (DND) have so little faith in the integrity and ability of the high command. They have come to believe that their leaders are building empires, following personal agendas, and developing too bureaucratic an outlook. They think there is too much talk about management and not enough about leadership. They think that civilians have too great a say in running the military and that there are too many generals and not enough soldiers. According to the survey, most serving members do not understand the department's changing mandate. There is a great deal of stress in their units. They are embarrassed by the negative publicity the Canadian Forces have received, especially following the murder at Belet Huen and the other revelations about the Canadian Airborne Regiment. They do not believe the public has much respect for the military. At the same time, the commitment of the soldiers to soldiering and the military as a vocation seems as strong as ever.

The majority (69 per cent) of Canada's soldiers today are "committed to DND as more than just a place to work." And 83 per cent are proud of the military's involvement in peacekeeping operations. Despite all their anxiety, the practical problems, and the lack of confidence in their leaders, some 62 per cent of military members believe they are "contributing to something important."[13] The majority of the men and women who make up the companies of infantry, the squadrons of armour, and the batteries of artillery still have confidence in themselves. It is the people at the top they're worried about.

Brig.-Gen. Roger Bazin (ret'd) was Roman Catholic chaplain general of the Canadian Forces until his retirement at the end of July 1995. Like all other chaplains in the Canadian Forces – they are more commonly referred to by the soldiers as padres – he served two masters: the army and the Church. He is disturbed by the trends and tendencies that have emerged among his charges in the last few years. Canadian soldiers have witnessed atrocities abroad, including the nearly genocidal slaughter in Rwanda and the torture and massacre of thousands of people in Bosnia, that are immeasurably more disturbing than what they saw in Cyprus or Germany. Family breakup is becoming more common than it used to be as stress levels increase among the soldiers. Bazin knows that some people in the army are saying morale is neither better nor worse than it's been for some time, but he believes that the chaplains are "more in touch" with what's going on and know better.[14]

If Bazin is right about the chaplains being in touch, then morale is, without doubt, a major problem in the army today. A Protestant chaplain at CFB Petawawa reported in April 1995 that "it has been a testing time for the morale of our army. . . . The stress levels within the ranks, the leadership and throughout the support agencies . . . is at an all time high." Maj. G. W. Scharf, senior chaplain for the 2nd Canadian Mechanized Brigade Group at Petawawa, told his superiors in early May 1995 that "the Chaplains at CFB Petawawa are getting burned out, largely due to cumulative stress . . . the troops are exhausted and their families are tired. The troops are continually going away, coming back and training to go again."[15]

This perception is shared by the Forces' command chaplains. Roman Catholic command chaplain Lt.-Col. Murray C. Farwell, for example, reported to the chaplain general's office in February 1995 that "people feel a frustration in most areas of every day life connected to the CF. The ordinary soldier has the impression that no one is looking out for his interest. Too many levels of command dilutes responsibility and accountability. Some of our most highly trained and motivated people are leaving the CF. This fact in itself is demoralizing for those who remain."[16]

Bazin's report on the state of morale in the Canadian Forces at the end of March 1995 stressed the crisis of confidence in leadership. "Le sérieux problème de moral dans les Forces canadiennes est mentione par tous les Aumoniers de commandement et . . . ils en identifient certaines causes: (a) le manque de confiance dans le leadership. . . ."[17] Bazin's beliefs are supported by one colonel of Land Force Central Area, who reported at the end of 1994, "[The soldiers] have lost confidence in the leadership and 'the system' that were heretofore sworn to protect them. The federal government, once their benevolent employer, has become to them a predator of wages and jobs but an increasingly voracious consumer of their energies." In his view, the continuing failure to reform the PER system "in spite of near universal complaint serves as one more cause for the loss of confidence and feelings of helplessness over an increasingly impotent military leadership and uncaring system."[18] "The Canadian Forces is becoming more and more like a big business," Bazin says. "Soon it won't be the Canadian Forces we knew for the last fifty years. Tradition is the soul of the Armed Forces, and I am afraid that we will lose the soul that makes it a living entity and become like Bell Canada."

That is the problem in a nutshell; the Canadian army today is a force divided against itself. Some of Canada's soldiers see themselves as managers and employees making a career in the military that would not be dissimilar to a career at IBM. Others join the military in the belief that soldiers are different, and special, and have a mission that cannot be defined in civilian terms. All peacetime armies face this problem in some degree, but it is particularly acute in Canada. Canadians as a whole know little or nothing about the importance of the military in the development of their nation, and few regard the application of military force by the Canadian government as necessary or even proper in any but the most extreme circumstances. Put simply, Canadians do not know what an army is for and are not sure they ought to have one.

In the United States and other countries with a realistic appreciation of the role military power plays in the pursuit of national interests, the military bureaucrats are usually contained by the warriors. It is the warriors who run things, because an army is for war. But in the Canadian army, the warriors are a beleaguered minority, merely a small part of what the government calls "the defence team." And they are more often "managed" as part of the team than commanded by other warriors. Within the Canadian military, the managers and the warriors are locked in a struggle for the hearts and minds of the soldiers, and the warriors are losing. It is, however, the warriors who know from history, and from their own sense of professional pride, that the principle of unlimited liability must lie at the centre of what soldiers do, or the army will lose both its direction and its soul. Effective military leadership and a moral and responsible armed force can be based only on the unremitting reaffirmation that armies exist to fight wars.

Maj.-Gen. Thomas de Faye agrees there is a "crisis of leadership" in the Canadian Forces today. He is uncertain whether that crisis is based on the actual failings of CF commanders or on a perception held by many members (a perception, he stresses, that could be wrong) that commanders are failing the troops. But then, as he admits, "perceptions are reality." That does not mean, de Faye points out, that "we don't have absolutely first-class leaders in the Forces."[19] That is, without doubt, true. The Canadian Forces devote considerable time, talent, and treasure to select, train, educate, and promote the best commanders available. In fact, excellent commanders can be found at all levels. What then, constitutes the elements of this crisis that de Faye and others speak of? It is a crisis of values, not of ability.

Militaries in all countries believe that soldierly values are ultimately instilled through training. That is why training invariably combines the teaching of fieldcraft, weaponry, small-unit tactics, etc., with the indoctrination of a specific military culture. In dictatorships, that indoctrination almost always flows from the desire of the rulers to instil a particular political viewpoint into young recruits, especially officer candidates. In democracies, the values taught are more apt to be informed by liberal-democratic notions. It is common to virtually all militaries, however, to teach a "military way" that is basic to everything else a soldier will learn.

In March 1993, Lt.-Gen. G. M. Reay, who had then just taken over from J. C. Gervais as commander of Land Force Command, sent a "state of the army" message to his subordinates. He warned that shrinking resources were having a severe impact on the army in several areas and most particularly training. "The sheer size of our current commitments is eroding our ... training and our training standards. This is acceptable in the short term but must be carefully scrutinized in the months to come. Collective training and all-arms cooperation are suffering."

An army's most important task in the absence of war is to train for war. An army that cannot provide its soldiers with the best training is an army that is needlessly jeopardizing their lives. Gen. Matthew B. Ridgeway, who succeeded Douglas MacArthur as commander of UN troops in Korea in 1951, wrote, "Good training should help a soldier get rid of the awful sense of aloneness that can sometimes overtake a man in battle, the feeling that nobody gives a damn about him."[20] The burden of proof for ensuring that the training is as good as it can be lies with the high command and those soldiers, from NCOs to company commanders, who run the training establishments. As former U.S. army chief of staff Gen. Carl Vuono said, "Poor training kills soldiers. . . . If the American Army is not well trained, you can't blame it on Congress, you can't blame it on the media, you can't blame it on the mythical 'they.' It's your fault, your fault, your fault and my fault because we didn't do our job."[21] Vuono and the U.S. army learned that lesson the hard way by sending hundreds of thousands of poorly trained and badly prepared soldiers to Vietnam in the 1960s and 1970s.

When most Canadian army recruit training was removed from the regimental depots following unification, it was centralized at CFB Cornwallis. After Cornwallis was closed as a training base, recruit training was decentralized to CFBs Petawawa, Valcartier, and Wainwright. Officer basic training was carried out at CFB Chilliwack, home of the Combat Engineers, but is now located at CFB Gagetown. This basic training is intended to acclimatize the new soldier or officer to life in the army and teach basic fieldcraft, weaponry, comportment, procedures, military law, and other fundamental subjects. Physical hazing or persecution of new recruits is not tolerated officially, although it still goes on "behind the barracks." The Canadian army believes, rightly, that the secret of successful training is to train a soldier hard and honestly. As

Col. Ian Fraser, onetime regimental commander of the Canadian Airborne Regiment, said, "Make the training tough, and make it challenging. Apply the traditional methods that have served us well for so long, give soldiers a feeling of accomplishment, and remember, for everyone that falls by the wayside, those that remain become stronger. The tougher the discipline and the harder the work is, the better your people respond."[22]

The combat arms have their own training facilities for advanced preparation beyond basic training. Most of the training is done at the Combat Training Centre at CFB Gagetown. Artillery basic training is taught at CFB Shilo. Combined arms training and major field exercises are held at Gagetown and Wainwright. Sometimes units are sent to the United States and elsewhere to train with other troops now that Canadians no longer take part in NATO field exercises in Germany.

There are several different ways that men and women can become commissioned officers in the Canadian Forces, ranging from the successful completion of a program of study and training at Royal Military College, Kingston, to commissioning directly from the ranks. No matter what route is chosen, basic officer training involves classroom study of subjects such as military history and basic logistics, as well as field exercises. The purpose is threefold: to "socialize" the prospective officer; to impart basic leadership and administrative skills; and to impart basic fieldcraft.

Maj. Romas Blekaitis is chief instructor at the Infantry School at the Combat Training Centre in CFB Gagetown. He has noticed a difference in the men and women he trains now, compared to those he saw just a few years back. "There is more of the 'me' generation coming through at the junior ranks. We have to turn it around. We have to teach service over self."[23] All recruit and basic NCO and officer training puts a heavy emphasis on socialization, that is, getting the recruit to absorb the military way of doing things and especially the ethos of the professional officer. There is evidence, however, that the process doesn't really work. Studies done both in the United States and Canada show that the extent to which a young officer embraces military values seems to be unrelated to the intensity of the socialization he or she receives. Officer candidates who attended four years of RMC, for example, where they were almost totally immersed in a military atmosphere, showed no greater affinity for the military way of life than those who had attended a civilian university on the ROTP (Regular Officer Training Plan).

The flip side to this finding is that the socialization process does not have a major impact on the development of fundamental attitudes and values in junior officers. One expert who studied this problem in the early 1980s concluded that the military ought not to be too confident about the extent to which it could influence the thinking of officer candidates. "While surface behaviours may change, it is doubtful that organization socialization can be credited for major attitude change."[24] Put simply, the attitudes and values that a candidate brings to officer training are far more important in determining the degree to which he or she will embrace the military ethos than any socialization he or she will be subject to at Gagetown or elsewhere.

And why not? Those who enter the military in Canada are not coming from the moon. They are modern Canadians, as much as the men and women who become tax accountants or carpenters. The military cannot hope to select as officers men and women whose opinions about the military and society, soldiering, discipline, and human rights reflect the conventional wisdom of the 1940s. Even if they did, their recruits would be so out of touch with the soldiers they are supposed to lead that they would be completely ineffective as leaders. The challenge, then, is to cultivate a military ethos that reflects the age-old traditions of unlimited liability and today's mainstream values and mores. In these circumstances, selection – choosing who is most likely to have the qualities necessary for effective command – is of the utmost importance. The task facing the Canadian Forces is to identify the men and women who already possess the required habits and beliefs, then reinforce them in training, while also passing on the knowledge they will need to become good officers.

The Canadian Forces believe leadership "can be developed by constant self-discipline and training" and that "the requirements of leadership . . .

may be studied, applied and mastered just as for any other human accomplishment."[25] Jacques Dextraze, chief of the defence staff from 1972 to 1977 and a decorated combat veteran and battalion commander in the Second World War and Korea, defined leadership as "the art of influencing others to do willingly what is required in order to achieve an aim or a goal." Dextraze believed there were four essential ingredients of good leadership: loyalty, knowledge, integrity, and courage. He elaborated on each quality:

(1) A good officer had to be loyal to those who were higher in the chain of command and to the troops under him. He knew what every successful officer knows – that there are no bad soldiers, only bad officers. He knew that a unit's ability to function would be greatly impaired unless every person in the chain of command gave loyalty and respect to every other person in the chain of command. But Dextraze also warned that when loyalty to those above clashed with loyalty to those below, "then loyalty upward must prevail, because in the final analysis it is loyalty to our country that really counts."

(2) A good officer had to have knowledge sufficient to do the job. A knowledgeable officer commands respect from both subordinates and superiors. Dextraze urged Canadian officers to set aside time for self-education. "You may be given more authority by promotion, but you are not, by the same act given additional knowledge or ability."

(3) An officer had to have integrity: "the refusal to deceive others in any way, no matter what the circumstances." To Dextraze, this was an essential ingredient of good military leadership. "As a leader, you must take decisions and accept the results. You are the one responsible for the success or failure of your own actions. You must admit your mistakes, at least to yourself, and profit by them."

(4) A good officer had to have courage: "the willingness to face danger in the knowledge that it exists." This last quality was easier to measure in war, Dextraze pointed out, because there were more opportunities to display it. But Dextraze also believed that courage was important in a peacetime army: "this 'quiet' courage is no less important than the battlefield kind . . . all of us in positions of responsibility are faced with making decisions that may call for a large measure of moral courage. Too

often in peacetime it takes courage 'to rock the boat,' and I must admit that our peacetime system sometimes seems to have a built-in bias against those who have the courage to speak out against what they honestly believe to be wrong."[26]

Dextraze thought of leadership as an art because it is not quantifiable. But there is another and complementary side to good military command, and that is management. If leadership is an art, management is a science based on the need to ensure that soldiers and material are deployed effectively and efficiently in a way that wins battles. Good management is as necessary as good leadership for success in war. A good leader can inspire his troops to superhuman feats, but if the troops are too few, or too badly equipped, or have too little food and ammunition, success may elude them despite their heroics. One of the keys to winning battles, according to Confederate Gen. Nathan Bedford Forrest, is to "get there first with the most men."[27] Napoleon is most remembered as a brilliant and daring tactician, but his military successes depended as much upon his innovations in supply and logistics as they did upon cavalry moves.

Even at the smallest unit level, commanders must be both leaders and managers. A section leader who inspires confidence in his riflemen does so not only because they respect his fieldcraft or his knowledge of small-unit tactics but because he makes sure they carry sufficient rations, ammunition, communications equipment, etc., to accomplish their mission. In the Canadian army, the relationship between leadership and management is described as such: "Management and leadership are complex variables. It is probably not correct to say either that management is a function of leadership, or that leadership depends on management. Both are very broad fields of study that widely overlap in many areas. . . . A commander will not be a leader if he does little to manage and inspire his subordinates."[28]

The ideal Canadian army commander, then, is one who exercises both leadership and management skills. The officer/NCO relationship is meant to help commanders excel at both. In an infantry battalion, for example, the onus for leadership falls mainly on the officers, while the responsibility for management falls mainly on the NCOs. Officers issue commands; NCOs implement them. Officers are responsible for the overall good order and discipline of their men; NCOs are responsible for their daily conduct. The officer should be the leader of men; the NCO, the repository of technical know-how. In the field, a platoon commander should seek the advice of his senior NCO before deciding how to assault a bunker or bypass an ambush. As one senior Canadian army NCO with almost twenty years of experience explains, "The lieutenant is the commander but the senior NCO gives him the technical expertise to do the job. We've got the technical expertise because we've been in for sixteen or twenty years, what weapon does what, say, or what combination of approaches would work best."[29]

Senior NCOs spend far more time learning the basics of the trade than officers do. One sign that a rookie platoon commander (lieutenant) might make a good officer is the respect he or she shows for the NCO's knowledge and experience, and his ability to use it, without getting confused about who stands where in the chain of command. A good senior NCO understands the chain of command and is prepared to be commanded by an officer who is both younger and less experienced as long as that officer has earned the NCO's respect. That won't happen because the officer knows more (he or she won't) or because the officer is physically tougher (that, too, would be rare), but because the officer demonstrates honesty, integrity, and decisiveness. In other words, the officer must convince the NCO that he or she – no matter how young or technically deficient – has what it takes to get the platoon home safely.

Too often in today's army, these military virtues are not rewarded. It is the managerial, ass-covering, political skills that lead to promotion.

It is probably true that military leaders in all countries and throughout history have complained about civilianization – civilians meddling in military matters. This is a different problem from that posed by the growth of a bureaucratic mentality among the soldiers themselves. The argument about the extent to which the Canadian army has become "civilianized," or has lost sight of the military ethos, will doubtless continue to rage for a long while. We are, after all, at peace and likely to remain so for the foreseeable future. Were this 1944, no one would waste time on the question. But even in peacetime, the issue is much overplayed. There can be no such thing as a "pure" soldier (except perhaps in the minds of Hollywood writers), especially in democracies where soldiers form an integral part of a legal-constitutional milieu. The best commanders are those who balance "civilian" and military values just as they harmonize leadership and management. The history of war in this century gives much proof that such harmonization is vitally necessary for victory. As U.S. military historian Williamson Murray pointed out, the German military leadership's chief failing in the Second World War was its inability "to analyze the strategic and political equation with honesty."[30] If Hitler's high command had had a broader view of the world – had they been able to see people and nations as much through the eyes of Ludwig van Beethoven or Johann Wolfgang von Goethe as those of von Moltke and von Clausewitz, the Second World War might have had a different outcome. They would then have understood the links between war and high politics and would have known that their ultimate objectives were political rather than military in nature. The high command of the western democracies, working in tandem with their political leaders, always kept the larger political and cultural context of the war in mind when planning high strategy. The German high command simply did what Hitler told them to do because they were, for the most part, political and cultural ignoramuses.

In the view of Canadian army chaplain Capt. Eric T. Reynolds, a good commander needs much more than the acquisition of soldierly skills. "Our military institutions must foster personal reflection, detachment and thought, in which each person seeks to understand the facts of the situation in question, tries to discover the basis for those facts, considers the forces at play, compares the possibilities offered, distinguishes the values involved, and weights the motives for the action to be taken. The greatest challenge for military institutions is that they, like their personnel, must learn to question themselves, share their solutions with others, discuss life-sustaining and life-enhancing values, seek consensus in basic questions, and practise open dialogue."[31]

If we accept that the human heart and the human spirit are, at

bottom, what sustains the soldier in battle, it follows that the commander who understands the essential humanity of his soldiers must invariably be successful. It has been said that an immoral man cannot be a
good soldier. He may well be a skilled soldier, but he cannot be a successful leader of soldiers, because a truly moral man recognizes war for the
profanity it is and approaches it with solemnity and a strong sense of
occasion, as a priest might approach an altar for a mass. A good
commander will embark on his bloody task determined to do it as expe-
ditiously as possible, knowing that if he and his men do not take a grip
on their own souls as they kill or are killed, they will lose their souls to
darkness and evil. That is why, as Reynolds says, "military institutions
have an obligation to develop an ethical competence that resides in an
aptitude for inquiry and dialogue, in the ability to exercise a creative and
critical spirit and in the on-going development of personal experience.
Our goal can be nothing less than the education and formation of the
'whole' person, and this is an ethical task in itself."[32]

What, then, is the central challenge to the Canadian army today? Is it
the struggle to maintain a military ethos as opposed to a civilian way of
thinking? Is it a contest of the art of leadership versus the science of
management? Is it a *kulturkampf* of old values against new ones, or of a
pre-Charter society against a post-Charter, pluralist, rights-driven
nation? It is, in fact, all of these and none of them at the same time. At
the heart of the Canadian army's deepest crisis lies the struggle to ensure
that the army's leaders are, first and foremost, true warriors whose
morality, integrity, and courage in leadership in battle and in peace set
the tone for the entire chain of command.

5

REGIMENTS AND FAMILIES

IN the fall of 1966, U.S. army Lieut. Barry McCaffrey survived his first tour of duty in Vietnam because of an intangible something called regimental pride. A paratrooper from 82nd Airborne Division, McCaffrey had been attached as a military adviser to a unit of South Vietnamese paratroopers engaged in a search-and-destroy mission near the demilitarized zone that separated North from South Vietnam. The South Vietnamese had run into a much larger force of North Vietnamese army (NVA) troops near the hamlet of Dong Ha. They were quickly surrounded and pinned down by mortar and machine-gun fire. The NVA assaulted the South Vietnamese hilltop position all night, slowly pushing the perimeter back. As dawn broke, low cloud hung over the valley – there would be no help from American aircraft and no evacuation by American helicopters.

As the NVA formed up for yet another assault, word came by radio that the South Vietnamese and their American advisers were to break into small groups and try to escape through the NVA lines. As the firing intensified, a South Vietnamese captain calmly walked over to McCaffrey's bunker for confirmation of the order; McCaffrey gave it to him. The South Vietnamese officer took off his helmet and replaced it with his red paratrooper's beret. The other South Vietnamese troopers did the same. "We're forming up the battalion for an attack," the captain told him. "It's time to die now."

They didn't die, at least not all of them. The hopeless attack of the South Vietnamese paratroopers against overwhelming odds caught the NVA off guard. So did an American AC-47 gunship that managed to slip under the clouds and pour a stream of Gatling gunfire into the NVA positions. McCaffrey was badly wounded but survived. The high-living paratroopers of the South Vietnamese army, by choosing to die with their guns blazing, had saved the day.[1] It is the stuff of a Hollywood B movie, but it has happened countless times in the history of warfare.

War calls upon human beings to go into harm's way not as a consequence of an accident or natural disaster but intentionally and with planning. A soldier who goes to war deliberately risks the annihilation of self and, at the same time, takes up the task of annihilating other humans. The death that is to be meted out in battle is not a fading away of life after years fully lived; it is brutal, dreadful, sudden, and violent. Why do sane men (and now women) undertake to kill or be killed in these circumstances? It is rarely because of a commitment to a political or religious cause, or pride in country. It is because the bonds of friendship and even love tie them to their comrades who are also going into harm's way.[2] In the Canadian army, the fostering of those bonds is the job of the regiment.

From the beginnings of organized warfare, armies have sought ways to bind soldiers together and engender within them a loyalty stronger than either their fear of death or their distaste for killing. In Canada and those nations whose martial traditions stem largely from Britain, generating loyalty has been a function of the regimental system. Other countries have developed alternative means, but the objective is always the same: to create an extended family that will nurture soldiers, give them a framework for life away from the battlefield, and ensure that when they enter battle, they will not be alone, even in death.

Soldiers fight best when they are part of a small unit in which they have close ties of affection and trust with one another and their commander. Most modern armies have used a "buddy" system in one fashion or another to attach an infantryman to his trenchmate. Tank crews of three to five persons bond easily. The squad or section of around ten soldiers similarly promotes battlefield intimacy. In the Second World War, German soldiers were constantly shifted from formation to formation whenever temporary *kampfgruppen* (battle groups) were formed, but their fighting ability remained unimpaired because their primary loyalty, inculcated in basic training, was to the squad or section, which was not broken up.

The U.S. army has succeeded in creating strong loyalties and traditions in formations much larger than sections or even battalions. The U.S. Marines stress allegiance to the Marine Corps above all other loyalties. Marines celebrate the birthday of the Marine Corps, honour Marine heroes of past battles, and always come to the aid of other Marines. It is a point of honour in the Marine Corps never to leave a dead Marine on the battlefield. Such cohesion is also found in the loyalties and traditions of famous U.S. army units such as "The Big Red One" (1st U.S. Infantry Division) and the "Screaming Eagles" (101st Airborne Division). In these units, the regiments and battalions are almost anonymous; loyalty to the corps (in the case of the Marines) or the division is the key to battlefield morale.

There is, however, strong evidence for the contention that soldiers fight better in small groups than they do alone or in large masses. In his now famous study of the U.S. soldier, *Men Against Fire*, American military analyst S. L. A. Marshall found that the majority of the men in U.S. line-combat units in the Second World War never fired their weapons at the enemy. A close analysis of a single battalion action in the Pacific revealed that only thirty-six men out of the entire unit could be identified as having used their personal weapons. "The really active firers," Marshall observed, "were usually in small groups working together." Marshall and others have suggested that this small-unit cohesion depends on the individual soldier's worry that those closest to him may think him a coward.[3]

In his book *Inside the British Army*, Anthony Beevor drew a connection between the British regimental system and the battlefield performance of the British soldier. "Unless he is a fanatic, a man facing death in battle needs more than an abstract cause to defend. His own family is far away, so the regiment takes on its emotional focus. And a soldier's fear of shaming himself in its eyes can balance his fear of the enemy. This tribal instinct has always been the basis of the regimental system. 'On a number of occasions,' said General Sir John Chapple, 'it has proved to be a rather stronger bond, dare I say it, than King and Country, God and the Cause, creed and caste.' "4

In the Second World War, the regimental system was found to be a mixed blessing in the Canadian Army. In the early part of the war, the army was loathe to move potential commanders from one battalion to another and was prone to promote COs only from within the regiment. Sometimes the result was not happy; a battalion did not receive the best possible CO, only the best possible CO from within its ranks. That practice was gradually dispensed with after the army became fully engaged from the summer of 1944 on. The demands of combat meant that competence usually took precedence over regimental protocol.

Another weakness of the regimental system was not so readily overcome: regimental loyalty tended to undermine loyalty to higher formations such as brigades and divisions. That was not especially serious at the section or company level, but sometimes led battalion commanders to isolate themselves from other battalions (or armoured regiments) in their brigades. Lack of cohesion in the 5th Canadian Infantry Brigade during Operation Spring in Normandy in July 1944, for example, contributed to one of the worst defeats suffered by a Canadian battalion in a single day of fighting. As the Black Watch (Royal Highland Regiment of Canada) attacked up Verrieres Ridge on July 25, it was decimated because its right flank had not been secured by its sister regiment, the Calgary Highlanders, who had themselves run into severe opposition. Acting Black Watch CO Maj. Phil Griffin led his men into the teeth of German fire because Black Watch tradition dictated that the regiment never retreat.

The Canadian army's basic administrative formation is the corps. There is a corps for every major branch of service – an armoured corps, an infantry corps, an artillery corps (called the Royal Regiment of Canadian Artillery), etc. These corps are administrative units that exist largely to hold reinforcements for field formations. They are not to be confused with those "corps" that are field formations of one or more divisions –

the First Canadian Corps in the Second World War, for example. Some of the administrative corps, particularly those of the combat arms, consist of regiments that, in the Canadian army, are used to connote both an agency to rally and raise troops and a field formation.

In both the armoured and infantry corps, there are regular force and reserve (or militia) regiments. Each of these regiments exists primarily to raise troops and instil in them that intangible but crucial something called regimental pride or *esprit de corps*. Militia regiments are almost always regionally based, drawing their members from a particular rural area, a single town, or even the district of a large city. This is no accident. It is done so that regimental loyalty can be built upon the already existing cohesion of friends, family, and neighbourhood. Permanent Force regiments are not so closely tied to a single locality but are still somewhat territorially based. In the infantry corps, for example, the Princess Patricia's Canadian Light Infantry (PPCLI) draws troops primarily from western Canada, while the Royal Canadian Regiment's soldiers come primarily from Ontario and the Maritimes. The French-language Royal 22e Régiment, headquartered at Quebec City, draws upon Quebec and the francophone areas of New Brunswick and Ontario.

In the Canadian armoured corps, a "regiment" is also a field formation consisting of three tank squadrons, a reconnaissance squadron, and a regimental headquarters squadron. Each of the tank squadrons has three tank troops. The infantry equivalent to the armoured regiment as a field formation is the battalion, which is made up of companies, the infantry equivalent to squadrons. In other countries (Germany, and Russia, for example), "regiment" is used to connote a field formation of infantry and is used instead of brigade, a term utilized in armies that have inherited the British tradition to designate a unit of two or more infantry battalions or armoured regiments. (The U.S. army has recently adopted "brigade" in place of "regiment.")

The parent regiment's main task is to direct soldiers to the field formations – battalions in the infantry, regiments in armour, artillery, etc. A regiment usually has more than one affiliated battalion. Currently, for example, the three regular force infantry regiments of the Canadian army have three battalions each. In the Second World War, virtually all

Canadian infantry regiments that sent soldiers to the fighting fronts had two battalions: the 1st Battalion was normally attached to the Canadian Army Overseas (i.e., in Britain, Italy, or northwest Europe), while the 2nd Battalion remained at home as a unit in the reserves. In the British army, which is much larger than the Canadian and draws upon a greater source of manpower, it is not unheard of for both armoured and infantry regiments to have six or seven battalions (or field regiments), or even more.

In the British and Canadian armies, "the regiment" is an extended family that reaches backwards in time and outwards in space to encompass those soldiers who have come to identify with its collective memories and traditions. Each regiment develops a culture that is partly rooted in the place from which it draws its members and partly in a set of values and mores that have been created for the sole purpose of making it different from other regiments. Above all, the regiment perpetuates the memory of the battles it has fought. The battle honours on the regimental standard commemorate those battles and remind members of the regiment's unique history. People die, but the regiment lives. As military historian Richard Holmes wrote, "A soldier may be able to accept his own death, the destruction of his section, even the annihilation of his battalion, knowing that the regiment will live on."[5] Lieut. Barry McCaffrey's South Vietnamese paratroopers donned their red berets and went out to die because the honour of their regiment would not allow them to slink away into the jungle.

This may be confusing to civilians, but it is axiomatic for Canadian soldiers. For the most part, their life and loyalty centre on the regiment – not on the army. As one captain in the Strathconas said, "Find somebody in the street who looks like a soldier . . . and say, 'What do you do for a living?' He might say, 'I'm a soldier,' but he's more liable to say, 'I'm a soldier in the Strathconas, I'm a soldier in the PPCLI.' Rarely have I heard people say, 'I'm a soldier in the Canadian Armed Forces, because that's too big for people. We belong to identified groups. I'm a Strathcona, been a Strathcona for thirteen years, that's my regiment, that's my family, that's my home."[6]

English regiments first appeared in the late sixteenth century, but did not truly flourish until after the English Civil War and the restoration of Charles II to the throne in 1660. Regiments were raised and led by colonels of the regiment ("colonel" derives from commander of the column), who usually paid much of the tab for their upkeep. These regiments were locally based and distinguished from each other in uniform, standard, and other accoutrements. Though usually numbered rather than named, they sometimes acquired nicknames or adopted the name of famous soldiers. The Duke of Wellington's regiment, for example, was named for the Duke, and the regiment's cap badge replicates the family crest.

The regimental tradition in Canada has been influenced by both of its "mother" countries, France and Britain. The first regular French regiment to be based in Canada was the Régiment Carignan-Salières, sent to fight the Iroquois in 1665. Canadian militia regiments pre-dated Confederation in all the British North American colonies, and when the first Canadian Permanent Force units were established in the 1880s, they were also organized along regimental lines. Much has changed in the Canadian army since the last century, but the process of forging regimental loyalty has been little modified.

Regimental cohesion depends on the features that set it apart. The formal dress of the Calgary Highlanders, for example (a militia regiment), tells much about the regiment's background. The regimental colours – green, yellow, blue, and red – have been borrowed from its affiliated regiment, the Argyl and Sutherland Highlanders of the British army. So has the kilt pattern. This was deliberately done in the early 1920s, soon after the Calgary Highlanders were formed, to give the regiment instant tradition. The Calgary Highlanders also inherited traditions from the 10th Battalion of the Canadian Expeditionary Force of the First World War, which is considered to be a parent regiment. Since the 10th Battalion's introduction to combat was the Battle of St. Julien's Wood in April 1915, the Calgary Highlander formal dress uniform includes a small oak-leaf badge.

Adopting distinctive mess dress, and hat and shoulder badges for its olive drab fatigues, is only the beginning. The regiment's music, its mess-dinner rituals, and its colours are all unique. It normally celebrates its own officially designated regimental birthdays and one or two famous battles with a mess dinner, a parade, and perhaps a drumhead church service. The Calgary Highlanders mark the Battle of St. Julien's Wood in the First World War in the second weekend of April and the Battle of the Walcheren Causeway in the Second World War in the last weekend in October; other regiments commemorate other battles and important events in their history.

Regiments maintain their traditions in similar ways. Young soldiers or junior subalterns joining the regiment receive indoctrination in regimental history. For one week each year, for example, the newly arrived junior officers of the PPCLI are given lectures from current and past serving officers or military historians about the regiment's founder, Sir Hamilton Gault, famous battles in both world wars, notable Patricias of the past, the regiment's operations in Korea, and home-defence tasks and peacekeeping. They are also taught the structure of the regimental association, regimental traditions and lore, and even the correct way to arrange their dress uniforms for formal occasions.

Regiments take great pains to preserve their own history. Regimental museums such as the Canadian Military Engineers Museum in Chilliwack, British Columbia, dot the country. In the Museum of the Regiments in Calgary, for example, the PPCLI has placed historical artifacts, uniforms of famous past serving members, paintings, photographs, dioramas, and other displays telling the Patricia story. There is a small room with the Patricia roll of honour on which the names are carved of those members of the regiment killed in action. Every Patricia is expected to visit the museum and learn the regiment's history. The PPCLI also maintains an archive with war diaries, photographs, and other important documents bearing on regimental history, all watched over by a part-time archivist who is usually a past serving member or NCO. The Patricias have had two regimental histories published; virtually all other regiments and some of the corps of the Canadian army have had at least one.

Regimental lore is compiled in a "regimental book," which is the bible of regimental tradition. A typical book will detail the story of the regiment's founder, the history of the regiment, its organizational structure, awards and honours, colours and dress, badges and other accoutrements, music, and the order of mess dinners. These dinners are central to the maintenance of tradition; attendance at them is compulsory for regular force personnel (though not always so for militia units). They are highly ritualized in structure, though semi-formal in execution. They invariably begin with guests gathering in the bar. The room is resplendent with colour and tradition. The jackets of the Canadian soldiers are usually red and adorned with medals, badges, and other insignia. There are striped pants, plaid pants, and kilts. Foreign guests and visiting officers from the air force or navy add to the variety of dress.

At exactly the posted time, a bugle is blown, or a tune played by members of the regimental band or the regimental piper, and the guests file into the dining room. The highly polished regimental silver sits on the tables. The guests sit in predetermined order, by rank, with the CO, the guest of honour, and visiting high-ranking officers at the head. The evening is managed by a PMC – the president of the mess committee – who introduces himself and calls upon the colour party to bring in the regimental standard. He then asks the padre to say grace, the guests are seated, and the meal begins. Certain subjects, considered controversial, are not discussed at the table. Dinner courses may be interrupted by toasts, music, or short speeches, all according to established custom. After the meal, there will be the toast to the Queen and other toasts, the passing of the regimental port, the lighting of cigars, even the taking of snuff, all done in precise order and according to a pre-set timetable. At some mess dinners, guests must pass the port from hand to hand and not allow the bottle to touch the table. At others, the toast to the regiment is made with one foot on the table. It is all laid out in the regimental book.

The messes themselves, particularly the officers' messes, are also repositories of regimental tradition. Plush chairs and polished wood panelling highlight display cases with trophies, standards, insignia, and the all-important regimental silver. The pieces are heavy and always polished to a high lustre. The Strathconas' collection includes silver cavalry figures and silver models of the main tanks used by the regiment since the start of the Second World War. On the walls are pictures of regimental vehicles, paintings of the regiment in battle or on exercise, photographs of the current and past COs, and photographs of the colonels of the regiments (honorary colonels in militia units).

Although all Canadian regiments, regular and militia, have somewhat different structures, they are more alike than not. The regimental family of the Strathconas, for example, is governed by the Regimental Society. It includes all regimental members whether currently serving with the regiment or elsewhere, as well as the Regimental Association and its branches, the Regimental Museum, the Mounted Troop, and the Cadet Corps. This last is made up of youngsters. The society's aims are to support the regiment and preserve its traditions, foster comradeship among regimental members, and collect and disseminate information (especially historical items) of interest to the regiment's members. The chairman is the senior serving member of the regiment.

A regiment's senior serving member is the highest ranking, currently serving, officer of that regiment. When Gen. John de Chastelaine was chief of the defence staff and Canada's only four-star (i.e., full) general, he was the senior serving member of the PPCLI. Senior serving members have no formal authority in the regiment. They are not part of the regimental decision-making structure, and they are certainly not part of the battalion chain of command. They are, nonetheless, very important to the regiment. They are considered regimental guardian angels, always on the lookout for the interests of the regiment, no matter where it is based or how far up the chain of command they climb. They are often sought out for advice, to put in a good word, and to influence decisions bearing on the welfare of the regiment.

In regular force regiments, the colonel of the regiment, usually a former high-ranking member of the regiment, presides over a committee of former regimental officers, former COs, and current COs, who are the official keepers of the regimental tradition and the makers of regimental – as opposed to military – policy. Their chief responsibility is to guard the good name of the regiment and to strengthen regimental tradition. Their duties vary from regiment to regiment. In Lord Strathcona's Horse, for example, the regimental guard advises the CO on the posting of regimental officers. The vice-president of the guard is known as the "Keeper of the Black Book," which records the careers of all regimental officers. The opinions of the guard on personnel issues are meant to provide regimental input to the otherwise almost completely centralized career-manager system. In the militia, the honorific head of the regiment is known as the honorary colonel; he usually presides over a regimental senate, whose duties are almost totally ceremonial.

The colonel of the regiment is, in theory, just a figurehead; in practice, he is likely to be a whole lot more. It is very rare that any major plans for the regiment would be instituted by army headquarters without consulting the colonel of the regiment. His opinion is often sought by the battalion COs on personnel problems, morale issues, and ceremonial matters. Like the senior serving member, he can be an important lobbyist for his regiment in the higher echelons of the army. Prior to the mid-1970s, a colonel of the regiment could be a serving member. (Now an officer must be retired for at least three years before he can accept an honorary appointment.) The late Lt.-Gen. Stan Waters was the colonel of the regiment of the Canadian Airborne Regiment while still serving at army headquarters in St-Hubert, Quebec. He was thus in a good position to protect the Airborne's interests from those who were trying to disband it or change its status in the 1970s.

In Britain, from whence Canadian regimental tradition stems, the regimental system is still so pervasive in virtually all aspects of army life that some observers have claimed the British army as such doesn't exist apart from its regiments. There, according to some reform-minded officers, "the paralysing effect of regimental loyalty at higher levels, its tentacles fastened on to almost every decision-making process, with rivalry, compromise and trade-offs maintain[s] the status quo."7

Regimental influence is not nearly as important in the administration of the Canadian army as it was, and still is, in Britain. Though Canadian regiments are, to some degree, territorially based as are those in Britain, they are not as venerable. The current regular force regiments did not predate the establishment of military forces in Canada, rather they followed them. In addition, unification of the Armed Forces, the establishment of the central career-management system, and the growth of the NDHQ bureaucracy have all tended to undermine regimental influence in strictly military matters.

Just how important are the regiments in Canadian army administration today? They obviously play an institutional role in strictly regimental matters and they do influence personnel decisions. Some members believe that regimental influence goes much further. Officers of one regiment always seem convinced that those of another constitute a hidden "mafia," which acts to advance regimental interests no matter what the impact may be on the army as a whole. This feeling, justified or not, is especially pervasive among English-speaking members, many of whom are convinced that the serving members of the Royal 22e Régiment form a sort of secret society pledged to advance the regiment's interests and the cause of bilingualism in the army. One former francophone CO of the Canadian Airborne Regiment scoffs at the notion, calling it "overblown" at the least. Nevertheless, the complaint points to one important drawback to the regimental system: rivalries are not always friendly.

The government, NDHQ, and army command have done much to gloss over French–English rivalries in the army, but those rivalries exist, and the feelings of distrust, especially of francophones by anglophones, are sometimes intensely bitter. Exacerbated by what many English-speaking officers saw as unfair affirmative-action programs that supposedly favoured bilingual francophone officers in the 1970s and 1980s, the resentment runs deep and adds to regimental rivalries between French- and English-speaking regiments.

In 1969, Minister of National Defence Léo Cadieux announced that five English-speaking regiments were being disbanded or taken off the active list and converted into militia units while three French-speaking regiments were to be activated. The move was intended to increase the proportion of francophones in the army. Two of the regiments – the Black Watch (Royal Highland Regiment) of Canada and the Queen's Own Rifles of Canada – traced their roots back to the 1860s. The Black Watch had had a distinguished record in both of Canada's major wars, raising three battalions for the Canadian Expeditionary Force in the First World War and one battalion for service with the 5th Canadian Infantry

Brigade in the Second World War. With headquarters in Montreal, it was the regiment of choice for old English-speaking Montreal families.

The Black Watch reverted to militia status following the Second World War, but was reactivated as a regular force regiment in October 1953. From then until 1969, the Black Watch supported two regular force battalions and a militia battalion. When Cadieux made his announcement, men cried. At the final parade, when the regimental colours and battle honours were laid up, many of those present wore black armbands as a mark of grief. The CO, Lt.-Col. "Scotty" Morrison, explained, "The troops accepted the news with grace and deep hurt . . . like a family that suffered a tragic loss of kinfolk." One Black Watch private wrote defence analyst Duncan Fraser that he was heartbroken to see his regimental home destroyed.[8] The Black Watch did not disappear; it remained in existence as a militia unit, but its soldiers were forced either to retire or to go elsewhere if they wanted to stay in the army. (Most who stayed went – "rebadged" – to the Royal Canadian Regiment.)

Soldiers can accept the fact that troubles may develop in a platoon, a company, even a battalion of a particular regiment. They understand that tough disciplinary measures sometimes have to be taken to get matters back on track in any unit. They can even accept that a battalion will be disbanded or, as in the case of the Black Watch, that the entire regular force component may be shifted away in a drastic downsizing. But many of those soldiers from Nova Scotia, for example, who rebadged into the Royal Canadian Regiment, (RCR), subsequently thought of themselves as having two regimental families, the Black Watch and the RCR, because the Black Watch still lived, even if in truncated form, as a militia regiment. When a regiment is expunged from existence by government order, as the Canadian Airborne Regiment was at the start of 1995, however, it is entirely a different matter. As one high-ranking officer declared, "The minister just didn't understand the notion of regiment, he didn't understand that you clean out the shit, but you keep the regiment alive in some fashion."[9]

For soldiers, killing a regiment is like wiping out a family; regiments are supposed to go on forever, and so are a soldier's ties to the regiment. "I remain a Strathcona, remain a member of the extended regimental family," declares Lt.-Col. R. A. E. Williams, administrative officer of CFB Calgary. "It is something I belong to, it is an extended family that is there and will provide support should it be necessary, if I go looking for it. It keeps me in touch with what is going on."[10]

In most regiments, especially ones that are as closely knit as the Strathconas or the R22eR, the support offered individual members comes in many forms. When one Strathcona was recently posted to CFB Calgary, members of his new troop found him a place to live and took an army vehicle out of the motor pool to help him move. Members and spouses will help with the moving, offer advice on local facilities, assist with the children, sell unused furniture at a token price or even donate it.[11] More importantly, they will make the new member feel welcome by including him or her in their social life. Since military people are, by definition, not loners, this is particularly significant. When the battalion or regiment is sent overseas, the regimental "rear party" is intended to help the stay-at-home spouse with all manner of chores from shovelling the walk to overseeing repairs to the family car. The rear party is normally made up of regimental members who have been left behind for one reason or another; sometimes they resent not having been included in the overseas operation and their unhappiness shows, but more often than not they help spouses cope under very difficult conditions.

Regiments are usually for life. From the time recruits are assigned to their new regiment until they die, the regiment is the framework of their lives. NCOs and officers to the rank of major almost always return to their regimental base after taking courses or being otherwise absent, and never remove their regimental cap badges. The soldiers at the Combat Training Centre at CFB Gagetown, for example, maintain their regimental affiliation and wear their regimental cap badges even though they may be posted to Gagetown, and away from their regimental base, for years. An officer who is promoted out of the regiment retains his or her regimental loyalty throughout the rest of his or her career, then usually joins the regimental association after retirement. As one officer said, "Belonging to a regiment makes a difference to the individual because they want to carry on the tradition. We have a proud past, and there is nothing we'll do to screw that up. I think there's a belief that if you are in the regiment, you move faster. Statistics might prove that out, but that [isn't the point]. . . . The regiment is where everybody prefers to be because it is the regiment. If you can go back to the regiment, you do."[12]

Sometimes that's just not possible – when a regiment is disbanded or a member is moved permanently for career reasons, for example. Then the process of "re-badging" begins. It isn't easy. "You feel like you are betraying your unit, your mother regiment," remembers one soldier who transferred from the 8th Canadian Hussars to the Royal Canadian Dragoons when the Hussars were brought back from Germany and deactivated (except for one squadron of demonstration troops). "In another way, you want to show these guys that you're a Hussar and this is how the Hussars operate. This is how I work. But slowly, you begin to integrate into the new unit. You slowly start to associate yourself as a Dragoon. Now I'm a Dragoon." Even so, this soldier still sometimes feels remorse at having given up his old identity. "Sometimes I think that maybe I was doing it a little too quickly, but I always put that aside. Where you come from, what unit you've been with, is irrelevant to the job at hand and the task that has to be done."[13]

There will always be debate about the benefits and drawbacks of the regimental system. In the United States, where the army went through more than a decade of angst and self-examination after the withdrawal and defeat in Vietnam, some reformers advocated that aspects of the regimental system be grafted onto the existing army structure. The personnel policies that the U.S. army had followed in Vietnam, particularly the rotation home of individuals who had completed twelve months "in country" (thirteen months for a Marine) had been a disaster. That policy, more than any other, had broken the cohesion that binds combat soldiers to one another. But resistance to the regimental system – with its home base, regimental depots for training, regimental rather than divisional or other loyalties, and, most important, battalion instead of individual rotation – has been strong in the United States. Some minor aspects of the system were introduced as part of the many reforms that transformed the defeated army of Vietnam into the victorious army of the Gulf War.

There can be no debate about the pervasiveness of the regimental system in the Canadian army, nor about the degree to which virtually all soldiers believe it to be an essential part of the Canadian military tradition. The regimental system survived the First World War despite Minister of Militia and Defence Sam Hughes, who insisted on an army of characterless, numbered battalions. The system survived the government penury of the 1920s and 1930s, sometimes supported almost wholly by members who contributed their meagre pay and summer-encampment allowances to a central fund to maintain their regimental mess and purchase dress uniforms. The system survived the wholesale cuts to the army budget after the Second World War, and it survived unification and the centralizing tendencies of NDHQ. Whatever the truth of the belief that regiments are vital to support men in combat, the soldiers of the Canadian army believe in it. That is why any perceived effort by the DND, by NDHQ, or by the army's high command to weaken the regimental system is taken by soldiers as an attack on the army itself. It is also why the disbandment of the Canadian Airborne Regiment "in disgrace" in early 1995 was taken personally by many soldiers who had no sympathy whatever for the killers of Shidane Abukar Arone.

The most serious threat to the regimental system today is posed neither by the government nor by NDHQ nor the army high command. It grows out of the daily lives of the soldiers and is symbolized by the loved one who sleeps beside them. The cohesiveness of the regimental family is being undermined by the needs of spouse and children. Nothing undermines regimental cohesion more than this divided loyalty; the desire to have a "normal" family life is one of the key factors driving soldiers away from the army today. More importantly, the soldiers who are leaving tend to be older, more mature, more stable, and – by virtue of their experience – more skilled than those who stay. The army has made an effort since 1991 to ease the conflict between a soldier's regimental family and his or her loved ones, but the task is far from complete.

Since the mid-1980s, the majority of Canadian soldiers have been married. This is normal in an all-volunteer force; the percentage of married members in the U.S. army is about the same. Men and women in the Canadian army have not been drafted for a couple of years of compulsory service; they have chosen the army as a career. Today, there are probably more marriages within the services than there were a decade ago (there were roughly one in five in 1986) simply because there are more women in the Forces. Ten years ago, only 20 per cent of military members had a working spouse; today, the figure is probably much higher. Few military families can get by on a single paycheque, and the participation rate of women in the workforce has grown considerably in the last decade.

Military marriages are beset by the full range of stresses that affect other marriages: worries about parenting and child-rearing, household economics, balancing the demands of career and home. But in the military, there is the added weight of long separations and worries about the dangers that a soldier's job entails, especially when assigned to an active war zone such as the former Yugoslavia. Stress levels are particularly high now for two reasons: the pay freeze and "over-tasking."

The Canadian Armed Forces have had no overall pay increases this decade, although some incentive bonuses are still paid. Yet prices have gone up, even for government-supplied goods and services. Take the case of base housing. These quarters are neither supplied to members free of charge nor subsidized. In fact, the Department of National Defence must rent base housing to military members at a rate equivalent to what those members would pay for similar quarters off base. Base housing has long ceased to be part of a soldier's compensation package, which is why some choose to rent, or buy, off base. Each January 1, rent for base housing is adjusted to meet increases (or decreases) in local rent rates as determined by the Canada Mortgage and Housing Corporation. In a region such as British Columbia where rents keep rising, the department will raise rents on base housing even though it is not paying its soldiers more money. It takes the not unreasonable position that since housing is not part of a soldier's pay, it cannot favour those living on base against those who live "on the economy." Equal treatment of federal workers, civilian or military, is, in fact, required by the Treasury Board, which makes the general rules for government departments and employees.[14]

Some soldiers and their spouses find it difficult to understand how the same department they work for can freeze salaries on the one hand and raise the cost of housing – and everything else supplied at the local Canex – on the other. The freeze and the price increases force military families either to economize or find other sources of income. Stories abound, true or not, that off-duty soldiers in major base areas are delivering pizza or pumping gas to make ends meet.

The money squeeze has put much additional pressure on military families, but it is the increased absences in recent years that are the source of the greatest stress. The army calls it "deployment": it is the dispatch of troops from home, usually for months at a time, and it creates "deployment stress," affecting both the physical and emotional well-being of soldiers and their families.

When soldiers are assigned away, their spouses are usually matter-of-fact, at least at first. They are, after all, married to soldiers and know that a soldier's career entails frequent separations. In the words of one soldier, "[My wife] had experienced separations before . . . she was used to a certain amount of separation from taskings and courses and exercises, [but] at one point in time in the mid-1980s, we were usually averaging nine months away from home, or a year."[15] It is a difficult, this being alone. "You get up in the morning, you fight with the kids and you get them going. And off to work you go. You come home, you have got to get supper. You have house chores to do. The kids are always nagging, 'Why isn't dad home, we want him, we miss him,' and it's, 'Well, he isn't here so let's try to do something without him."[16] When the mission is to an especially dangerous place, the strain of departure is worse, especially on the younger children. "The youngest guy was upset about it . . . he wasn't too happy. He asked a lot of questions like are you going to get shot at, or are you going to come home? . . . I always made a point when I phoned from Bosnia to talk to him."[17]

The stress of departure and absence is rarely shared equally in a military marriage. When a soldier is sent to a place like Bosnia, after all, he is going to the job; this is what he signed up for. And once there, he will enter a self-contained support system with other soldiers who largely share his outlook on life. As one former army officer recently said, "When you're not out in the field, you're not doing your job. You're not doing the whole job. You're just sort of getting ready to do the job. Being out in the field and doing the job is where you get your greatest satisfaction."[18]

Back home, however, things are very different. The spouse, usually a wife, must assume the entire burden of running the family and cope alone with all the stresses and strains that entails, in addition to her normal routine or outside job. Resentment can build easily. Said one spouse, "A lot of times now I get angry at him for having to go just because in my opinion he is gone to wherever he has gone and to me it is, 'Well, you get a holiday, you are gone out there, you are doing your job, but once you are done for the day, you are done for the day, you don't have to worry about anything else.'"[19] On one occasion, a mother was playing ball with her children when she accidently hit her son in the head with a bat. For days she worried about the results of the medical tests. The boy was okay, but "by then I was a nervous wreck! It didn't help that my husband had just sent me a picture from Cyprus of him and some friends sitting around having a drink with the sun in the background. The whole thing made me so mad, [but] it really wasn't his fault."[20]

Returning from deployment can put almost as much stress on military families as going away. It is difficult for husband and wife to re-establish emotional, physical, and sexual intimacy after a long absence. The first few days may be like a honeymoon, but then reality sets in. "The first couple of days they are back are, of course, wonderful. You have fantastic sex . . . [then] there's normally a blowout – a release of everything that's been building up for the last couple of weeks or months or whatever."[21]

Being together again means that both parents experience a loss of independence and self-reliance; they have to start making compromises again on the most mundane family issues. Sometimes that is very difficult. To add to the tension, children, especially younger ones, are often confused by the sudden arrival of a "daddy" or "mommy" who has been little more than a voice for a large part of their young lives. "My daughter was eighteen months. She became very attached to her mother," said one soldier. "When I got back, it took about a month,

month and a half, before she would come to me when she was hurt or something."[22] It is a difficult time for both spouses. The strong marriages weather the storm; the weak ones tend to fall apart.

Alcoholism and the use of illicit drugs has declined dramatically in the army over the last decade, but there is some evidence that spousal abuse is still a problem. According to the 1993 Report of the Canadian Panel on Violence Against Women, wife-battering occurred frequently in military families. The report's authors blamed it on the military culture with its supposed "atmosphere where violence against women is tolerated and even fostered."[23]

No doubt there is wife-battering in the military, as there is in society as a whole, and it is not to be tolerated. But the panel is wide of the mark in its bald assertion that armies are comfortable havens for wife-beaters. The Canadian Forces have started to put mechanisms in place to aid the victims of family violence and to help married members cope with the pressures on their spouses. In 1991, the Military Family Support Program (MFSP) was established by then Associate Minister of National Defence Mary Collins. The program is designed to ensure a "coordinated, consistent and effective CF community approach to military family support" and particularly to help prevent military family breakdown. The most visible component of the program is the Multi-Service Family Resource Centre, whose board of directors consists of a majority of civilian spouses of military members. The centre marshals both professional and voluntary services to tackle a wide variety of military family problems.

It is hard to judge how effective the program has been in alleviating the worst stresses on military marriages. Some soldiers and their wives are reluctant to use the facilities for fear that they will be targeted for early release. Others find little solace when they do because old attitudes – "you are married to a soldier and that's all there is to it" – persist. But regardless of how successful the MFSP is, some of the realities of military life will not change and neither will the underlying stresses on military marriages. It is not easy being married to a soldier, and some spouses will always decide to bail out no matter what support mechanisms are in place.

Loyalty is the essence of soldiering. It is the various and sometimes contrasting loyalties of the soldier to the regiment, to the chain of command, to country, to abstract values such as duty and honour, and to spouse and children that form his or her daily frame of reference. Once those loyalties were far clearer than they are now: A soldier's first love, first loyalty, first obligation, was supposed to be the army. But that was in the old army. The challenge to the Canadian army today is either to be satisfied with younger recruits who don't care about these things or to attract and retain those somewhat older career soldiers who are likely to be married and have children.

Following the defeat of the United States in Vietnam, and the ending of the draft, a coterie of American army leaders set out to revise their approach to the waging of war. They concluded that the U.S. army had to be rebuilt, almost from the bottom up, to fight and win its first battle in any war. That meant greater professionalism among both officers and ranks, a much higher quality of recruit, better training, and a sustained effort to improve the overall quality of army life for both the married and unmarried soldiers.

The Canadian army can do no less, and must do more than it is doing now to make life more bearable for military spouses and their children. Improving the lot of soldiers' families will have a direct beneficial impact on their ability to fulfil their duty to the chain of command. At one level, the conflict between regiment and family will remain, but at a more fundamental level, there need not be any real dichotomy, as the U.S. army has demonstrated. The challenge to the government and to the Canadian army is to make sure that the venerable, and all-important, loyalty of a soldier to the regimental family neither precludes nor undermines today's equally important loyalty of a soldier to his or her spouse and children.

6

CALL TO DUTY: BOSNIA

IN November 1995, the last Canadian soldiers to serve with UNPROFOR (United Nations Protection Force) left the former Yugoslavia to go home. In Canada, meanwhile, a new contingent of about one thousand Canadian troops was preparing to leave for Bosnia as part of NATO's newly established sixty-thousand-strong IFOR (implementation force). Spearheaded by American troops with a large contingent of British and French soldiers, IFOR was assigned the task of overseeing the Dayton Peace Accords that U.S. President Bill Clinton engineered in late 1995. Some Canadians complained that their contribution to IFOR was too small. But, as Ottawa pointed out, Canada had already supplied more than ten thousand troops for UNPROFOR since the first Canadians had arrived in 1992. More to the point, ten Canadians had been killed there and more than one hundred were wounded or injured – at a time when the Americans had been nowhere near the action.

Master Cpl. Phil Friday was one of those Canadians who served with UNPROFOR. He will not soon forget his arrival at the start of May 1994. It was like the opening scene from the film *Platoon*. "We got off the plane in Split [Croatia], and the British were loading a coffin on a transport to go back to Britain. It was, like, 'Welcome to Bosnia.' It was a good warning. It really hit home to a lot of the guys. Be on your toes, keep your eyes open and your head down. The Brit got drunk and walked past a checkpoint. He was told to stop, but kept walking and they shot him. I told myself right there, that's not going to be me. I am going to do everything I can to get through this."[1]

For Friday, the arrival in Split was the beginning of the last leg of the journey to Visoko, Bosnia. Visoko is about twenty kilometres northwest of the then-besieged Bosnian capital of Sarajevo. Friday was one of the 778 members of the Lord Strathcona's Horse (Royal Canadians) Battle Group assigned to Visoko for a six-month tour of duty. Visoko was head-quarters of CANBAT 2, one of two Canadian battalions stationed in the former Yugoslavia as part of UNPROFOR.

Canada's initial presence in Yugoslavia had been small but significant. It began when Brig.-Gen. Lewis MacKenzie, now retired, arrived in Sarajevo as chief of staff of the UN contingent in early March 1992. The site of the 1984 Winter Olympics, and a supposed example of the peace and harmony that had been achieved between Yugoslavia's once-warring ethnic groups under the country's liberalized Communist regime, Sarajevo was a mess when MacKenzie arrived. The end of the Cold War had brought peace to most of Europe, but had brought a frightful civil war to Yugoslavia, when Catholic-dominated Croatia, then Bosnia and Herzegovina with its Moslem majority, declared themselves indepen-dent nations.

At first the war centred on Croatia, as the Serb-dominated Yugoslav army tried to end the Croatian secession. Then Bosnia blew up when the minority Bosnian Serbs, backed by the Yugoslav army, tried to secede. They laid siege to Sarajevo and fought the Bosnian Moslems for control of the city. MacKenzie was not successful in stopping this fighting, but he did temporarily lift the siege of Sarajevo by arranging the reopening of the airport and the road from the airport to the city.

The first substantial Canadian contingent to arrive in Yugoslavia (twelve hundred troops) moved into Croatia as part of UNPROFOR in March and April 1992. Their mission was simple – patrol the zone of separation between Croatian and Serbian soldiers that had been worked out in a UN-brokered cease-fire agreement. It was to be a classic UN peacekeeping mission, not much different from the many that Cana-dians had served in since the very first in the Sinai Peninsula in 1956-57. The aim was to separate the two sides, to make it easier for them to move from the battlefield to the conference table. But in June 1992, the mission changed. Largely at MacKenzie's behest, the Canadian battle group was moved to Bosnia to help secure the Sarajevo airport and escort relief convoys from there into the city. A second Canadian battle group arrived in October and was based in Croatia. In February 1993, the first battle group moved from Sarajevo to Visoko, its chief mission to escort UN relief convoys. At its height, the Canadian army had nearly three thousand soldiers in the former Yugoslavia performing a variety of vital operations from the clearing of mines to the separation of hostile forces.

By the end of 1992, the three-corner civil war – pitting Bosnians against Serbs, Serbs against Croatians, and Croatians against Bosnians – had intensified into one of the most vicious conflicts since the end of the Second World War. All sides resorted to unspeakable atrocities, including the massacre of prisoners of war, mass rape, and the murder of civilians. There was no peace to keep, especially in Bosnia. UN peacekeepers, who had been initially welcomed by the population, were increasingly targeted as one side or the other accused them of bias. That was the situation in the spring of 1994 when Phil Friday and the Lord Strathcona's Horse (Royal Canadians) Battle Group arrived on the scene.

Neither the United Nations nor the Canadian government ever defined precisely what UNPROFOR was supposed to achieve in Bosnia. Probably, they didn't know. The original separation-of-forces mission that Canada's troops were to perform in Croatia was doable, but Bosnia was a mess from first to last. And yet Canada stayed. Peacekeeping had become a religion of sorts to Canadian foreign-policy makers, so no one challenged Canada's presence there. Asked time after time by the Parliamentary Opposition to explain why Canadian soldiers were in harm's way in the middle of a vicious civil war, the governments of Brian Mulroney, Kim Campbell, and Jean Chrétien never came up with an answer that made sense. Canada appeared to be keeping its troops in Bosnia because they had been sent there in the first place.

That doesn't mean that some (maybe most) of the soldiers who went there didn't see some greater purpose in what they were doing. It was easy to think that the mission was important when starving children were being fed with each UN food convoy, or when the peacekeepers could stop the fighting long enough for men and women to emerge from their shelters to get food and water or to plant their fields. But that did not mean any higher Canadian interest was being served or that the cost to Canada in money and lives was worth any gain, moral or otherwise, to the nation or its citizens.

It isn't supposed to be that way. Canada has a well-established policy regarding troop contributions to peacekeeping operations, UN or otherwise, which presumably ensures that a Canadian national interest will be served by our participation. The first and most important principle of that policy is that the mission must have "a clear and enforceable mandate." There was no clear and enforceable mandate in Bosnia from almost the beginning of UNPROFOR. What this meant in practical terms is that Canada's troops trained, equipped, and prepared themselves for a standard peacekeeping operation when Bosnia was anything but. This had an especially significant impact on the rules of engagement (ROEs) that Canadian soldiers were supposed to follow there.

For all practical purposes, ROEs don't exist in war. When one side finds enemy forces, it tries to destroy them, as quickly as possible and with as much violence as it can bring to bear. The only rule is Carl von Clausewitz's, that moderation in the fighting of battles is a recipe for disaster. But rules of engagement are vital when an army is deployed to perform a non-fighting mission such as a peacekeeping operation. Those rules dictate when a soldier is permitted to use force and how much force is allowed in given circumstances. For example, if a convoy comes under sniper fire from a village in a war, an appropriate response from the convoy might be to call down artillery on the village. It would, in other words, use whatever force was necessary to eliminate the threat. But if a convoy of peacekeepers comes under sniper fire, the rules of engagement would probably dictate that the convoy return fire only if it can definitely identify a muzzle flash, and only by directing fire precisely at that location.

Rules of engagement are supposed to be drawn up according to a number of criteria. What are the diplomatic objectives of the mission? What are the possible dangers to the peacekeepers? What does Canadian or international law say is an appropriate mode of behaviour? The rules are supposed to balance the need of peacekeeping troops to defend themselves with the requirement that they act as a neutral party to the conflict. The rules can be quite complex. They can dictate matters as elemental as the circumstances in which personal weapons may be loaded. Before any such rules can be drawn up, it is essential to know what the mission is.

Two sections of the UN Charter provide for the use of troops: Chapter VI and Chapter VII. In a Chapter VI mission, the UN deploys troops in classical peacekeeping style to help bring about a diplomatic settlement of a dispute. Normally, the parties to the dispute have agreed on a UN presence to keep their forces apart. There is little or no physical threat to the UN forces because they are there with the agreement of both sides. In a Chapter VI operation, therefore, UN troops are almost always lightly armed. They carry personal weapons. They may be equipped with a variety of light to heavy machine guns and light cannon. They do not deploy the full panoply of deadly weapons available to most armies today.

A Chapter VII operation is very different. It is undertaken at the behest of the UN to maintain or restore international peace or security. When the UN sanctions a Chapter VII operation, it is effectively declaring war against a transgressor. It will use troops offered to it by member nations to achieve some major international objective, such as restoring the independence and territorial integrity of Kuwait after it had been invaded, occupied, and annexed by Iraqi forces in 1990. In a Chapter VII operation, the rules of engagement regularly allow the use of deadly force by UN-sanctioned troops in a much greater variety of circumstances than is the case in a Chapter VI operation. Those troops, accordingly, are much more heavily armed than peacekeepers would be. The UNPROFOR operations in Bosnia were carried out under Chapter VI of the UN Charter. The rules of engagement under which Canadian and other UN troops operated were not much different than those that had been in use in Cyprus, for example, even though Cyprus – with only a few exceptions – was a sun-drenched picnic compared to Bosnia.

UN troops in Bosnia were in an active war zone and were often targeted themselves. The Canadians, for example, performed operations such as mine clearing and convoy protection, which were no different than those they might have carried out in a war. They also saw, heard, and smelled the sights, sounds, and stench of war, even when they were not being shot at. Twenty-four hours after leaving a peaceful and prosperous Canada, they were in the midst of a grievous slaughter; twenty-four hours after leaving that slaughter, they were back in Canada. It was as close to war as Canadian soldiers had been since the end of the Korean conflict in 1953.

It took almost four months for the Strathcona Battle Group to prepare for the mission dubbed Operation Cavalier III. The battle group was assembled by Brig.-Gen. Jim Cox, commander of the 1st Canadian Mechanized Brigade Group headquartered in Calgary. A Canadian battle group consists of an armoured regiment or an infantry battalion as its core, augmented by other units. For this mission, the Strathconas were joined by a company of infantry, an engineer squadron, troops from a service battalion, and medical and other support troops. Some 15 per cent of the contingent were reservists who had to be brought up to regular force standards through an additional three months of refresher training. Although these reservists almost always arrived at their assigned units with serious deficiencies in training and preparation, the ninety-day workup seemed to do wonders for their skills. One report noted that these men and women were "virtually indistinguishable" from their regular force counterparts in the field and that, "at the rifle man level, their performance [was] excellent."[2]

In February, the battle group travelled to Camp Pendleton, a U.S. Marine Corps training facility in California, to sharpen the skills they would require in Bosnia. At Camp Pendleton, too, they were given the rules of engagement and the standard operating procedures (SOPs) they would apply in the course of their duties. The troops were given live-fire training, first-aid refresher courses, and training in camp security. Particular emphasis was laid on convoy escort and cease-fire monitoring.

At that time, the army thought the Strathcona Battle Group's basic task would be to escort UN relief convoys. That turned out not to be true. After the conclusion of a February 1994 "peace plan" for Sarajevo – one of a series of ineffectual cease-fires – the battle group's mission was changed. It was assigned to patrol separation zones between the hostile forces in the northwest quadrant of an "exclusion zone" set up around the Bosnian capital. Consequently, the battle group's six-month tour in Visoko was mainly spent manning outposts located between Serb and Moslem forces and reporting to UN command on how well the two parties to the supposed cease-fire were doing killing each other. Operation Cavalier III put the Canadians square in the middle of some very dangerous situations.

As winter began to abate in the foothills of the Rockies, the Strathcona Battle Group returned to Calgary to prepare its heavy equipment for ocean transport to Croatia. The men and women of the battle group were due to fly to Split in three airlifts, called "chalks," on April 26 and May 3 and 10. From there, they would be trucked over narrow mountain roads to Visoko, where they would take possession of the CANBAT 2 base from the departing troops of the 5e Brigade mécanise du Canada.

Master Cpl. Phil Ward had been a Canadian soldier for twelve years before leaving for Bosnia on Operation Cavalier III. A member of the Strathcona anti-tank (TOW) troop, he had been stationed in Germany for four and a half years before returning to Canada in 1993. Ward and the other soldiers of TOW troop were trained to destroy enemy tanks using the wire-guided TOW missile and guidance system that had been retrofitted on a number of M-113 armoured personnel carriers. Though the Strathconas are an armoured regiment trained to use the Leopard main battle tank, tanks were not called for in this mission. If necessary, they would defend themselves against hostile armour with the TOWs.

When Ward had been assigned to Germany, his wife had gone with him; she would not be going this time. They decided to part at home rather than join the gaggle of husbands, wives, and kids saying their goodbyes at the base. "We both felt that it would be a lot easier for us to say goodbye in our own house," recalled Ward. "That way, if something did happen to me over there, the last time she would have seen me is in our own house, not on an army base. . . . We didn't want to do the sappy goodbye thing. . . . I filled up my coffee cup, went out the door, gave her a kiss goodbye, and she stood at the back door of our quarters. I waved goodbye to her, and as I backed out the driveway, I looked back at the house and she was crying."[3]

The troops assembled in one of the large drill halls at the Harvey Barracks, home to the Strathconas, with wives, children, and sweethearts hugging and kissing and saying their goodbyes. A taped line on the floor divided the hall in half. As the soldiers said their farewells, they grabbed their personal kit and walked across the line; families were not allowed to follow. Soon the crowd was sorted out, with families on one side and soldiers ready to depart on the other. The troops then filed out, boarded buses, and were driven to the Calgary airport. Some of the families followed in their cars all the way to the airport gate, which was swung closed behind the buses. The buses pulled up to the chartered jets and the troops climbed aboard. After a long flight, with stops in Montreal and Paris, they landed in Croatia and spent a night in Split.

The next morning, the trucks began the arduous climb into the mountains. As they left the peaceful Croatian coast behind, the sights of war became more common with each passing kilometre. Cpl. James Strayer remembered, "As we got deeper and deeper into Bosnia, we saw a lot more. In one of the big cities on the way, half the city was destroyed. . . . Then it really hits you. You wonder, 'Holy shit, am I going to be involved in this?' There's just a million and one questions going through your head. You're wondering what is going to be happening and how is this going to turn out. There is fear, there is definitely fear."[4]

The countryside around Visoko is much like it is in the Laurentian Mountains of Quebec, with wooded mountains, streams, and thick forests. The valley floors are dotted with villages and farms, many now gutted from the fighting. Most of the buildings are modern structures built in the last few decades because the area was devastated during the Second World War. In the summer, daily temperatures can reach as high as the low thirties, but the mountain nights are cool, with temperatures usually dropping to the mid-teens. In the fall and winter, heavy snow blankets the area and the narrow roads are often impassable. From their checkpoints and observation posts (OPs) south of Visoko, the Canadians could see as far as Sarajevo when the weather was clear. They could also easily hear the gunfire and see the smoke from the mortaring and shelling that never really stopped in and around the city.

On May 12, the Strathcona Battle Group assembled at Visoko. The next few days were taken up with the many tasks of the handover. The departing troops did their best to familiarize the Strathconas with the lay of the land and to identify the local warlords. Despite the cease-fire, Moslems and Serbs continued to snipe at each other with rifles, machine guns, and even mortars. It didn't take long for the battle group to learn to keep their heads up and their eyes and ears open. Sgt. Bob Harkies of the reconnaissance squadron later recalled, "You never had to motivate the guys to pay attention, never. I never had the case of a guy falling asleep on watch or anything like that. . . . I heard every bullet, crack, and thump that was within five kilometres of me. By the end of the tour, you could tell in the middle of the night what each was. I could open one eye and say, 'That was four hundred metres away and doesn't really concern me' or 'Son of a bitch, that was right over the OP.'"[5]

Although most of the battle group was assigned to man OPs for up to eight or nine days at a time, some of the reconnaissance troops were tasked to patrol the roads in the vicinity of Visoko. Phil Friday's squadron covered almost ten thousand kilometres in the first week alone. They were horrified to see the result of the "ethnic cleansing" that all three sides – Serb, Croatian, and Moslem – were wreaking on each other. "You go through towns where the town itself, maybe there are few bullet holes here and there, but the town itself is in good shape, except for every odd house which would be burned right out, burnt right to the ground," recalled Friday. Most of the Canadian soldiers had once thought the Serbs alone were guilty of conducting a race war. They soon changed their minds. "The Moslems are just as guilty as the Serbs, and the Croats are as guilty as the Moslems and the Serbs," Friday concluded. "Everybody is guilty over there."[6]

Virtually no Canadian soldier who served in the former Yugoslavia was untouched by the ferocity of the religious and ethnic hate that fuelled the conflict. When they talk about what they saw, they remark on the deep acrimony and mistrust all sides had for the others and for anyone they perceived as supporting their enemies. That made life especially difficult for peacekeepers, who daily discovered the burned and mutilated remains of Moslem, Serb, or Croat women and children in the ruins of their homes but still had to keep their emotions in check and deal even-handedly with the people. When they came home, few Canadian soldiers had a good word to say about any of the inhabitants of that much troubled region, or at least about the armed men who called themselves soldiers but who slaughtered innocents in the name of religion or ethnicity.

Cpl. Tracy Meisner Coulter was one of the very few Canadian woman to serve in Bosnia in a combat unit. During Operation Cavalier III, she was attached to the Strathcona TOW troop. The Moslem soldiers in the vicinity were uneasy in her presence; as far as they were concerned, a woman's place was at home or working in the fields and certainly not in a front-line combat unit. But although she received many strange looks, she never ran into any real trouble. "We never had any problems at check stops. They kind of looked at you funny when you were driving by.... Or if I wasn't driving that day for some reason, you'd get out of the vehicle and they'd take a second look. Kind of weird for them to see a female in combat."[7]

At first when the Canadians set up a patrol routine and began to man their checkpoints and OPs along the cease-fire lines, life in the area was quiet. There were cease-fire violations almost daily, but they usually consisted of a few rounds fired by snipers. The farmers returned to their fields as the days grew longer and warmer and a semblance of normal commerce and regular life resumed. To a limited extent, the trust of the locals in the UN also returned, although it was not at all unusual for the Canadians' white-painted vehicles to be stoned when they passed through certain villages. Almost always, children ran alongside the vehicles begging for candy or cigarettes, but the patrols were under strict orders not to halt lest they be delayed by small crowds. A stopped convoy, strung out on the main road of a village, was a tempting target for anyone with a machine gun and a bad attitude towards white paint and blue helmets.

There were land mines everywhere. The simple act of walking could bring instant death or mangled limbs to soldiers who momentarily forgot where they were. There is supposed to be an international convention governing the laying and marking of minefields, but it was almost completely ignored in Bosnia. Any innocent-looking field, path, or gravel road could hide them. Some of the mines had to be cleared by the battle group's combat engineers before the Canadian troops could travel freely in their patrol zones. That was a singularly dangerous job. Many of the mines were made of plastic and difficult to detect with electronic mine-sweeping gear; others were booby-trapped so that the deactivation of one mine would result in a chain explosion of several others.

Among the outposts used by the Strathcona Battle Group were two known as Kilo Fox-trot and Charlie One. Because Kilo Fox-trot was several kilometres from Visoko, on the top of a mountain, the soldiers usually spent eight or nine nights there. Kilo Fox-trot was the first OP that Jim Strayer's troop was sent to. "With all our observation equipment, spotting scopes and binoculars and everything, you could get a pretty good look at Sarajevo," Strayer recalls. "There was always shooting in the background, out in the distance, but it was always a kilometre or two away. So we had a lot of cease-fire violations to report, but they were distant, not a direct threat. It didn't involve you. You were on the outside looking at it and that made it easier, for everybody back home as well . . . but then we ended up moving to Charlie One and the difference was night and day."[8]

Charlie One was in a hot zone about three kilometres from the battle group's main camp. The danger meant that the Canadians followed a different routine. They rarely stayed in place for more than twenty-four hours at a stretch. Strayer remembers, "You are watching the [Moslem troops] shooting from a bunker twenty metres from you rather than hearing the shots from two kilometres away . . . rather than looking at it from the outside, I'm in it." At first the sniping didn't really involve the Canadian troops, even though Charlie One loomed just over the main Moslem positions. But then the Moslem troops began to use the Canadians as a shield. "They would know that we were twenty metres from their positions and they would use it to their advantage. They would shoot in the direction of the Serbs and know that the Serbs weren't going to return fire. And sure enough, that was the way it was, for a while."[9]

But only for a while. By midsummer, the cease-fire violations all along the separation lines were becoming more routine, and far deadlier. Machine-gun, mortar, and rocket-propelled grenade (RPG) fire was starting to become commonplace. The Serbs were losing their already stretched patience with the tactical situation at OP Charlie One. They were starting to shoot back, and the Canadians were in the middle. Towards the end of June, battle group commander Lt.-Col. Ray Wlasichuk sought and obtained permission from UN command to fire illumination rounds from his 81-mm mortars in case shooting broke out at night. It was his way of demonstrating to both the Moslems and the Serbs that the Canadians had some serious firepower available if they needed it.

In the early morning hours of Sunday, July 4, two Canadian armoured personnel carriers (APCs) and eight soldiers were in position at Charlie One when Moslem troops opened up at the Serbs from the bunkers just below the Canadian positions. With an extraction plan in place in case his soldiers were directly attacked, Wlasichuk ordered the heavy mortars to begin firing. Jim Strayer was there: "It was frustrating. The rounds were going everywhere, and we were going to have to just sit like guinea pigs until it blew over. I couldn't believe it when it really started happening. I remember thinking it was a bad shoot and that they'd better not start shooting anything but illumination rounds or we will be in a world of hurt. Everything was off."[10]

Cpl. Tracy Meisner Coulter was inside one of the APCs and began calling corrections to the mortar crews. "We were really hyped up for it because . . . we're sitting in the middle of this and we don't know what the heck is going to be the response or anything. We were just waiting. Everybody was just sitting there and waiting and thinking, 'Come on. Come on, just do it and let's find out what the result is.'" When the illumination rounds finally started to pop over the Moslem positions, the effect was stunning. "I am sitting and I can't see much because I just have little periscopes . . . the flare goes off and it illuminates the Moslem trenches really well. I'd say five hundred to a thousand metres beyond us. The guy in the turret starts laughing, and we're asking him, 'What are you laughing at?' and he says, 'They're like little ants scattering.'"[11]

As the flares popped and hissed under their parachutes, the Moslem riflemen were caught in the open and dove for cover. The firing died down. Wlasichuk's emergency reaction force, made up of a platoon of infantry and a squadron of armoured vehicles, waited at their start line (the point from where an advance would commence). A fog blanketed the area and sporadic rifle shots split the dark. One sniper in particular seemed to be deliberately shooting into the Canadian positions. Strayer was in the turret of the APC. "I used the thermal [a night-imaging device] to find the sniper's location," he recalls. "Finally, a muzzle flash and we knew where he was. I had him in my sights and we were given the okay to fire if he shot again. It was quite a feeling for me because I had him in my cross-sights. . . . I knew one more shot and I will take a life."[12] But the sniper didn't fire again.

As the night wore on, the tempo of shooting increased from the Serb positions. At least four hundred rounds of automatic fire were aimed at, or over, Charlie One. Then, at about 5 A.M., a Serb-launched RPG round exploded near one of the Canadian APCs. Section leader Sgt. Tom Hoppe sprang into action. He ordered the exposed vehicle to move away from the ridge line while he radioed battle group HQ to warn them that his group might need immediate rescue. That was easier said than done; the road to Charlie One was under Moslem control. As the convoy moved up the road, it came under intense rifle and automatic-weapons fire; Master Cpl. Frank Cananco was hit by a bullet fragment. With the road effectively blocked, the convoy was forced to withdraw, and a stronger relief effort was organized. But by 6:30 A.M., the fog began to lift and the firing around Charlie One died down.

The firefight around Charlie One on the night of July 3, 1994, was barely noticed in Canada. People were too busy enjoying the first week of the summer holiday to care. But eight Canadian soldiers had come perilously close to being killed or wounded. For Hoppe, Meisner Coulter,

Strayer, and the others, it was all in a night's work. They are professional soldiers. They go where they are sent, do the best they can, and accept the risks inherent in soldiering as part of the job. They trust their lives are not being endangered needlessly and that the missions they are sent to perform are doable and necessary, at least to somebody. The fact is, however, that they ought not to have been on Charlie One in the middle of a deadly firefight. They had been sent to Bosnia to police a cease-fire, not to act as human shields for two armies bent on killing each other. And they had been sent without adequate backup, with ROEs that were too restrictive for the mission, and with both equipment and intelligence that were dangerously out of date.

When a Canadian battle group returns from an operation, it files a post-operation report to Land Force Command. The report for Operation Cavalier III details the many deficiencies of equipment and procedure that were revealed in the battle group's six-month mission to Bosnia. Maps are vital to any military operation, but there was "a major problem" with them. The maps supplied were of two different scales, which made it difficult to plot positions on a single grid. Nor were there adequate aerial reconnaissance photographs, which can often make up for deficiencies in maps. Poor coordination between NATO and the UN command undermined the battle group's ability to call in help from NATO fighters or helicopters. In addition, the chain of command in Bosnia was complex, cumbersome, confusing, and slow. It took too long for information to move. The battle group sometimes received orders from officials not authorized to issue them or received several different and confusing orders from different agencies of the UN command at the same time. That might not have mattered in a situation of relative quiet, but it was a serious handicap as the summer wore on and the fighting between the Moslems and Serbs became more intense.

The battle group had to cope with a number of serious shortages of both manpower and equipment. The combat engineer squadron was about half the size of engineer units in other national contingents and lacked important command and control personnel. The heavy equipment supplied, such as front-end loaders, dump trucks, etc., was "not suitable for op[erations] on steep approaches to OPs" and was not armoured, a key deficiency in a high-threat environment. The Cougar, a wheeled armoured vehicle that was the mainstay of the mobile patrols, was not equipped with a stabilized turret and could not bring its 76-mm gun to bear quickly in an emergency. That was important because "the threat in this theatre can materialize in seconds from any direction." Mine-detection gear was inadequate. Too often the only way to find these deadly devices was for the engineers to get on the ground and probe for them by hand, a risky business that ought not to have been necessary. There were also shortages of Kevlar helmets and flak vests while those "drawn in theatre were for the most part in poor condition." Even the rainwear leaked.[13]

Canadian soldiers perpetually live with second-rate, old, or patched-up kit; they take a perverse pride in their ability to make do with what they have and do a good job of it. Far more serious than any shortage or deficiency of equipment were the inadequate rules of engagement. The Strathcona Battle Group was in the middle of a war. As the weeks and months dragged by, the fighting intensified and the Canadians were increasingly being targeted by one side or the other. The soldiers on patrol, or manning OPs, ought to have been able to instantly call on the battle group's 81-mm mortars, TOW missiles, or 76-mm guns to defend themselves against hostile fire. Nothing is more effective in knocking out a heavy machine-gun firing into an OP than a barrage of mortar fire. Yet the Canadians had to sit and take it – and hope to survive – because their rules of engagement were designed for a Cyprus-type of situation, not an active civil war. In the words of the post-operation report, "Situations develop too quickly and req[uire] immediate return fire to adequately protect our soldiers." The battle group commander should have been authorized to use heavy weapons when necessary without having to clear the decision with some higher authority. He had no such authority.

The complete inadequacy of the Canadian rules of engagement became more apparent with the passing of each day. On the night of July 15, Sgt. Tom Hoppe and his TOW troop were again positioned at Charlie One. This time they had three M-113s parked above the Moslem trenches. A

UN flag was flying, illuminated by a spotlight. Cpl. Darren Magas had just dismounted one of the vehicles at about 11:30 P.M. and had entered a tent to begin his break. "The Serbs opened up machine-gun fire just over top of the tents . . . this was about 150, 200 rounds . . . it was just non-stop," he recalled. "I was in the tent beside another guy trying to slap the old boots on really quick. You are screaming at him and you can't hear what he is saying, that's how loud it was."[14] Master Cpl. Phil Ward was outside the tents when the shooting began. He yelled at the men inside to stay down, then dashed around the corner of the position. "I could see a muzzle blast from just behind the tree line, this went on for about five or six minutes, but I couldn't get a clear view of the guy so I didn't return fire." Ward then climbed into one of the APCs and got the engine started. With the bullets cracking around him, he waited for someone to get the other two moving. The machine-gun fire intensified as the Moslems began to shoot back at the Serb positions. Both sides poured fire into Charlie One. Trooper Jason Skilliter ran out of his tent, grabbed his machine gun, and sprawled on the ground facing a Moslem bunker. Then he opened up at the bunker's firing slit. When the shooting from the bunker stopped for a moment, he and Hoppe ran to the other two APCs, got them started, then began to move them back out of the line of fire. With Ward's APC as rear guard, Hoppe and Skilliter then led the troop off the hill and out of danger. Hoppe and Skilliter were later decorated for their bravery.

By the first week of August, the Canadian sector had become an all-out war zone. The battle group's war diary for the first five days of that month tells a harrowing story:

01 August 94
Between 1000-1030 hrs 5 x mortar rounds impacted in the town of VISOKO. . . . At 1537 hrs the BiH [Bosnian Army, i.e., Moslems] began to fire mortar rounds at BSA [Bosnian Serb Army] positions. . . . The camp state of readiness was changed to State Yellow at 1610 hrs due to the threat of BSA retaliatory fire. Heavy exchanges of SA [small arms], HMG [heavy machine gun], and mortar and artillery fire developed. BSA stated that if the BiH did not stop immediately

they would "let loose with everything." At 1641 hrs air raid sirens sounded in VISOKO. At 1705 hrs the BiH were reportedly shelling ILIJAS. By 1713 hrs the intensity of HMG and mortar fire had increased and at one point 15 x mortar rounds impacted south of OP C2 at a rate of one every 20-30 seconds.... This is probably the first time the Strathconas have been jammed in an operational theatre since KOREA....

2 August 94

at 1930 hrs ... both OP MIKE and OP PAPA found themselves in the middle of a savage firefight between BiH forces in BANJER and the BSA at CEKRCICI. This continued throughout the evening. ... Fighting continued throughout the night with all OPs reporting firefights and artillery fire.

3 August 94

Fighting between the BSA/BiH continued into the night with mortars, artillery, heavy machine gun and rocket propelled grenade [RPG] fire.... the BiH captured key ground which in time may permit them to launch further attacks to the southeast.... The BSA formally requested CANBAT 2 ... to imposition troops between them and the BiH. This is the first time, to the writer's knowledge, that the BSA have requested UNPROFOR assistance.

4 August 94

Today the BG [battle group] attempted to deploy B Sqn Cbt [combat] Team to the DASTANSKO SALIENT in an attempt to interposition troops between the warring parties. The BiH denied the BG access through OP M and laid spike belts across the road. It is believed the BiH wish to deny us access due to the success they are enjoying in the DASTANSKO SALIENT.... Tensions are on the rise around the OPs and all positions are noticing an increase in the number of firefights and artillery impacts, but none have come close, as yet!

5 August 94

A very interesting day! Early this morning the BSA took 4 weapons from a weapons collection point [WCP] in ILIDZA, west of SARA-JEVO. These weapons were a T-55 tank, two M80 armoured personnel carriers [APCs], and a self-propelled anti-aircraft gun. . . . Authorization was granted for the use of airstrikes against BSA targets inside the Exclusion Zone [around Sarajevo] and at approximately 1630 hrs a NATO A-10 aircraft engaged and destroyed a BSA M-18 Hellcat tank destroyer! . . . The BiH have gone so far as restricting our movement through OP M and the KISELJAK POCKET stating that they no longer trusted the actions of the BG due to our . . . attempted deployment of the combat team. The AOR [area of responsibility] remains volatile and unpredictable as fighting continues between the BSA and the BiH.[15]

The shooting abated the next day and in the weeks that followed partly because of the UN's diplomatic efforts, but mostly due to the threat of further NATO air strikes. But it did not stop completely. On the last day of the month, Sgt. Tom Hoppe was given another chance to show his bravery under fire. He and seven other soldiers were positioned at an OP between ridges occupied by the Moslems and the Serbs when shooting broke out. "There was a lot of drinking going on," Hoppe later told *Maclean's* magazine. "These guys would get totally blotto and take potshots at us. It was irritating." Hoppe and the other Canadians were not the only targets, however; he soon noticed gunshots hitting around three young boys who were trying to take cover near the entrance to a cemetery about forty-five metres from the Canadian position. Hoppe told his APC driver to cover him and began running towards the children; the M-113 moved beside him blocking him from the gunfire. When he reached the cemetery gate, Hoppe dashed out from cover, grabbed the boys, and shoved them to safety through the rear doors of the APC. Later that year, Hoppe received both the Medal of Bravery and the Meritorious Service Cross from Governor General Ramon Hnatyshyn to become one of the most highly decorated Canadian soldiers since the Second World War.[16]

The final serious incident to befall a member of the battle group took place just weeks before the return to Canada when Warrant Officer Tom Martineau was shot by a Moslem sniper while on duty at OP Romeo 5. Phil Friday was one of the first to reach him. "I was sleeping and Corporal Jensen comes in yelling that Martineau had been shot," he remembered. "When I first woke up, I couldn't believe it. I remember thinking that this is some stupid drill." Friday grabbed his rifle and flak jacket and started walking up the hill towards where Martineau had been positioned; about halfway up he started running. Then he saw Jensen and two other men, one a friendly Serb soldier, pulling Martineau down from the APC. "He was just limp so I grabbed the other leg, pulled him down the front of the vehicle, and laid him on the ground." Friday asked Martineau where he had been hit and was told the left side. "I still didn't believe he was shot for some reason. Then I pulled my hand away and it was all covered in blood . . . I got out my knife, cut away his shirt, and all I could see was a perfectly round hole about six inches below his armpit."[17]

With the help of a number of Serb soldiers, Martineau was bandaged and carried down the hill to await an ambulance. The call went in at about 11:30 P.M., but the vehicle did not arrive for almost an hour; it was only five minutes away as the crow flies, but the ambulance had to cross from the Moslem to the Serbian side. When Martineau finally arrived at the hospital, Sgt. R. D. Mackwood first thought he looked in good condition, but knew that a small bullet hole on the outside often meant major internal damage: "They opened him up, had a look in. . . . The bullet, of course, did tremendous damage to him and lodged into his lower back." Martineau's spleen had disintegrated and there was extensive damage to other organs. He survived, and was evacuated out, but his active career as a Strathcona was over. "Tom always had a dream," Mackwood remembers, "of coming back to the regiment. But as time goes by, it becomes less and less likely."[18]

The Strathcona Battle Group returned to Canada at the end of the month, the last flight arriving in Calgary on October 29. When close to eight hundred soldiers return from a mission as harrowing as this one, there are probably as many different personal reactions to what they had been through as there are members in the battle group. For Master Cpl. Roger Laverdure, the mission as a whole had been a waste of time. "After about the third month, everybody was fed up," he later recalled. "We weren't doing anything, really, besides counting bullets."[19] But whatever the ultimate value of the operation to Bosnia, to Canada, or to the world, Sgt. Bob Harkies, for one, learned much about himself while he was there. "It proved to me after seventeen years in the army that I could do what I was trained to do. . . . I was perfectly willing to shoot a twelve-year-old boy who pointed a rocket launcher at me. My .50 [-calibre heavy machine gun] was cocked and he was history. The only reason I didn't shoot was when he finally turned it at an angle, I caught a glimpse down the tube, there was no rocket in there. If there had been a rocket in it, he was wearing fifty bullets. I don't care if he was a twelve-year-old boy, I got six guys in the back [of the APC] and a rocket is pretty impersonal."[20]

No one was killed from the battle group. But in the same period that CANBAT 2 was struggling to fulfil its mission in Visoko, a Canadian soldier of CANBAT 1 was not so lucky. In June 1994, Cpl. Mark "Izzy" Isfeld, a thirty-two-year-old husband and father, and a member of the Combat Engineers, was killed while clearing mines in Croatia. It was Isfeld's second tour. He was walking in front of an APC when the vehicle drove over a mine linked to six others in what the engineers referred to as a necklace. Only one other mine exploded; it was the one that killed Isfeld. Before he left for his second tour in that unhappy place, Isfeld had told his mother, "Every mine I lift, someone else won't die." He lifted lots of mines and saved many lives. He was the tenth, and last, Canadian soldier to be killed there.[21]

Returning from a six-month tasking to Cyprus or the Golan Heights was never easy; coming back from six months in the cauldron of Bosnia was even more difficult. For decades, Canadian soldiers had been returning to Canada from peacekeeping missions that took them to the middle of active war zones or that made them observers of the terrible aftermath of war. Now, in Bosnia, they had themselves been the targets of hostile fire and had had to shoot back. What had gone unrecognized in more than four decades of Canadian peacekeeping missions was now discussed more frequently: the soldiers didn't always come back in the same frame of mind as when they had left. More and more soldiers coming home from the former Yugoslavia found that they could not talk to their loved ones, that they had recurring nightmares, that their nerves were shot, that their memory had become faulty, or that they were mired in depression. A new term was coming into usage: critical incident stress (CIS) reaction. This was a variation on the better known "post-traumatic stress disorder" that has been commonly identified with returning American Vietnam War veterans.

The army now believes as many as one out of six Canadian soldiers who served in Bosnia suffers from some variation of CIS. The military defines CIS as a "normal reaction to an abnormal event." In peacekeepers, the reaction is usually delayed. "They get back home, everyone's happy, and after a month, the bubble bursts and it takes six months to a year for them to recover," says Canadian Forces psychiatrist Lt.-Cmdr. Greg Passey. They've seen terrible things that no one at home could possibly imagine, even in the worst nightmare. When CBC reporter Eve Savory recently prepared a story on CIS for "Prime Time News," one soldier told her of seeing children nailed to a wall, another of collecting and burning bodies and taking days to get the blood cleaned from his shoes.[22]

CIS most often affects those, like the soldiers sent to Bosnia, who suddenly find themselves in the midst of terrible events without adequate time to prepare themselves. It causes acute anxiety and alienation and can be as debilitating as clinical depression. The army is now providing briefings on CIS to Canadian peacekeepers about to go abroad, and every unit has people trained to spot the early symptoms and to alleviate it. But those who are most deeply affected by CIS usually need professional help to recover. And although they are starting to get that help, they are not getting it as quickly as they ought to. One recent report prepared by Roman Catholic command chaplain Lt.-Col. Murray C. Farwell documented the situation: "Several chaplains have indicated there is a problem in obtaining the required medical help for returning military personnel who are suffering critical incident stress syndrome. The number of channels before receiving authorization for assistance is unwieldy. The problem is especially evident in the Reserves. Presently, a soldier must go through five levels of command before reaching the specialist that can help him." According to Farwell, the process is "cumbersome, frustrating and time consuming and is in many cases the determining factor for a soldier refusing the help that he initially sought."[23]

When the Canadian press and public first heard the shocking revelations of the murder of Shidane Abukar Arone in Belet Huen, Somalia, on the night of March 16, 1993, there was an immediate and understandable outcry. Since then, almost every facet of that mission has been exposed to the view of the Canadian public. Most Canadians know more today about the scandal of Somalia than they do about Vimy Ridge, Normandy, Kap'yong, or Visoko. But the greater scandal, one which took place at the same time as the Somalia mission, was that thousands of Canadian soldiers were sent into a place where their lives were recklessly risked by politicians who appear not to have cared for their welfare. At the same time, these soldiers were virtually ignored by the media, which sniffs out every whiff of scandal in the Canadian army but dismisses missions such as the one to Bosnia as just another army job to be taken for granted. The Canadian participation in UNPROFOR has been one of the country's best-kept secrets. To the everlasting credit of the men and women who went to Bosnia, the vast majority did what Canadian soldiers have done for over a hundred years: their very best, without complaint, until time and circumstance brought them home again.

PART THREE

THE CANADIAN

AIRBORNE REGIMENT

———◆◆———

From first to last, the Canadian Airborne Regiment needed the best leaders the army could give it. In wartime, elite status is bestowed on virtually anyone who trades fire with the enemy. The battlefield is the great leveller among soldiers. But in peacetime, paratroopers usually think and act (and are sometimes treated) as the elite of the infantry because of the unique mental and physical challenges that they must overcome.

Paratroopers are considered by some in the military as the essential soldiers. They are trained to move, shoot, and manoeuvre quickly, without the benefit of support from armour or artillery. In the Canadian army, a stint in the Airborne became a virtual requirement for higher infantry command. In the first decade and a half of its existence, the Airborne's unique composite structure and special status virtually guaranteed that Canada's infantry regiments would send it a fair share of their very best soldiers and leaders.

That started to change in the 1980s when the army's leadership crisis began to take hold. When more and more inadequate commanders filtered into the regiment at all levels, discipline and good order suffered. By the end of the 1980s, enough troublemakers had found a niche in the regiment to require a thorough housecleaning. That did not happen. The murder in Somalia was the result.

7

THE PEGASUS TRADITION

THE Pegasus Bridge is a bridge no longer. Until the night of June 5, 1944 – the night before D-Day – it was known as the Benouville-Ranville Bridge. It spanned the Caen Canal and the Orne River between the hamlets of Benouville and Ranville, just a few kilometres south of the Bay of the Seine. But on that fateful night, the men of the 6th British Airborne Division landed there and at points to the east, seized the bridge, and held it until relieved by British ground troops nearly twenty-four hours later. From that night on, the bridge was known as Pegasus Bridge, in honour of the first British troops to liberate French soil.

When representatives of the Allied nations who took part in the Normandy landings gathered in June 1994 to mark the fiftieth anniversary of that fateful battle, the Pegasus Bridge was only a memory. Despite loud protests from veterans' groups and local residents, the old bridge was torn down in 1993 and replaced by a modern span. But not all the protest was in vain. Embarrassed by the charge that France did not especially care to preserve a memorial to British paratroopers, Paris agreed to reconstruct the old bridge in a field nearby. As late as the spring of 1996, however, the remnants of the bridge lay where they were unceremoniously dumped when the structure was torn down.

Pegasus, the winged horse of Greek mythology, is one of the two symbols that signify the British airborne tradition. The other is the maroon beret. Both symbols were adopted by Canada's paratroopers because the only parachute unit formed in Canada, the 1st Canadian Parachute Battalion, was attached to the 6th British Airborne for the duration of the Second World War. The 1st Canadian Parachute Battalion, Canada's pioneer paratroop unit, played an important role on the night of June 5, 1944. Attached to the 3rd Parachute Brigade of the 6th Airborne, the Canadians were assigned to destroy a German head-quarters at Varaville, about seven kilometres east of the Benouville Bridge, blow two bridges over the Dives River, and cover the flank of the 9th British Parachute Battalion as it attacked and destroyed a coastal battery at Merville. The overall divisional objective was to secure the Allied left flank before the troops hit the shore on D-Day. At the other end of the Normandy beaches, American paratroopers of the 82nd and 101st Airborne Divisions were to land to the west of Utah Beach to secure the other flank of the Allied invasion zone.

The British paratroopers assigned to attack the Benouville Bridge landed by glider some twenty minutes after midnight on the morning of June 6. They completely surprised the defenders and seized the German guard posts and gun positions at both ends of the bridge. Then they hunkered down as the Germans began to react to the threat in their midst. Through the long night the British troops beat off attack after attack. As dawn broke, they heard the thunder of the Allied naval bombardment of the landing beaches over the crackle and thump of the small-arms and mortar fire that marked their own intense battle.

The 526 paratroopers of the 1st Canadian Parachute Battalion were supposed to land in a small drop zone about one kilometre east of Varaville. They were to come in two waves, with C Company landing first to guide the rest in. They took off from England in twenty-six C-47 transports at twenty-five minutes to midnight; three other C-47s towed gliders filled with heavy equipment to the drop zone. Things started to go wrong almost immediately. Many of the C-47s got lost on the way in, and the men and their equipment were scattered over an area about forty times larger than planned. Eighty-four were quickly captured by the Germans. Much of the equipment the battalion had counted on to survive against German armour was lost in fields that the Germans had flooded in anticipation of an invasion. Despite their casualties – the Canadian battalion suffered 113 in the first twenty-four hours, including 19 killed, 10 wounded, and 84 taken prisoner – they did the job demanded of them. The bridges over the Dives were blown, the headquarters at

Varaville was captured, and the 9th British Parachute Battalion received the flank protection it needed when the Merville battery was destroyed.

By mid-day on June 6, the battalion completed a pull-back to the crossroads at Le Mesnil. Their job: help the rest of the division mount a defence against the expected German counter-attack. It soon came, as one British war correspondent later reported, "The Germans came at us with tanks and men, again and again. At night they pushed patrols forward, probing and seeking our weak spots. Every day men died, men were wounded and our ranks thinned. But the Germans got nowhere: their dead were found in the woods, along the lines, in the cornfields … everywhere."[1] German losses were formidable, but when the Canadian paratroopers were temporarily pulled out of the line eleven days after D-Day, less than one-third of the original contingent answered the call to muster.

The idea of armed men dropping from the sky to surprise and envelope a defending force is at least as old as the Renaissance. Leonardo da Vinci speculated on how such a feat could be achieved. Until there was some practical way of transporting troops into the sky over enemy territory, however, the notion of airborne assault was nothing more than science fiction. The rapid evolution of aircraft and aerial combat after the outbreak of the First World War produced the two elements necessary to give life to the idea: aircraft capable of carrying heavy loads, and the parachute. By the end of the war, the Germans and the Allies were launching bombing raids on each other using multi-engined aircraft capable of carrying several thousand pounds of bombs while pilots routinely wore parachutes to bail out of stricken aircraft (as did balloon-borne observers).

Only four years after the end of the war, the military of the then-newly constituted U.S.S.R. tried dropping soldiers from aircraft by parachute. German army advisers attached to the Soviet forces took the idea back to Germany. Both countries pushed ahead with the development of airborne forces, perfecting the use of anchor and static lines (instead of the rip-cord), and experimenting with ways of exiting from aircraft in flight. In the late 1930s, the German air force began to assemble an airborne corps. They used gliders to transport the heavier weapons and other equipment paratroopers could not carry. This idea was later taken up by the British and Americans, who included at least one glider regiment or brigade in each of their airborne divisions.

The deployment of German paratroopers in the opening battles of the Second World War stunned the Allies. In the spring of 1940, the Germans employed airborne troops with great effect in the invasion of Norway and the Low Countries, and later – in 1941 – in the conquest of Crete, where they suffered very heavy casualties. The Allies quickly began to train and organize their own airborne forces, although they were, at first, unsure how to deploy them effectively. Early American airborne doctrine called for the insertion of small airborne units just behind enemy lines, but there were those who advocated the use of massed airborne troops in large-scale operations far behind the front.

Airborne forces offered both advantages and disadvantages over regular infantry. They could, in effect, vault over enemy defences to attack the enemy's rear. They could seize important tactical objectives such as bridges, road junctions, or airfields. Their very presence as a tactical threat could force the enemy to hold back reserve forces better used at the front. But by their very nature, airborne troops were also highly vulnerable. If their aircraft were spotted en route to the drop zone, they could be slaughtered by anti-aircraft fire or fighter planes before they were committed to battle. If they were dropped too close to enemy formations in daylight, they were easily shot while still swinging in their parachute harnesses.

Night drops seemed to be the answer to some of these problems, but aerial navigation by night was a crude affair in the Second World War: aircraft often got lost or released troopers or equipment too far from the drop zones. Allied airborne forces suffered all these problems during the war as, for example, when a mass night drop laid on for the invasion of Sicily in 1943 resulted in major losses of aircraft, gliders, and paratroopers.

The most important drawback of airborne troops was that they could be only lightly armed. Gliders enabled paratroopers to take some ground vehicles – the four-wheel-drive jeep in particular – and heavier weapons, but nothing like the firepower available to regular infantry. An airborne brigade, for example, had none of the field artillery, none of the armoured support, and little of the heavy-mortar and machine-gun support available to its regular infantry counterpart. Nor did it have a secure line of supply to bring up food and ammunition or to evacuate casualties. Under the best of circumstances – when a successful drop enabled airborne troops to concentrate quickly and get at their jeeps, mortars, machine guns, radios, and supplies before the enemy did – an airborne force was not capable of holding out behind enemy lines for more than about three days.

Nowhere was the vulnerability of airborne forces proved more dramatically than at the Battle of Arnhem in September 1944. In that fight, the 1st British Airborne Division was dropped some one hundred kilometres behind German lines to seize a Rhine River bridge at Arnhem, in eastern Holland. The force was practically annihilated by German armoured troops when Allied ground forces failed to reach it in the planned forty-eight hours.

Because airborne formations were neither trained nor equipped for prolonged combat, they proved to be a major drain on men and resources. Successes at Normandy in June 1944 and in the massive Rhine-crossing drop of Operation Varsity in March 1945 notwithstanding, British, American, and Canadian paratroopers spent far more time out of combat than did their regular infantry comrades. The 1st British Airborne Division was held in reserve from June through September 1944, for example, while British infantry and armoured divisions were chewed up in the slaughterhouse of Normandy. There was, thus, an inclination on the part of Allied military planners to design missions for which airborne soldiers might be used, almost to prove that the men and equipment that composed those forces were not being squandered.

Canada entered the airborne era in 1942 when plans were first laid for a Canadian parachute battalion of 618 officers and men. The unit was originally to be used for the defence of Canada. This idea was too limited to merit the expenditure of sufficient funds, however, and so overseas deployment was authorized. The unit was to operate in conjunction with British and other Commonwealth forces. The men were all volunteers and came from units in Canada and the United Kingdom. They were sent to Fort Benning, Georgia, for initial training, then to Shilo, Manitoba, where the Canadian Parachute Training Centre was eventually set up (it was later moved to Rivers, Manitoba). They trained on American equipment and learned the American style of doing things, and when they arrived in the United Kingdom in the summer of 1943, they had to relearn much to conform to British equipment and procedures.

While the Canadian parachute battalion was being formed, a second parachute unit containing Canadian troops was also being established. This was the Canadian section of the First Special Service Force (FSSF), which later became famous as "The Devil's Brigade." The first commander of the FSSF was U.S. Col. Robert T. Frederick, who foresaw a joint Canadian–American unit of parachute commandos. The force was activated at Helena, Montana, in July 1942 and was supposed to take part in the campaign to recapture the Aleutian island of Kiska, but Kiska was found abandoned and the force was sent to Italy instead. From the fall of 1943 to the winter of 1944, the force distinguished itself in a number of daring commando operations during the long ordeal at the Anzio beachhead and in the liberation of Rome.

Although the FSSF never jumped into action, it suffered inordinately heavy casualties in its short, illustrious career. In one six-day action at Monte la Difensa, Italy, in December 1943, the force sustained 511 losses in killed, wounded, missing in action, and battle exhaustion. Frederick himself was twice wounded. In early December 1944, the force was disbanded; the American members were transferred to U.S. airborne units while the Canadians were either absorbed into the infantry or transferred to 1st Canadian Parachute Battalion.

In the United Kingdom, the 1st Canadian Parachute Battalion was mated with the British 8th and 9th Parachute Battalions of the 3rd Parachute Brigade. They saw action with the 6th British Airborne Division in Normandy, in the Battle of the Bulge, and later in the Rhine crossing in Operation Varsity on March 24, 1945. This was the last major parachute drop of the European war. The battalion CO, Lt.-Col. Jeff

Nicklin, was killed in action on the first morning when he was snagged in trees just above a German machine-gun position. As part of 2nd British Army, the Canadian paratroopers participated in the race to outrun the Russians to the German–Danish border. They reached the Baltic – and joined up with the Russians – on May 2, 1945. The unit was disbanded five months later.

The Canadian paratroopers of the Second World War are much older now. They have lost the exuberance of youth. "We were just fairly average guys," declares George Robertson. "Parachuting to me was a way of getting from A to B, just a different mode of transportation. Flying in was not nearly as dangerous as coming over the beach, though we were conscious of our isolation." Dan Hartigan has a similar recollection: "Calling us 'elite' made us angry during the war. . . . We were all fighting the same enemy to the best of our ability."[2]

There were certainly some wartime paratroopers who thought of themselves as an elite – as better trained, physically tougher, and more daring than regular infantry. But the claim was hard to sustain. There was nothing special about the fact these men were volunteers, because all but a tiny handful of Canadian soldiers who saw action in the Second World War were volunteers. (That was not true in the U.S. military, which was largely manned by conscripts.) More important, those Canadians who fought in units such as the PPCLI in Italy or the Calgary Highlanders in northwest Europe saw far more action (if they escaped death or serious wounds) than any airborne soldier, and everybody knew it.

By the beginning of 1946, Canada's two wartime parachute units were gone, but the idea of using parachute troops in the defence of Canada was very much alive in Ottawa. The Canadian military was struggling to find ways of mounting a credible defence of the nation in an era of rapidly shrinking budgets and with no immediate enemy threat to the nation. Thus was born the Mobile Striking Force (MSF) and the radical idea that virtually all of Canada's active (i.e., permanent or regular force) army ought to be air-transportable.

By the end of 1946, Canada's wartime army of almost 500,000 had been reduced to some 15,500 regulars and a somewhat larger force of reserves. The active force troops were organized into three infantry battalions, two armoured regiments, artillery and engineering regiments, and a number of other support units. Some of the soldiers manning these units had received parachute training during the war, others took the jump course at Shilo to qualify for their paratrooper wings. Parachute pay was better, and jumpers were thought to be showing more initiative in preparing for an all-round career in the army. The army's initial intention was to create a Canadian Special Air Service Company consisting of one jump platoon from each infantry battalion. In 1948, with the deepening of the Cold War, this intention was expanded; henceforth, all three infantry battalions would be jump-trained and combined into a Mobile Striking Force (MSF). The MSF was to be a reserve capable of being airlifted at a moment's notice to any place in the Canadian north. There it would counter landings from Soviet paratroopers bent on seizing forward airfields for the use of Soviet bombers. In the summer of 1948, the PPCLI became the first of the three battalions to begin jump-training.

On paper, the Mobile Striking Force seemed a good idea. The Canadian military planners of the late 1940s were convinced that there would be no full-scale invasion of the continent upon the outbreak of any hostilities with the U.S.S.R., and so only a small defence force was needed. But there were major problems to overcome: the MSF was not intended to be based together as an integrated brigade group, and neither the numbers, nor the type of aircraft most suitable for the airborne role, were available. Large-scale exercises such as Eagle, in August 1949, and Sweetbriar, in February 1950, were a mixed success. The outbreak of the Korean War in June 1950 and the raising of a Canadian brigade group for service there (the 25th Canadian Infantry Brigade), and the subsequent raising of a second brigade group for NATO (the 27th Brigade), relegated the MSF concept to the back burner.

As the U.S.S.R. acquired the A-Bomb (1949) and the H-Bomb (1953), along with effective long-range delivery systems, the need for the MSF became less and less obvious. By 1958, the brigade-sized MSF had been reduced to one jump-trained company from each infantry regiment. The newer, smaller, airborne unit was named the Defence of Canada

Force. From 1958 to 1968, it was the sole manifestation of airborne forces in the Canadian Army.

In April 1966, Lt.-Gen. Jean-Victor Allard, commander of the new Mobile Command in Paul Hellyer's soon-to-be-unified Armed Forces, sat down with Col. Don Rochester, base commander of CFB Chilliwack, to discuss a new idea. Allard was one of Canada's most distinguished soldiers. He had been a brigade commander in the Second World War and Korea, and he had been accorded the signal honour of commanding a British division attached to NATO in Germany. A supporter of Hellyer's plan to unify the Canadian Armed Forces, Allard would soon become CDS.

Rochester had also had a notable military career. He had joined the Royal Canadian Engineers after graduating from the University of Toronto in 1941 with a BSc in Engineering. He served in Canada, northwest Europe, and the Aleutians during the war and elected to stay in the army when the fighting ended. He had passed the jump course in 1946 and had taken up skydiving as a hobby in 1962. Before being posted to CFB Chilliwack, site of the Royal Canadian School of Military Engineering, he had taught at the United States Army Command and General Staff College at Fort Leavenworth, Kansas, and commanded the Canadian contingent of the United Nations Emergency Force in the Gaza Strip.

Allard's idea was a radical one. He wanted to create an all-volunteer airborne regiment that would specialize in commando tactics – much like the British Special Air Service (SAS) – and act as Canada's premier force-in-readiness for the defence of Canadian territory or for overseas operations. This unit would be directly under the command of the Commander Mobile Command. Such a unit was needed, he believed, because it took as long as two months to train, equip, and deploy a Canadian brigade group. In his words, "The light and rapid airborne regiment was meant to 'fill the bill' between the time our government acceded to a request for intervention from outside and the arrival of the main body of troops."[3] Allard knew of Rochester's love of parachuting and suggested that he become the first commander of the new unit. Not long after, Rochester was posted to Mobile Command in St-Hubert, where he began planning to bring the new formation into existence. Allard had originally wanted to call it the Canadian Commando Regiment, but when it was formally activated in 1968, it was named the Canadian Airborne Regiment (CAR).

Allard also thought of the CAR as an operational training unit. He wanted the tougher physical training, the sharper mental attitude, the higher level of fieldcraft, and the better knowledge of small-unit tactics and rapid deployment that the troops in the regiment would learn to be diffused throughout the Canadian infantry. And so the members of the regiment would be required to return to their parent units two or three years after joining the Airborne. Allard wanted every officer and NCO in the Canadian infantry to do a stint in the Airborne in order to be eligible for promotion. It was important to the Airborne's mission that time not be wasted training new recruits in the basic arts of their chosen specialization. Raw recruits were accordingly barred from volunteering. Anyone who wanted to join the Airborne had to have served at least four years in the army and be of corporal rank or qualified to be corporal. Every volunteer had to have his jump wings.

What Allard did not want the Airborne to become was a formation of permanent paratroopers "utilized alongside all the other units, but for special missions." As he wrote in his memoirs two decades later, "This regiment . . . did not follow the Victorian regimental system, since men had to be 'fast in fast out.' . . . There was thus absolutely no question of training professional paratroopers, except for the instructors. . . . This regiment was . . . designed to fill a gap in our strategy for modern warfare. In the minds of its planners, it was never intended to remain in the fighting line for more than a few weeks."[4]

In the spring of 1967, Rochester received specific instructions regarding the mission and terms of reference of the Airborne from Lt.-Gen. W. A. B. Anderson, commander of Mobile Command. The CAR was to be organized and equipped "to perform a variety of tasks including: a. The defence of Canada; b. The standby role in response to the UN; c. Peacekeeping operations; d. Missions in connection with national disaster; e. "Special Air Service (SAS)" type missions;[5] f. *Coup de main* tasks in a general war setting, and g. Responsibility for parachute training in the Canadian Forces."[6] To this end, "all elements" in the Airborne were to be parachute trained, the regiment was to be kept in a high state of readiness, and it was to be prepared to operate on a self-sustaining basis for up to two weeks at a time. The training requirements for members of the regiment were similar to those of "elite" or "special forces" units in the American, British, and other militaries. They became proficient at mountain climbing, scuba diving, underwater demolition, clearing underwater obstacles, deep penetration patrols, HALO (high altitude, low opening) parachute descents, etc.

Rochester was given considerable leeway in shaping the new unit. He was to recommend its base site, fashion its operational and training doctrine, suggest final forms of organization and establishment, and decide the regiment's personnel policies. He was also given permission to "recommend to the Commander Mobile Command any special terms of reference which in [his] opinion might expedite the bringing into being of the Canadian Airborne Regiment as a fully effective operational component of Mobile Command."[7]

There were many officers at Mobile Command who did not share Allard's enthusiasm for the new unit, although Anderson appears not to have been one of them. Through the years, Canadian proponents of the Airborne have chalked up this opposition to regimental and personal jealousy, as well as to the inevitable budget rivalries. In fact, however, Allard's concept does not appear to have been well thought out. There was and is a real argument that although a modern, all-round military ought to retain some airborne capability, a unit such as the Canadian Airborne Regiment was operationally obsolete from the day it was formed.

The perfection of the helicopter as a troop carrier has doomed the mass airborne formation. That must have been apparent to Allard by the mid-1960s. When the Israelis invaded the Sinai Peninsula at the start of the Sinai–Suez War in October 1956, they began their campaign with a parachute drop close to the strategically vital Mitla Pass. The Anglo-French invasion of the Suez Canal Zone only days later also started with a parachute attack. But there have been very few major parachute operations since then. In the Vietnam War, the United States deployed the 101st Airborne Division and one brigade of the 82nd Airborne, but only one parachute drop was ever mounted there (in February 1967) and only because of the unavailability of helicopters for a particular mission.

In the early 1950s, prominent Second World War American paratroop commanders such as James Gavin, Maxwell Taylor, and Matthew Ridgeway speculated about the possible demise of mass airborne operations. Gavin was particularly adamant that helicopter-borne forces, deployed as "air cavalry," were the wave of the future. He and other helicopter advocates carried the day. The United States's first dedicated helicopter division was formed in April 1965 when the 1st Cavalry Division was redesignated as the 1st Cavalry Division (Airmobile). Equipped with close to four hundred helicopters for troop carrying, medical evacuation, resupply, command and control, and air-ground support, the entire division was fully mobile. It was capable of striking behind enemy lines in search-and-destroy operations, mounting vertical envelopment assaults, and undertaking other missions once reserved for paratroopers.

In the Arab–Israeli Six-Day War of 1967, the Israel Defence Forces proved the effectiveness of heli-borne assaults when it loaded paratroopers onto helicopters to successfully attack key Egyptian defence positions at Abu Agheila and Ras el Sudr close to the Israeli border. Later that year, the Americans changed the designation of the 101st Airborne Division to 101st Airborne (Airmobile). The change was a sign of the times and a sign, too, of the importance air cavalry had already assumed in Vietnam. Today, there are few nations that do not provide at least a modicum of helicopter assault training for their infantry if they do not, in fact, possess dedicated airmobile units.

Helicopter insertion has major advantages over the dropping of paratroopers from aircraft. It is true, on the one hand, that helicopters are more vulnerable to groundfire when approaching a landing zone, but most large-scale parachute drops are made at altitudes of three hundred to five hundred metres, well within the range of effective anti-aircraft fire. On the other hand, helicopters afford good concentration of troops on the ground. They can bring far more supporting equipment and supplies into the initial assault, and do it more quickly and with greater accuracy than if dropped by parachute. Helicopters can evacuate the wounded, and, when armed with missiles, cannon, or heavy machine guns, give close support to assaulting troops. Since the advantages of airmobile over airborne formations must have been pretty clear by 1968, why did Canada choose to go the airborne, rather than the airmobile, route? Indeed, why create a new unit in the first place? The answers are difficult to document, but easy to surmise.

Morale was low in Mobile Command in early 1966 following the removal of the Canadian Guards from the order of battle and the reduction of the Black Watch and the Queen's Own Rifles. As a result of the changes Paul Hellyer was introducing, regiments were to lose their training depots and all recruits were to be given their basic training at one facility – CFB Cornwallis near Digby, Nova Scotia. No soldier reared in the Canadian regimental tradition could have been happy with these changes. Creation of a new, supposedly elite, unit to which soldiers could aspire for greater physical challenges and to achieve a higher level of training and skills might help raise morale.

Then there was the Canadian Army's fixation on parachuting. This preoccupation first arose when the army was forced to make do with a modest force (the MSF) for the defence of Canada at a time of huge cuts in the defence budget. But even after the Mobile Striking Force receded in importance, many officers and NCOs continued to qualify for their jump wings both for personal reasons and in the belief that it would help their career. In the smaller postwar army, this was a reasonable assumption: competition for the better jobs was fierce, especially because virtually all the officers who stayed on after 1945 were forced to take reductions in rank and wanted to work their way back up the ladder. Since lots of officers had jump wings, there was a built-in inclination to think that parachute training was, in itself, a good thing.

Then there was cost. Although organizing and maintaining an airborne unit is not cheap, especially when the costs of aircraft and aircraft facilities are added to those of the jump school and the parachute-packing establishment, it is cheaper than starting and operating a comparably sized airmobile unit. To go airmobile means purchasing helicopters that are costly to maintain and can't be used for much else. In contrast, aircraft such as the CC-130 Hercules, Canada's standard transport aircraft since the late 1960s, can be used for many other purposes when they are not dropping paratroopers.

Airborne probably struck Allard and others as more versatile than airmobile. In the CAR's original specification, after all, troopers were to be taught both paratroop and commando tactics so they could be employed on virtually any mission, anywhere. Helicopters were (and for the most part still are) short-range delivery vehicles. They do not give an airmobile unit a long-distance strike capability. But, although paratroopers can be flown long distances, they can't necessarily be dropped there. To fly a battalion-sized force to a drop zone a thousand kilometres from home and dump it out the back of the aircraft without some closer-to-hand means of supporting it would mean certain defeat. The U.S. army's thirty-six-hour standby force is a brigade of the 82nd Airborne Division, located at Fort Bragg, North Carolina. When it was moved in haste to Saudi Arabia to counter a possible Iraqi invasion in August 1990, it was airlifted, not air-dropped.

In the Canadian Army tradition of "making do" during peacetime, the Canadian Airborne Regiment was supposed to give Canada an additional military capability without adding significant numbers of additional troops or even creating a new formation. The CAR was new in the sense that it would be started from scratch, but all its manpower was to come from existing units, and, to paraphrase Jean-Victor Allard, it was not supposed to be a new stand-alone formation with its own regimental base, its own history, and its own traditions. In the end, that turned out not to be the case, however, because the only way Don Rochester and subsequent commanders could weld such a disparate unit together was to create a regimental tradition.

According to one former high-ranking officer, Allard's primary reason for creating the Canadian Airborne Regiment was fear of an outbreak of revolutionary guerilla war in Quebec where the Front de libération de

Québec (FLQ) had been conducting a campaign of bombings and armed robberies since the early 1960s. Dan G. Loomis is a retired major-general. His book, *Not Much Glory*, advances the thesis that Allard so feared a Vietnam-type war in Canada that he reorganized the entire structure of the army to meet the threat. Two of his most notable moves, in Loomis's view, were to set up Mobile Command (now Land Force Command) headquarters at the former RCAF base at St-Hubert and to place virtually all other Canadian army units near to airfields for quick move to Quebec in case of emergency.[8]

Whether or not Loomis is entirely correct, he is surely right about the inclination of Allard and other military leaders to think that Canada needed some sort of anti-guerilla, anti-terrorist military capability. They were not alone in that thinking.

In the mid-1960s, military hierarchies in the democratic countries suddenly discovered terrorist and guerilla warfare. For a time, they were seized by the problem of how to counter it. That preoccupation was especially evident in the U.S. military. The Americans seemed to swallow whole the notion fed to them by intellectuals attached to the Kennedy presidency that a "people's war" might be virtually unstoppable. The appropriate response, according to the wisdom of the time, was to form special forces of one's own, such as the U.S. Navy Seals, the U.S. Army Green Berets, and the already established British SAS and SBS (Special Boat Service). Allard and other army leaders wanted Canada to possess a comparable force. Rochester was specifically instructed to visit the John F. Kennedy Special Services Forces Center when he toured Fort Bragg and to make contact with the British SAS.

There was one more less tangible, but no less important, reason for forming the Canadian Airborne Regiment. Since the initiation of airborne forces before and during the Second World War, virtually all armies have held up the paratrooper as the essence of the combat-ready soldier. Paratroopers were (and still are in some armies) held to be special. They are supposed to be tougher, more self-reliant, better trained, and more purely physical than other soldiers. Because para-troop units are almost always volunteer, they are self-selecting: they are made up of men who can be presumed to love soldiering for its own sake. Maintaining a parachute unit is a good way, perhaps the best way, to identify the action-oriented soldiers who are thought to make the best infantry and the best future leaders of any army. In the United States, for example, most of the chiefs of staff who commanded the army in the 1950s had led airborne units in the Second World War. Although the airmobile concept has clearly won out in the U.S. army, several thousand soldiers a year still take airborne training and join the 82nd and 101st Airborne Divisions. In the 1960s, the leadership of both the Canadian Army and the Canadian defence establishment believed that the army's prime mission was to be ready to fight wars – the administrative mind-set so evident today was not yet entrenched. It was, therefore, natural for some army leaders to think that officers, NCOs, and soldiers who passed through the Canadian Airborne Regiment might form the nucleus of a Canadian combat-ready army for the 1970s and 1980s.

Don Rochester's first choice for the location of the Canadian Airborne, CFB Edmonton, offered several advantages. There was a Canadian Forces air facility close by at Namao that would give the regiment virtually instant access to the new CC-130 transports based there. This would expedite the training not only of paratroopers but also of the air force air and ground crews. Edmonton's Griesbach Barracks were available, 1 PPCLI having been relocated to CFB Calgary. Edmonton offered all the amenities of a major city, and, most important, it was far away from Mobile Command at St-Hubert, which gave Rochester and subsequent regimental commanders much-needed leeway in shaping the new regiment. Edmonton was close to possible theatres of action, in the far north and along the Yukon–Alaska border. And finally, Edmonton had a significant francophone minority living in the suburb of St. Albert that would make it easier for francophone members of the regiment to educate their children in French.

This last factor was of particular importance because Allard – and the federal government – had one other reason for favouring the formation of this new unit: to advance the cause of bilingualism in the army. Whatever shape the CAR was to assume when activated, both Allard and

Anderson insisted that one of the two airborne infantry units was eventually to be francophone. This unit, 1er Commando, at first contained a number of English-speaking men, but was later composed entirely of volunteers from the Royal 22e Régiment. Initially, one English-speaking company of 1er Commando was established in Edmonton while the rest of 1er Commando was being organized at CFB Valcartier. In the spring of 1970, the contingent from Valcartier joined the rest of the Airborne in Edmonton and all non-francophones were rotated out of the unit.

When the Canadian Airborne Regiment was formally activated on April 8, 1968, it was a queer duck. Neither a battalion nor a brigade, it was a self-contained command unit that harboured other command units within its structure. In the Canadian Forces, a "unit" is formally established through the issuance of a Canadian Forces Organization Order (CFOO). A CFOO describes the name, structure, size, mission, and other essential characteristics of a unit. That unit has a "commanding officer," who is solely responsible for its good order, discipline, and performance. In this sense, an infantry battalion is a unit, but an infantry company is not. In having a number of "units" within its structure, therefore, the Canadian Airborne Regiment as established in 1968 was like a mini-brigade, but with roughly the same number of troops as the regimental battle group the Strathconas sent to Bosnia in 1994.

The Canadian Airborne Regiment was originally to contain a light armoured unit too. When the regiment was formed in 1968, however, this unit was dropped from the Edmonton establishment, largely because no air-droppable armoured vehicle was available. A No.3 Commando, stationed in Europe, was only technically attached to the CAR, although it had no airborne capability. However, attached units of communications and signals troops, engineers, artillery, and service and support troops gave the regiment considerable breadth and flexibility. With the exception of some members of the service and support unit, everyone – from cooks to clerks – had to be jump-qualified.

The two infantry commandos, 1er and No. 2 Commando, made the infantry unique. The first was manned by the R22eR, the second was a mixed bag of officers and men from the PPCLI and the Royal Canadian Regiment (RCR). Until changes were made in the organizational structure of the Airborne in 1977, all the units – infantry and otherwise – were commanded by majors, but these were majors with a difference. They were "unit" commanders rather than company commanders, as they would have been in the regular infantry. It was they, therefore, who had primary responsibility for the conduct of their troops in and out of battle and who were responsible for discipline within their units. It is a sacred principle in virtually all armies that a CO holds sway in his unit. His superior might suggest this or that course of action, but he is not supposed to interfere in the operation or administration of subordinate units. In armies, micro-management is not just a generator of excess paper; it is a killer of soldiers and a main reason why battles are lost.

The total establishment of the Canadian Airborne Regiment was 878 men; 556 of them in the two commandos. In an effort to give the commandos the maximum flexibility and firepower, they, too, were at first organized in a non-traditional way. Each commando consisted of three seventy-three-man rifle companies and each rifle company was divided into two rifle platoons of twenty-four men each and a twenty-one-man headquarters platoon. The rifle platoons were further divided into rifle squads (later renamed "sections") of eleven men and each squad into a five-man fire team. Each member of a fire team was armed with an automatic rifle except for the light machine gunner; two members carried light anti-tank weapons. The fire team was led by a master corporal. The fire team concept, pioneered by the U.S. Marines, was designed to provide maximum flexibility at the smallest possible unit level. When fire team and squad weapons were combined with a platoon's three medium machine guns, three Carl Gustav anti-tank weapons, and four light machine guns, the amount of sheer firepower in an airborne company was much greater than that built into an average infantry company, even though the latter contained more men. Later, when the Airborne Regiment was downsized, more conventional Canadian forms of organization were adopted, as the commandos were subdivided into platoons and sections.

As every good CO must do, Rochester began early to put his stamp on the Airborne. Some of the measures he initiated would remain virtually unchanged until Col. Ian Fraser took command in 1975. Rochester assumed that members of the regiment would arrive with basic combat skills. He, therefore, saw his job as threefold: to make each member of the outfit as physically and mentally tough as possible; to provide individual and unit training in new skills such as skiing and mountaineering; and to provide individual and unit training in paratroop operations in a variety of terrains and climates. At the base, extensive and intense physical training was reinforced by the order that everyone always move "on the double" outside barracks, hangars, or administrative buildings. This order applied even to regimental ceremonies.

As each group (or "serial") of volunteers arrived, its members were given refresher jump training before being hustled off to courses in swimming, unarmed combat, skiing, mountaineering, and rappelling (down cliff faces and from helicopters). Rochester himself went on every jump and accompanied the men on many of their training exercises. In the fall of 1968, the Airborne held its first full regimental exercises at CFB Wainwright and in the forests near CFB Chilliwack (in place of a cancelled exercise in Jamaica). In the following year, the first winter jump and exercise were held near Watson Lake, Yukon, and the unit finally got to jump into the jungle of Jamaica. On one exercise in the early summer of 1969, they were transported to Tofino, on the west coast of Vancouver Island, to launch a mock attack against a British SAS company.[9]

The demanding physical regimen, the accelerated cycle of exercises, and the "on-the-double" spirit that Rochester infused in the regiment helped bring its disparate men and elements together. But Rochester also knew that some effort would have to be made to develop a regimental tradition. In one sense, this ran counter to Allard's original intention that the regiment not be considered a separate or stand-alone unit in the army and that its members rotate back to their parent formations. Rochester really had no choice, however, if he was to create the *esprit de corps* that was necessary to motivate his soldiers to reach beyond themselves in every task they performed. As one internal document stated, "A great deal of the effectiveness of the Cdn AB Regt will depend on its internal loyalty and esprit. This can not be fragmented to parent units, corps or branches."[10]

Rochester took a two-track approach; the Canadian Airborne Regiment would create its own sense of loyalty and traditions but would also inculcate affinity to the larger traditions and values of airborne soldiers in general. The maroon beret was adopted with a unique hat badge that combined parachute, wings, and maple leaves. The Pegasus symbol was appropriated as an informal sign of the regiment. The two Canadian parachute units of the Second World War – 1st Canadian Parachute Battalion and the First Special Service Force – were declared to be predecessor formations. Special regimental days were organized with parades (accompanied by the Edmonton Police Pipe Band) and talks on subjects of importance to the regiment in general. A regimental coin was minted, and Airborne members were expected to carry that coin at all times, even after they left the regiment.

In the end, though, it was the jumping itself and what that jumping meant both operationally and symbolically that created the necessary *esprit*. In wartime, jumping out of airplanes is, in reality, just another route to the battlefield. In peacetime, jumping is a test of courage, a deliberate confrontation with death. It is real, not just an exercise. It is because it is real that those soldiers who jump out of airplanes usually come to think of themselves as an elite. They face dangers other soldiers don't. And they share something other soldiers know nothing about. In the Airborne, everybody was expected to jump, regardless of rank or specialization. They became equals when hooked to the static line. Each soldier in a jump "stick" (the group of jumpers who exit one side of an aircraft) was responsible for checking the equipment of the man in front of him and for making sure that his mate's chute line was properly hooked up. Their lives depended on one another as much when they leapt into space as when they hit the ground and were alone and isolated behind enemy lines.

It takes a special kind of person to meet the mental and physical challenges that airborne soldiering entails. They are action-oriented, certainly. Many are the type of men who might otherwise seek adventure as mercenaries in foreign armies. They are the sort that joins fighting organizations such as the French Foreign Legion to live by the raw creed of "march or die." One expert studying French paratroopers summed up their lives as a "rejection of materialism, the exaltation of asceticism, violence and risk, of action for action's sake."[11] Writing of British paratroopers, Anthony Beevor concluded, "For a dedicated para, life outside has little meaning. Some of those who leave come back in because they are hooked on the notion of belonging to an elite. . . . The paras are conspicuously proud of being unlike other regiments." The society they build within the regiment is one of muscular and meritocratic men.[12]

Paratroopers join armies to fight. When there is no fighting to be done, jumping is the primary substitute. Overcoming the fear of death in the jump gives them individually and collectively their basic creed. That creed is remarkably similar throughout the world of military parachuting: a paratrooper is supposed to be mentally and physically fit at all times. He is an elite shock trooper, always neat and courteous, attentive to his equipment and weapons, has high morale, fights fairly, always fights on to the objective. He is a fighting man in a team of fighting men. He never surrenders.[13] This is the ideal, of course. Like all creeds, it is sometimes honoured in the breach more than in the observance.

Because these men are usually young, intensely physical, and combative by nature, discipline is often a problem within paratroop units. Don Reekie was RSM of the Canadian Airborne Regiment in 1976-77. He recalls that the Airborne "was a difficult organization to command. It had strong individuals. They all wanted to do the Entebbe thing every half-hour." Entebbe was the site of a daring Israeli rescue mission in the mid-1970s. "They were the thoroughbreds of the army, and they always needed to be properly led and properly disciplined."[14] Violent incidents have dogged both the British Parachute Regiment and its American counterparts in the last decade or so. The problem is not confined to Canadian units.

Rochester recognized that discipline might be a problem, but thought that the members of the regiment would be "so elite and so dedicated to their cause, that normal disciplinary measures would not be needed. Minor hell-raising in the line of duty could be overlooked and serious problems arising from inactivity and indolence could never occur."[15] He believed, in other words, that unit pride and the high level of physical activity demanded of the troopers would preclude the emergence of serious breakdowns in discipline. He had another factor working in his favour: the majority of the men who volunteered for the Airborne in the first two decades of its life were first-class soldiers.

Ron Irwin joined the army in 1966. It was all he ever wanted to do. One year after joining, he was posted to the jump company of 1 RCR. He turned down three chances to go to Germany so that he could take the jump course. He wanted to wear the high jump boots and the maroon beret of the Airborne, and he volunteered to join the regiment soon after it was formed. "The single best thing was when they gave us our own badges," he recalls. "We were accepted as part of a family and we had to continue the traditions of our forebears." He particularly enjoyed the closeness and the camaraderie that came from the shared danger of the jump.[16]

Irwin was one of the regiment's younger members when it formed in 1968. Most already had several years of soldiering behind them. Bob Burchell, for example, had joined the army in 1959 at seventeen and, after a long stint at CFB Gagetown, decided to take the jump course at Rivers, Manitoba. This was in the early 1960s. He was "scared to death" the first few times he leapt from the aircraft, but he qualified and returned to Gagetown in 1964. When he heard that the Canadian Airborne Regiment was being formed, he volunteered and reported to Edmonton the day the Airborne's RSM, R. J. Buxton, plunged to his death when his chute got fouled. Burchell loved the spirit of the unit, the risks inherent in the job, the intense mental and physical challenges. He found a much stronger bond and greater commitment to soldiering in the Airborne than he had in his parent regiment, the RCR.[17]

Irwin and Burchell and most others went to the Airborne because they believed it was a step-up from regular soldiering. It offered greater challenges and demanded a higher state of physical prowess. More important, it imbued its members with the notion that whatever happened, each was personally obliged to give his very best performance each and every time he was called upon. That's what most impressed Dollard Rousseau. Rousseau came to the regiment in 1968 after sitting behind a desk for most of his army career. "You worked hard together and you played hard together, and you did all the hairy assed, gung-ho shit that the Airborne does."[18]

No paratrooper ever forgets the sequence of events that leads to the jump. It begins where it ends: on the ground. The jumpers report in, get their names checked off, and gather together in their "chalks" (the traditional name for an airplane load of paratroopers). If it is a full-equipment jump – and most jumps are – there is kit to be rigged and adjustments to be made. Platoon and section commanders circulate among their troops, going over last-minute details of the coming operation. To an outsider, the scene appears chaotic, but there is an unseen order to the proceedings. At the appointed hour, the seeming chaos comes to an end as the jumpmasters assume control of their "sticks."

There are two sticks in each chalk: the port stick and the starboard stick, each named for the side of the aircraft on which the troopers will sit and the door from which they will jump. Each stick has its own jumpmaster, but one of them is the senior man and is responsible for the entire chalk. It is on his command that the troopers will launch themselves into the air.

Every man is inspected to ensure that he is wearing his identity discs and that rings are either removed or taped over so that hands won't be snagged and torn on the aircraft's door. Everyone is treated the same. The regimental commander and regimental sergeant major are required to observe the same rules as everyone else.

The sticks file by huge cardboard shipping boxes and pick up their parachutes: first the main chute then the much smaller reserve. Then everyone waits for the command that will start the sequence of events leading to the jump.

"Get dressed for rigger's check."

Working in pairs, people don their main parachutes. Once everything is snugged into place, the riggers work their way down the line, checking each jumper's chute. These people are the experts on military parachutes. They cut their teeth on the packing tables at the Canadian Forces Parachute Maintenance Depot, at Edmonton, under a huge sign that reads: "Our job – their safety, Our aim – perfection." The rigger's official motto is: "I will be sure – always," and they are. If there is so much as a hint that there is something wrong, even something as minor as a frayed thread in the stitching of the harness, the entire ensemble is returned unused to the depot.

The final ground check is done by the jumpmaster, but not until each jumper has clipped his reserve parachute to his chest, slung his rifle and snowshoes over his shoulder, rigged his rucksack on a quick-release assembly and lowering line below his reserve chute, and snugged everything in with his waistband. Some soldiers carry special loads such as mortar components or a machine gun.

No one rushes into this final preparation. When it is complete, any possibility of personal comfort disappears until the trooper is finally hanging under the parachute. The jumpmaster's check gives new meaning to the word "thorough." Each one has graduated from a course where the pass standard is 100 per cent. This is well known throughout the Airborne community, and every trooper is comfortable in the knowledge that his life is in the hands of people who have "met the standard." This element of trust exceeds that found in any other military unit. It is an "Airborne" thing.

In a no-nonsense, staccato tone, the jumpmaster issues the final briefing. He outlines the details of the jump to come and reviews the drills that will be followed in the event of an in-flight emergency. The common theme in all these briefings is the closing statement: "You have now been manifested and you will jump in accordance with my command and all orders applicable to this chalk. Have a good one." From this point on, if a trooper changes his mind about jumping, he forfeits membership in the unit.

A jumper does not walk to the airplane, he waddles. He has more than fifty kilograms of paraphernalia attached to his body. Even the RSM loses his "parade-ground manner" and becomes a mere mortal. The jumpmasters and the aircraft loadmasters work together helping the jumpers up the ramp and strapping them, one by one, into their seats. The men with the heaviest loads have to be lifted on board. The CC-130 is a workhorse, not a fancy airliner. The smell of JP4 jet fuel and hydraulic fluid is everywhere. The jump seats are actually like one long, webbed lawn chair. They are constructed to be folded out of the way as soon as they have served their purpose. They are not designed for comfort. Depending on the type of operation, time of year (paratroopers take up more space when they are wearing bulky arctic clothing), and the amount of extra gear the troopers are carrying, there will be from forty to sixty-four jumpers on board. There is hardly room to shift in one's seat, let alone get up and walk about.

The flight to the drop zone can be brief or it may take several hours. For the jumpers, it always seems longer than it really is. The Hercules is a powerful plane, and the drone from its four 4,020-horsepower engines makes normal conversation all but impossible. The flight is often bumpy. On tactical approaches, the aircraft fly low and in close formation, and make tightly banked turns. Even the heartiest soldiers sometimes need an airsick bag.

Many things can go wrong. If the navigator miscalculates the release point, the troopers can be dropped over a lake or into the trees. If the wind shifts at the last moment, they can land far from their drop zone. There is always a medic and an ambulance at the drop zone.

The veterans do not think of these things. They blank negative thoughts from their minds. They no longer feel the abject fear felt by the neophytes. That fear has been replaced, however, by a special kind of apprehension, and they are never as comfortable as outward appearance would indicate. The real veterans know that apprehension keeps them alert and aware of everything around them. When they lose it, it will be time to quit jumping.

The red light comes on. The drop zone is now only ten minutes away. "Seat belts off – look this way."

All eyes are on the jumpmaster. He holds out both hands, palms forward, and shouts "get ready." The troopers echo the command. From now on, all commands are repeated. All jump commands are also accompanied by an appropriate hand signal. Even the loudest of parade-square voices is no match for the four turboprops.

"Stand up."

This is not a precision drill movement. Cramped muscles must be coaxed into action and protruding rucksacks and parachutes clash. The seats must be detached from the floor and swung up on hinges against the aircraft fuselage, and everyone pitches in to accomplish this task. Then they all face to the rear, and the jumpmaster once more has their undivided attention. The drop zone is now nine minutes away.

"Hook up."

With one click more than forty snap fasteners lock onto the anchor-line cables.

"Check static lines."

Each jumper pushes his snap fastener back along the cable so that the man behind him can trace all 4.5 metres of yellow nylon line from the hook to the point where it attaches to the parachute deployment bag. At the same time, he checks the static line of the man in front of him. No one cuts corners when it comes to checking static lines. A misrouted static line can cause a jumper to remain attached to the airplane. Only three Canadian paratroopers have been "hung up" in almost forty years, and all three were successfully hauled back into the plane. No one wants to be the fourth.

"Check your equipment."

Each jumper checks himself, starting with his static line and working down from there. At the same time, the jumpmasters move to the front bulkhead and work their way to the rear, giving each of the troopers one final check. At the end of each check, they look each man in the eye and state, "You are good to go, jumper. Have a good one." By the time every-one is checked, the drop zone is less than three minutes away.

"Sound off for equipment check."

Starting at the rear of the stick, the jumpers shout "okay" and slap the person in front on the back. The two number-one jumpers shout "star-board stick okay" and "port stick okay." The senior jumpmaster gives the thumbs up to the senior loadmaster, who advises the flight deck via his intercom link. Up front the two pilots, the navigator, and the flight engineer are going through their own checklist. The air deflectors in front of the jump doors must be extended, and the wing flaps must be at exactly the right setting. Using their air-to-ground radio, they speak to the pathfinders on the ground. These men jumped in by free fall two nights earlier to secure and mark the drop zone. The aircraft navigator computes last-minute adjustments based on the current wind speed and direction over the ground. Everything is coming together as the big mottled grey and green plane makes its way to the drop zone. The experienced jumpers are now watching the senior loadmaster.

"Prepare for slowdown," he shouts into the senior jumpmaster's ear as he makes a pushing motion with both hands. Everyone braces himself as the plane decelerates to exactly 130 knots airspeed. The lead pilot makes the final corrections to line up with the release point over the drop zone while the remaining aircraft in the formation fine-tune their positions. All systems are go and it is time to open the doors. The drop zone is now only two minutes away.

It is the two loadmasters' responsibility to open the doors and snap the jump platforms (thirty-centimetre-wide steps that extend outside the aircraft) in place. The two doors slide smoothly upwards in their rails and the engine's roar jumps a few decibels. The burst of fresh air is felt halfway down each stick, and an aura of heightened excitement flows forward in the plane. The troopers pull on their static lines and stamp their feet. Shouts of "Airborne" and "let's go" echo off the bulkheads. The mood is infectious, and any doubts felt during the approach flight have been absorbed into the air rushing past the open doors. The atmosphere is the same in every plane in the formation.

Again the loadmaster grabs the jumpmaster's shoulder and shouts in his ear. The jumpmaster blows across the palm of his right hand and holds up eight fingers. Wind speed across the drop zone is eight knots. The message is passed down the line. The troopers share knowing glances and give each other the thumbs up. Eight knots is not excessive. It should be a good jump.

"One minute."

Both jumpmasters swing into the door to do their final check. Secured by safety lines, they ensure the wind deflectors are extended, feel to make certain that the safety pin is still in the door, and stamp hard on the jump platform. On the ground, the Pathfinder platoon commander, in his role as drop-zone controller, acknowledges the one-minute warning. He confirms the wind speed and direction, takes one last look across the drop zone, and states, "You are cleared to drop."

Back in the aircraft, the seconds tick by at a rate so slow it defies measurement. The loadmaster shouts "fifteen seconds," then "stand by." The number-one jumpers in each stick swing into the door and crouch in readiness. Everyone else shuffles forward two steps. Then all five red lights in the plane turn to green, and the first two jumpers leap from the door and into the slipstream. Like giant snakes, the sticks slither out the two doors. Each jumper throws his static line towards the jumpmaster, makes a sharp ninety-degree turn, and springs out trying to get as far away from the plane as possible. Every chin is held tightly to the chest. Knees are locked in place, as are elbows, and each jumper bends at the waist adopting the position that has served Canadian paratroopers well for decades. The static line jerks the deployment bag off each trooper's back and the prop blast fills each canopy with air and drives it away from the aircraft. Like a plumb bob on the end of a line, each jumper swings under his canopy. The sequence takes less than three seconds. If a man refuses to jump, he is asked a second time. If he declines again, he is taken out of the stick and brought to the front of the aircraft. By the time his mates return from the exercise, he and all his personal effects will be gone from the base.

If it is a "clean" exit, there will be no "riser burns" on the jumper's neck and no twists in his suspension lines. Few exits are totally "clean," however, and twists are a common occurrence. Behind each aircraft are several jumpers pulling on their risers with both hands and kicking violently to speed up the spin that will clear their lines. All the jumpers are now in a different world. It is a world totally devoid of sound. The strain on the body caused by fifty kilograms of gear is replaced by a feeling of total weightlessness.

As each aircraft reaches the release point and disgorges its human cargo, the air fills with parachutes. Military chutes cannot be steered as such. All a jumper can do is reach high on his risers and pull down, causing his canopy to spill air. This will normally change his drift sufficiently to avoid a mid-air collision with another jumper. While it is not impossible to land with one's rucksack, rifle, and snowshoes still tight to one's body, this practice is not encouraged. It is much safer to lower the equipment on a five-metre-long lowering strap and let it land first, and that is the drill. The equipment is never released above seventy metres.

The descent takes about forty seconds, and if something goes seriously wrong with the main chute, there is barely time to go to the reserve. If there is any hesitation, the trooper will die within seconds. Suddenly the ground is there, and in a flurry of "ground rush," the troopers hit it. This is the trickiest part of the whole operation. The inexperienced invariably endure aches and pains for days after the jump. The old masters have perfected the self-control required to totally relax and not reach for the ground. They arrive on the drop zone "fit to fight."

On the ground, it takes a while to come down from the adrenalin high. There is a feeling of exhilaration, almost of euphoria. The camaraderie is never stronger than during those first few moments after landing. It is a moment that does not need to be shared with the rest of the world. It is a moment when only those who have earned the title "paratrooper" are present. It is, however, a moment that passes quickly. After all, a parachute is nothing more than a means of transportation. It is time to get on with the job at hand.[19]

It is the nature of airborne units that comradeship in the aircraft is followed by comradeship on the ground. In a line-infantry battalion on exercise, the usual practice is for officers to tent in their own area and for senior NCOs to do the same. That's not what happens in an airborne unit: officers, NCOs, and men live together and depend on one another. This habit of intermingling can lead to disciplinary problems if officers and NCOs have not earned the trust and respect of the troops. If senior staff are not held in high regard, the unit's leadership will pass to the most forceful, the physically strongest, possibly even the most rebellious men in the unit. Someone must always lead. When it is the wrong person, the unit is heading for disaster. When it is the right person, the officer trained and tested for leadership, then the chain of command will be safe even though all five men living in a tent share responsibility for getting the firewood, keeping the stove going throughout the night, or getting meals ready.

The underlying principle in airborne units is "one man, one kit." Each individual bears prime responsibility for his own health and well-being, his weapon and equipment. Every man carries his load and does his job. No man asks another to share his burden. Each man is supposed to know that by taking care of himself, he is also taking care of the unit. This is especially true in winter exercises, which are invariably 80 per cent survival training and 20 per cent combat training. "If I got frostbite because I didn't take care of myself," John McNeil remembers, "that was my problem, but it was everyone else's problem also, because we all depended on each other for survival."[20]

Arctic jumps tax the men to the limit. The jumpers are weighed down by thick arctic gear to protect them against the subzero temperatures and high winds, especially during the jump itself. They wear woollen masks and heavy gloves, and they hope for deep snow to cushion their landing. The toboggans that will carry their survival gear go out the door first; if they don't hit near the RV, precious time will be lost finding them in the subzero cold. After the men hit the ground, they hitch themselves to the toboggans, load their kit, and move to the RV. They can't move too fast in the cold or they will sweat; when the sweat freezes, their inner clothing will freeze too. They are well aware that exposed flesh dies quickly and that they may not know it is happening until it's too late. It is the section leader's job to make sure his men are protecting themselves from the cold. Every few minutes they peer at each other to check for frostbite.

Everything is difficult. Because the snowmobiles don't always work, the men often haul their supplies themselves. It is an art just to get into a sleeping bag without freezing. Routine tasks such as setting out a listening post or mounting an ambush are mentally and physically taxing. Eating is vital, but the food can rarely be heated. After a few days, the exhaustion takes its toll and the men move about like zombies.[21]

In the first years of the regiment's existence, the men developed a fierce pride in the Airborne. They played hard in the bars and clubs of Edmonton, but they also worked hard on exercises in the frozen north and elsewhere. Many were permanently bitten by the Airborne bug and left determined to return. Many did. Some managed to stay and formed a more or less permanent core within the regiment. This was, in some ways, a dangerous development. All the officers and virtually all of the NCOs served only the regular stint of two to three years, and in this situation, the "regulars" sometimes elicited more respect from newer members of the regiment than did those who were higher up in the chain of command.

As Don Rochester had forecast, there were few serious disciplinary problems in the Airborne. Some of the older NCOs had faced enemy fire in northwest Europe, Italy, or Korea. The campaign ribbons on their chests commanded respect and helped them maintain order. Just as important, the three infantry regiments generally made sure that a fair share of their best officers and men were sent to the Airborne. That was how Jean-Victor Allard had planned it and that was how it worked, for a time. The Airborne still had rough edges when Rochester turned command over to Col. R. G. Therriault in August 1969, but the Pegasus tradition was alive and well in the Canadian Forces.

8

THE BEST SOLDIERS, AND THE WORST

JULY 1974. The Canadian Air Command Boeing 707 descended through the dark night towards the Royal Air Force base at Akrotiri, the British Sovereign Base area on the shore of Episkopi Bay, just to the west of Limassol, Cyprus. On board were reinforcements from the Canadian Airborne Regiment in Edmonton on their way to help shore up the UN peacekeeping force on Cyprus (UNFICYP). With stop-overs for refuelling, the flight from Edmonton had taken almost twenty hours. The men were tired and jet-lagged but excited at the prospect they would shortly be in an active war zone.

Canada had been sending soldiers to Cyprus since 1964 to help the UN keep warring Greek and Turkish Cypriots apart. Cyprus was always dangerous; more than twenty Canadian soldiers were killed there in the almost three decades of the Canadian mission. But most of the time, duty on Cyprus was a pleasant change from the routine of base life and training, not to mention the cold of a Canadian winter. On duty, they joined the other UN contingents in patrolling the cease-fire lines between the two communities and manning observation posts to log and report cease-fire violations. Off duty, they enjoyed the sun and the beer and the girls of the island, toured its ancient sites, or visited the other timeless attractions of the eastern Mediterranean.

In April 1974, 1er Commando Groupement of the Canadian Airborne Regiment went to Cyprus on the regiment's first overseas posting. The contingent consisted of 1er Commando augmented by 1 Airborne Engineer Field Squadron and a logistics company. Everyone expected the tour to be routine. On July 15, 1974, however, Cyprus President Archbishop Makarios was thrown out of office in a coup launched by

Cyprus National Guard officers determined to unify the island with Greece. Turkey accused the coup leaders of being puppets of the Greek government; five days later, Turkish infantry began landing on the north coast of the island while Turkish paratroopers began dropping onto the Maesoria Plain, just north of the capital of Nicosia. One Canadian Airborne officer later recalled, "At 0700 a dramatic illustration of the invasion occurred as I watched the Turkish airborne operation from the upper floor of the Ledra Palace Hotel. Turkish aircraft were dropping parachutists north of Nicosia. It was a beautiful, still, cloudless morning, and watching the sky fill with parachutes was an awesome sight, especially to our Canadian Airborne Regiment members."[1]

Within days some forty thousand Turkish soldiers crowded onto the island to force a partition that has lasted to this day. As they poured in, they pushed forward in a bid to take control of all the territory where the Turkish Cypriot community lived and to dominate key points such as the international airport, just west of downtown Nicosia. Mortar and artillery rounds were soon exploding inside UN positions, and Canadian and other UN troops were caught in the crossfire. The peacekeepers began to sustain casualties. UN headquarters in New York asked Canada and other contributors to UNFICYP to augment their forces on the island; National Defence Headquarters responded by sending a reconnaissance troop of the Lord Strathcona's Horse and the rest of the Canadian Airborne Regiment. As Canada's designated quick-reaction force, the Airborne was a natural choice. If nothing else, the regiment's ability to deploy quickly would get a thorough testing.

Ron Irwin was one of the paratroopers aboard that Air Command 707. "We landed at night in a sovereign base area and were driven by truck to Nicosia," he recalled. "The heat was overpowering and the air sultry and sticky. They handed us our ammunition, took our maroon berets, gave us the blue helmets, and sent us out in a truck convoy. We arrived in Nicosia at first light. It was very quiet and there was little traffic on the roads. You could see bullet holes and shell damage from the fighting."[2] The entire transfer took less than three days. It was inevitable that foul-ups would occur. Former regiment member Ralph Goebel remembered that the UN was seemingly caught off balance. "They were initially very unprepared to receive us. We had to beef up on additional weapons and vehicles to at least defend ourselves properly. They were even short of ammunition." The men were given about ten rounds each in case they came under fire in the first few hours after their arrival.[3]

The Airborne and the rest of the Canadian UNFICYP contingent were sorely tried in the days and weeks after the Turkish invasion. Backed by British armoured cars, Canadian troops managed to prevent the Turks from taking control of the airport and the UN headquarters at the Ledra Palace Hotel. The dangers were real and immediate as the fighting raged. Capt. Normand Blaquiere and Sgt. Joseph Plouffe of 1er Commando were seriously wounded by Greek Cypriot machine gunners when they tried to escort a group of Turkish Cypriot civilians back to their lines. When other Canadians rushed to rescue their two comrades, they also came under fire. Supported by a British armoured car, the Canadians then opened fire on the Greek position while Capt. Alain Forand crawled out to the two wounded soldiers. He managed to drag one to safety and organized the rescue of the other. Forand, Plouffe, Blaquiere, and three other members of the rescue party were later decorated for their bravery.

After the initial fighting died down, the Canadians were hustled out to patrol the new cease-fire lines, man observation posts, or escort refugees from the Greek area to the Turkish area or vice versa. Members of each community were doing their level best to make sure that members of the other community got out, fast. Ralph Goebel still remembers, "They term it ethnic cleansing now. . . . The biggest instance we found was where they cleaned out this village and there were 126 villagers found in a mass grave."[4] For most of the paratroopers, the jobs to which they were assigned were deadly and boring at the same time. Wearing blue helmets and flak jackets, they stayed put in their OPs in the heat of the day, peered through their binoculars, and watched and listened. When a shot rang out, they reported it to UN headquarters. Otherwise, they stood and watched and sweated under the Mediter-ranean sun. Sometimes, though, they themselves came under fire. "One day we were in our OP and a shot rang out," Ron Irwin remembered.

"Then there was another and another, and pretty soon they were coming in short bursts as a firefight started up. We could hear the bullets snapping by our position and see the leaves dropping from the trees and bushes around us." Then someone opened up with a .50-calibre machine gun. Irwin and the other man were ordered to evacuate their position immediately. "Do you want us to bring the starlight scope and the radio?" Irwin yelled into the phone. "Just get out now" was the reply from headquarters. The two Canadians crouched low and ran. "We were kind of giddy," Irwin recalls. "We wondered what we were going to do. We were scared, all right."[5] Irwin and his buddy escaped unscathed from that shooting incident, but two other Airborne soldiers were less fortunate. 1er Commando Pte. Gilbert Perron was killed by a sniper on August 6 while investigating an alleged Turkish violation of the cease-fire agreement. Para Claude Berger was also killed by a sniper on September 19 while feeding livestock abandoned by refugees. Berger's death, coming long after the main fighting had subsided, cast a pall over the regiment. Irwin remembered, "You could hear a pin drop in the mess hall the next day. The attitude was 'the fuckers killed one of ours.' You realize that you can really get killed and it's a whole bunch different from before. A part of your family is gone. Until then, you'd been on the outside looking in."[6] The heat, the boredom, and the apparent randomness of the shootings added to the normal frustrations of peacekeeping. Don Thomas, a combat engineer with the Airborne, had no illusions about the role the Canadians were being asked to play. "You are stuck in the middle," he said. "When push comes to shove, they [the Turks or the Greeks] will do what they want. They'll bypass you, or they'll take your OP. Your hands are tied."[7]

The Airborne stayed on Cyprus until December 1974, when it was relieved by the 1st Battalion of the Royal Canadian Regiment. Canadians seemed to take little notice of the regiment's return to Edmonton; some of the paratroopers felt like forgotten men. And yet they were justifiably proud of the tasks they had performed under difficult conditions. More than thirty of them had been wounded and two killed in an operation that had started as a regular peacekeeping mission but ended up as a vicious little war. More to the point, the Airborne had proven beyond doubt that given the airlift capacity, it was ready to go virtually any-where, anytime, when called upon to do so, and to do a first-class job.

The Canadian Airborne Regiment was barely two years old when it undertook its first operational mission – to help secure Montreal in the dark days of the 1970 October Crisis. Separatist terrorists had kidnapped British trade commissioner James Cross and Quebec cabinet minister Pierre Laporte. Prime Minister Pierre Elliott Trudeau responded by invoking the War Measures Act and dispatching Canadian army contin-gents to Montreal from CFBs Valcartier and Edmonton. On the after-noon of October 15, two Hercules transports left Edmonton loaded with men from 1er Commando, bound for Mobile Command headquarters at St-Hubert. Airborne regimental commander Col. R. G. Therriault had received a warning order from Mobile Command less than twelve hours before. Eventually, the entire Airborne Regiment was flown in and based at the St-Hubert airfield to act as a mobile reserve for the troops actually patrolling the city streets.

The paratroopers didn't know what to expect when they arrived; news from Montreal had been confusing. Maybe the terrorists had pene-trated base security. Would they be shot at? Who could they trust? As they ran down the ramps of the Hercules transports in the dark and rain, there was fear, apprehension, and confusion. This was Canada, this was Montreal. Surely their first shots fired in anger would not be directed against other Canadians? But there were no shots fired by the Airborne. Organized into four quick-reaction tactical teams, they guarded the airfield at St-Hubert and took part in some of the patrolling in Montreal, to the north of the city, and on the south shore. Then in mid-November, as the crisis lessened, they returned to Edmonton to prepare for an Arctic exercise.

Given the bilingual nature of the Canadian Airborne Regiment, Therriault had been a logical choice to succeed Rochester as regimental commander. He was chosen by Gen. Jacques Dextraze, as was appropri-ate, given the Airborne's status as an independent force directly respon-sible to the commander of Mobile Command. In making the selection,

Dextraze set a precedent: thenceforward, command of the Airborne would alternate between English-speaking and French-speaking officers. Therriault had had a long and distinguished army career. He had joined the militia in Quebec City in 1944 when he was only seventeen and transferred to the R22eR in 1949. He saw action in Korea as a platoon leader, then gained extensive operational and staff experience before being posted to the Airborne. He made his first jump with the regiment in August 1969 on his forty-second birthday.

Therriault was impressed by the Airborne's mobility, by the fact that it could go anywhere in Canada on a defensive mission, for example, on short notice. But he also noted that it wouldn't be able to do much when it got there: it simply did not have the raw combat power. Therefore, he concentrated on the opportunities the Airborne presented for spreading the specialized knowledge its members would learn throughout the other units of the army. His tenure as regimental commander was marked by long-range exercises to the high Arctic, the Caribbean, and Vancouver Island, as well as intensive training in mountain warfare and helicopter assault techniques.

Therriault's successor, Col. Herb Pitts, was the last of the Airborne's commanders who had combat experience. After graduating from RMC in 1952, he went to Korea, where he served with the 1st and 3rd Battalions of the PPCLI, receiving the Military Cross for gallantry. His term as regimental commander of the Airborne was marked by the presentation of the regimental colours in June 1973. On that occasion, the unit officially adopted Canada's two Second World War-era paratroop units as predecessor regiments. The occasion was a major ceremonial event held in Edmonton's Clarke Stadium. Despite high winds, Pitts insisted that a full regimental jump go ahead. It was a spectacular display of parachuting. "My heart was bursting with pride," he later wrote.

The early to mid-1970s were the salad days of the Airborne. Physically isolated from other army units, with its own base, air support facilities, and the entire resources of the jump school and the parachute-packing centre at its disposal, the Airborne's regimental commanders were able to arrange exercises from the jungles of the tropics to the ice and snow of the Arctic. It was high adventure and it was fun. The training was tough, the men were dedicated, and Edmonton was just the place for them. With its many bars, restaurants, and women, the paratroopers played as hard as they worked. There was lots of off-duty drinking, but in those years, soldiers were expected to drink. So what if a bar fight broke out now and then? Paratroopers were supposed to be aggressive.

Within the regiment, order and discipline were maintained without serious incident. From the regimental commander on down, the Airborne seemed to know exactly how much leeway to give its soldiers. Only the best and most experienced officers and NCOs from the regular infantry regiments served in the unit. There were more volunteers than the regiment could take. The other regiments looked at the Airborne as an excellent training establishment: send a major to the Airborne from the RCR, the thinking went, and he will gain valuable command experience. Then, when he comes back to the RCR, he will be ready for promotion to lieutenant-colonel. By the mid-1970s, a stint in the Airborne was *de rigueur* for advancement to higher rank in the army either as an officer or as an NCO.

With the possible exception of Don Rochester and Herb Pitts, no one had a greater influence on the Canadian Airborne Regiment in its first decade than Col. Ian Fraser. Fraser had joined the army in 1952 and attended Acadia University as an ROTP cadet. Both his father and older brother had been soldiers, his dad with the Royal Flying Corps in the First World War, and his brother with the Cape Breton Highlanders in the Second World War. Coming from New Glasgow, a military town if ever there was one, he never really considered any other career. When he graduated from university, he joined the 2nd Battalion of the Black Watch. From then until he took the jump course at Rivers, Manitoba, he attended staff college, commanded a company in the field, and began organizing tattoos – military displays. (After retiring from the military, he became famous as producer and director of the Nova Scotia International Tattoo.) Fraser was posted to the Airborne in 1975 after commanding the 2nd Battalion of the RCR and spending one year as the CO of the Infantry School at CFB Gagetown. He thought of the Airborne as "the ultimate thing to run" and the best command in the Forces.[8]

Fraser was not comfortable with the Airborne's structure: he would have preferred a standard battalion-type of organization. He thought the regiment looked "too American," too much like a U.S. army regimental combat team, but changing the regiment's structure was not part of his mandate. He therefore put his best efforts where he thought they would do the most good – into vastly improving airborne training while ensuring that new members had the skills they required on which to build. He thought discipline generally needed tightening up and that unit morale needed a boost after the letdown that followed the return from Cyprus. With the help of his new RSM, Don Reekie, a twenty-three-year-career NCO, he set about making the Airborne the crack outfit it was designed to be.

Fraser's major innovation was the "maroon beret course."[9] A physically demanding two-week regimen of exercise, jumping, basic fieldcraft, and weapons handling, the maroon beret course became the Airborne's initiation rite. Every man who joined the regiment had to pass the course to receive his beret. Every man rejoining the regiment also had to pass the course, no matter how many times he had passed it on previous postings.

From Fraser onwards, NCOs, officers, and even the commander of the regiment and the COs of the commandos were required to undergo the course. In this way, Fraser could be sure that the training the men got in the Airborne would be built on a standard, common foundation. It was an essential feature of the Airborne, reinforced by the maroon beret course, that those who joined would already possess infantry skills and that no time would need to be wasted teaching them how to be soldiers before they learned how to be paratroopers.

From almost the beginning of his posting as regimental commander of the Airborne, Fraser was bedevilled by rumours, stories, and leaks emanating from Mobile Command in St-Hubert and NDHQ in Ottawa that the Airborne was going to be disbanded or, if not, that it would be reorganized or moved out of Edmonton. The one thing Fraser knew for sure was that NDHQ and Gen. Jacques Dextraze, now CDS, had directed Mobile Command to study and prepare a plan for the reorganization and repositioning of the army in Canada. The government was bent on saving defence costs by closing bases and reducing manpower, but reliable information was hard to come by and rumours were rife. Fraser used all the channels available to him to find out what was happening, even while he was preparing to deploy the Airborne to St-Jean, near Montreal, for security duties during the 1976 Montreal Olympics.[10]

Dextraze was indeed determined to move the Airborne out of Edmonton. His original plan was to station 1er Commando in Ottawa, with an airhead at Uplands airport, and the rest of the regiment at CFB Petawawa, about 165 kilometres northwest of Ottawa. Since there was no airhead at Petawawa, one would have to be built. In the meantime, No. 2 Commando and the rest of the regiment would use CFB Trenton, a four-hour drive away. The CDS had probably made this decision as early as the beginning of 1976, but he had difficulty getting cabinet approval because of the intense political opposition to the closing of the Griesbach Barracks in Edmonton.

Dextraze intended to reposition the Airborne at the centre of a new army formation he ultimately called the Special Service Force (SSF).[11] Akin to a light brigade group at first (its configuration was later changed to that of a mechanized brigade), the SSF was originally to consist of the Airborne, a light armoured reconnaissance regiment, a light infantry battalion, and attached arms including engineers, artillery, signals, and support troops such as military police. Dextraze envisioned the SSF as Canada's strategic reserve capable of quick deployment by air to any world trouble spot. Unsuited for the sort of high intensity air/land battle that would accompany a full-scale Warsaw Pact assault on NATO in Europe, the SSF was designed primarily for UN-style operations. The SSF was to serve another key purpose: it would become the Canadian army's major formation in Ontario, balancing the 1st Canadian Mechanized Brigade, with headquarters in Calgary, and the 5e Brigade mécanise du Canada, based at Valcartier. The SSF would ensure that the army's presence in Ontario was as substantial as it was elsewhere in Canada.

There was considerable speculation in army circles that Dextraze wanted a combat-ready force within easy striking distance of Montreal in the event of another outburst of separatist violence. One former high-ranking officer who was in on the planning process for the SSF denies this, saying, "Politics never entered the equation."[12] True or not, Prime

Minister Pierre Trudeau was reluctant to have the Airborne based in the national capital region and vetoed the idea that 1er Commando be located at Uplands. In the end, it was moved to Petawawa with the rest of the regiment. The formal announcement of the move came on November 26, 1976, and within a year the transfer had been carried out. Fraser and former Airborne COs such as Herb Pitts were worried that Dextraze wanted to dump the Airborne altogether – it was a costly formation and the military was under considerable budgetary pressure. In Fraser's view, the Airborne ought to have been put on the same organizational basis as the three regular infantry regiments, with three airborne battalions of its own. That would have served two purposes. It would have ended the Airborne's hybrid structure and ensured the Airborne's future as a permanent part of the Canadian Forces.

There is no solid evidence to indicate what Dextraze's long-term plan for the Airborne was – extinction or continuation. There was clearly a great deal of confusion on the subject in the army high command, at NDHQ, and in the government. In the end, the unit was preserved, although the move to Petawawa placed it under the command of the CO of the SSF, a brigadier-general, and consequently it lost its independent status in the chain of command. At the time of the move to Petawawa, the Airborne was also stripped of 1 Airborne Battery and 1 Airborne Field Squadron (which were placed under command of 2 Royal Canadian Horse Artillery and 2 Combat Engineer Regiment, respectively). This downsizing was partly compensated for by the later disbandment of No. 3 Mechanized Commando in Europe and its reactivation in Petawawa in 1979 as a true airborne commando akin to 1er and No. 2 Commandos. The total establishment of the Airborne shrank to 750 all ranks. When the new COs of the three commandos were appointed in 1977, they were appointed at the rank of lieutenant-colonel with all the powers and duties of battalion commanders even though their commands were much smaller.

The establishment of No. 3 Commando as an airborne unit brought only a slight modification in the way men were selected for the Airborne. Now No. 3 Commando was to be manned and commanded by soldiers from the Royal Canadian Regiment, and No. 2 Commando by men from the PPCLI. 1er Commando remained the exclusive province of the R22eR. The CO of the regiment would still be selected by the army commander, but instead of rotating between French- and English-speaking officers, a three-way rotation began with each of the three regular infantry regiments getting an opportunity to nominate the Airborne CO. Given the strength of the regimental tradition, it was a virtual certainty that the officer named to be CO by the eligible regiment would, in fact, get the appointment. Other officers – platoon commanders (captains) and commando commanders (lieutenant-colonels for a short time, then majors again) – were suggested by each regiment to fill positions in "its" commando. Everyone had to be a volunteer. The Airborne would inform the appropriate regiment of vacancies in its commando, and the parent regiment would then ask for volunteers. It then selected the soldiers it wanted to send, and the Airborne decided which men it was prepared to receive.

The Airborne's move to Petawawa, and the structural changes that accompanied that move, had both immediate and far-reaching consequences that neither Dextraze nor anyone else in the army command could have foreseen. At CFB Petawawa, the status-conscious paratroopers were thrown together with other army units on the same base. Consequently, normal regimental rivalries became even more concentrated both on the base and in the bars and other soldiers' hangouts in the town itself. There was not much for an off-duty soldier to do in Petawawa and few places for high-strung young paratroopers to blow off steam after vigorous and demanding training. The CO and the other Airborne staff now worked under the authority of a brigade commander and had to deal with the army bureaucracy for just about every requirement. What once took hours now took days.

In Edmonton, the Airborne had trained constantly for its specialized missions, but in Petawawa, as part of the SSF, it shared all the usual taskings demanded of other army units. That was fair, but it reduced the regiment's training time and combat readiness. At Edmonton, both airbase and drop zones were close by, but there was neither airhead nor drop zones at Petawawa. The regiment was isolated from the airmen and aircraft it worked with so closely and depended on so much. Even worse, the men had to be driven for four hours before they could board the aircraft, and sometimes the weather closed in between the time they mounted the trucks and the time they arrived at the airbase, which further complicated training.

In a high-strung unit like the Airborne, constant, intense training is an absolute requirement for good morale and proper comportment. Airborne units all over the world tend to attract both the worst and the best of soldiers. The best want to prove their mettle. The worst want to throw their weight around. It's not hard to tell them apart.

The best believe in the airborne creed, that the mental and physical toughness of a paratrooper is a product of both airborne training and disciplined behaviour. They know that looking fierce, or behaving like a bully, or acting like some caricature of a deranged Hollywood sociopath is the very opposite of what a well-trained paratrooper must be if he and his unit are to survive the trial of combat.

The worst are those who want to act out the "kill them all and let God sort them out" fantasies they see on TV, in movies, and in video games. They believe that war is a game that the meanest and the roughest always win. They are the ones who wear bandoliers of ammunition over their shoulders, not because they need the bullets but because it looks warlike. They are the ones who carry the deadly looking commando knives and tie bandannas around their heads. They are the ones who sport menacing tattoos. Most dangerous of all, they don't begin to understand that their aggressive posturing is the antithesis of a soldier's role in a democracy.

The worst were always a problem for the Airborne. Even before the move to Petawawa, a number of the paratroopers began to affect biker-gang behaviour both on and off base, and heavy tattooing became common.[13] Good officers and NCOs know how to handle such men, and the job was much easier, as Rochester had known from the start, when the troopers are kept busy doing what they like best – intense soldiering. A CO like Fraser and an RSM like Don Reekie brooked no nonsense from the wanna-be Rambos in their midst, always a minority, and kept the others working and training hard. That was also true, always, of the majority of officers and NCOs who led the Airborne from beginning to end. But at

Petawawa, and as a result of the restructuring of the regiment, it became easier for the worst soldiers to thrive and for their anti-social behaviour to spread and fester among their more impressionable comrades.

The erosion of training opportunities at Petawawa, the hothouse atmosphere on the base and in the town, and the deterioration of the bond between the men and their junior leaders all contributed to the decline of discipline.

Even before Petawawa, Fraser had noted a tendency for platoon commanders to be "bloody sloppy disciplinarians . . . scared green of their section commanders and their pl[atoon] W[arrant] O[fficers]." He found young officers drinking with their NCOs and using their first names when addressing them in front of the troops.[14] This kind of behaviour, and the careless thinking it betrays, constitutes a serious threat to the chain of command. The tendency to familiarity was always greater in the Airborne than in other army units because of the nature of parachute operations. It worsened at CFB Petawawa.

The confining atmosphere, lack of adequate recreation facilities both on and off base, and reduced training opportunities at Petawawa exacerbated the Airborne's chain-of-command problem. Increased association with foreign paratroopers added to it. The unit was making more jumps in the company of foreign troops and their influence was clearly perceptible. The conduct of some of those foreign paratroopers reinforced the attitudes and influence of the self-proclaimed tough guys in the Canadian Airborne. The British paras were known for their anti-social attitudes and violent behaviour. In the opinion of one former Airborne officer, many of them were no better than "street thugs." The French Foreign Legionnaires with whom 1er Commando trained were often little better. But the main foreign influence on the Canadian Airborne Regiment came from American units, especially the 82nd Airborne Division at Fort Bragg, North Carolina. In the mid- to late 1970s, the U.S. military was having trouble maintaining enlistment quotas as an all-volunteer force. It became a haven for the uneducated, the criminal, and the anti-social elements of American society. As the Canadians trained with these men, a growing tendency developed for some of them to emulate their anti-social behaviour.

Some of that copy-cat comportment was essentially harmless, but the lawlessness, disrespect, and outright racist behaviour of some of the American paratroopers, especially white Southerners, were not. "Somewhere in there, this goddamned macho business got started," former Airborne CO Herb Pitts believes.[15] In his view, it was a problem that could and should have been managed. Jim Cox, former CO of 1st Canadian Mechanized Brigade Group and himself a former Airborne officer, echoes Pitts's views. "The American influence was partly responsible for the development of 'airborne' as a culture with its 'death from the skies' attitudes," he maintains. This tendency was strengthened by the increased special operations training that the Airborne received after the move to Petawawa. Instead of concentrating on keeping its fine edge as a ready-reaction military force, the Airborne was increasingly called upon to engage in what Cox calls "airborne plus": "black" operations; long-range penetration training for the types of missions carried out by U.S. Navy Seals in Vietnam; British SAS-style anti-terrorist preparation. Cox thinks this period was the Airborne's fork in the road.[16]

In July 1977, Col. Ian Fraser handed command of the Airborne to Col. Jacques Painchaud, then in his twenty-second year in the army. Painchaud had taken the jump course in 1963 and, when CO of 2 R22eR, had insisted that all his officers also take the course. He demonstrated his continuing belief in the importance of jumping by taking Fraser's maroon beret course when he was posted to the Airborne and retaining it for all other newcomers to the regiment. It was left to Painchaud to solve some of the major problems that developed in the regiment following the transfer to Petawawa and to preserve as much of the regiment's special status as possible. He pushed his superiors, especially Army Cmdr. J. J. Paradis, to restore some of the manpower taken away from the regiment when it transferred from Edmonton. His job was made no easier by the recurrent rumours that the army, or the government, was still considering doing away with the unit. It was no secret that the Airborne would have no role to play in the event of a war in Europe, and constructing the new airhead was going to be expensive – this at a time when cutbacks in defence spending were the order of the day. The new chief of the defence staff, Admiral Robert H. Falls, questioned the utility of a parachute unit and challenged the army to justify its existence in terms other than mere tradition.[17]

The issue of the Airborne's future came to a head in the spring of 1978 when Minister of National Defence Barnet Danson told the Empire Club in Toronto that he saw no need for elite troops in the Canadian military. Although Danson had not specifically mentioned the Airborne, Painchaud was disturbed by the remarks and attacked Danson in what he thought was an off-the-record conversation with a reporter. Within a day, a headline in the local paper screamed, "DANSON MUST RESIGN – PAINCHAUD." Painchaud was summoned to Ottawa and relieved of command, eventually to be posted as director of infantry.

Painchaud was replaced by Kent Foster, who oversaw the integration of the newly reorganized No. 3 Commando into the Airborne at Petawawa. Under his leadership, the CO positions of the three commandos were reclassified to major from lieutenant-colonel, and the links between the three regular infantry regiments and the three commandos were strengthened. That meant that each of the three regiments bore a heavy responsibility to ensure that the soldiers – both officers and NCOs – it was sending to the Airborne represented what Foster calls a "fair share of the best available."[18] Foster left after two years, satisfied that he had put the Airborne on a solid foundation in its new home and that he had refocused the unit on its most important task – showing its strengths through superior performance in training, in exercises, and, if need be, on the battlefield.

By 1980, the Airborne's place in the Canadian order of battle seemed secure after several years of uncertainty. An airhead was finally built at Petawawa and closer drop zones secured. Training picked up, exercises were mounted continuously, and missions to Cyprus were laid on in 1981 and 1986. The Airborne had become an essential posting to qualify for further promotion. The decade ought to have been one of triumph and, on the surface, it was. When the regiment returned to Canada from Cyprus in the fall of 1981, CO Col. R. L. Cowling told his troops that they had carried out their duties in "an exemplary manner" and had "excelled" in operations.[19] In fact, the 1981 Cyprus mission gave the first dark hints that something was going wrong.

At one point during the tour, some sixty soldiers from 1er Commando descended on a Nicosia disco armed with clubs and bats and savagely beat men and women in a crowd that numbered in the hundreds. It was retribution for an alleged slight to one of the members of the regiment. Former Airborne Sgt. Danny Pelletier was among the attackers. "Everyone had to be punished – women and men were fair game," he said. When one man stood up to claim that he was an Italian diplomat, "we just assaulted him [too]," Pelletier remembered.[20] Even given the tendency among some Airborne officers and NCOs to allow their charges more leeway than they would in line-infantry battalions, this ought to have been treated as a serious incident by itself, let alone a sign of deeper troubles. It was not.

In 1982, Col. Ian Douglas took command of the Airborne. A twenty-five-year veteran with extensive command and staff experience, he was disturbed by the growing slackness within the regiment, part of which he chalked up to its structure. "I was the commander, but they [the commando commanders] were the COs," he recalls. But, whatever the cause of the problem, Douglas was reluctant to micro-manage the commandos or give their COs direction in matters of discipline. He tended to attribute the erosion of discipline in the unit to failures in the manpower selection system and to a growing tendency among junior officers to be too lax. In violation of a fundamental principle of the regiment, an increasing number of young men with no prior army experience were coming to the Airborne right out of battle school. More and more troopers were wearing items that were not regulation. Biker dress and behaviour began turning up in town and even on the base. Douglas let much of it pass, though he did ban his men from wearing such paraphernalia on the base.

By early 1983, discipline at CFB Petawawa had deteriorated to such an extent that Brig.-Gen. R. I. Stewart, CO of the SSF, was forced to take action. In an extraordinary memo sent to base COs in May 1984, Stewart proclaimed, "The problem in a nutshell is that we have far too many cases of ill disciplined behaviour, assault, disobedience, disrespectful behaviour; theft of public and personal property by soldiers; impaired driving offences; vehicle accidents; inadequate control of stores, ammunition/pyrotechnics, weapons and equipment that result in theft; and a general laxness in properly controlling soldiers, all of which contribute to erosion of disciplined/soldierly behaviour."[21] He put the bulk of the blame for this breakdown on "the more senior leaders," whom, he believed, were failing to ensure that the junior leaders and others understood and maintained an acceptable standard of behaviour.

Overall, Stewart blamed infiltration of the values of "the permissive society" for the trouble. He ought to have blamed the entire chain of command. It was obvious, and made more obvious by subsequent events, that the Airborne, and maybe the entire army, needed a close examination. If the army as a whole was getting too lax – too ready to accept unsuitable recruits, too willing to pass those recruits through battle school to the infantry regiments, too tolerant of unacceptable behaviour – that was bound to be even more true of the Airborne. It, after all, reflected what the rest of the army was. If the paratrooper is the essence of the soldier, he is the essence of the bad soldier as well as the good.

Stewart's solution to the growing number of disciplinary problems at CFB Petawawa was to tighten administrative procedures, including control of property, to reinstitute regular inspections, and to mete out appropriate punishment.[22] But nothing seemed to work. Thefts – particularly weapons thefts – increased. Then, in the summer of 1985, a series of violent incidents occurred off base involving paratroopers and knives. In early August, a civilian was murdered by a machete-wielding paratrooper. The murderer had been in the regiment for only a month. He was less a representative of the unit than an example of the raw material the unit was getting. Nevertheless, it was time for drastic action. Army commander Lt.-Gen. Charles Belzile ordered Maj.-Gen. C. W. "Bill" Hewson, chief of intelligence and security, to investigate.

Although Hewson's investigation was aimed specifically at finding out what was behind the growing problems plaguing the Airborne, his report was meant to reflect much that was going wrong in the army as a whole. At the root of the problem lay a weakening of the all-important bond between the soldiers and their junior leaders. In Hewson's view, this was primarily caused by over-tasking of young officers away from their units. But there were other major problems as well. Because too few soldiers were volunteering from the standing units, the Airborne was taking a growing number of soldiers directly from battle school. They were receiving neither the seasoning nor the screening they ought to have had before joining. The army was too often remiss in not uncovering pre-service criminal records. Too many men were able to extend their postings to the Airborne almost indefinitely. This meant that while officers were in for short periods, some NCOs and others were long-term members who knew the ropes. The "Hellyer corporals" were really just privates, but army regulations classified them as NCOs, which restricted the ability of an officer or senior NCO to discipline them. The problem was made worse in the Airborne because most of the troopers were "Hellyer corporals." There was a distortion of authority within the regiment because the regimental CO had five COs under him, each responsible for discipline in his own unit. Consequently, discipline was applied unevenly and authority too thinly dispersed. Disciplinary action had been inadequate on too many occasions. Senior officers too often escaped responsibility for disciplinary breakdowns and junior officers became their scapegoats.

Hewson also suggested that the social climate in Petawawa lay behind the Airborne's troubles: there were too few ways for single soldiers to blow off steam; there was too much drinking; there were too few available women. Hewson warned the army that "lacking effective leadership from junior officers and NCOs, the majority of officers [*sic*] must turn to something else. Many look to the informal leaders amongst themselves; unfortunately, some of these informal leaders cannot cope with the challenge in a responsible manner and problems can occur."[23] Prophetic words.

By the mid-1980s, the Canadian Airborne Regiment was not getting the strong leadership it needed. Although the majority of the officers, NCOs, and troopers were fine soldiers, responsible leaders, and conscientious professionals, enough rebels were infiltrating the regiment to cause severe problems. They could have been dealt with; many probably were. But some were not because the junior leaders who should have straightened them out, or sent them packing, didn't, and their superiors either looked the other way or did not care. The latter was more interested in keeping the peace than in solving problems, more interested in a good PER than in alienating troublemakers.

Belzile forwarded Hewson's report to the CDS, indicating areas that needed action at the NDHQ level, and those that Land Force Command might deal with. While acknowledging that the murder that had prompted him to call in Hewson was a serious matter, he also knew that it was neither the first time a Canadian soldier had committed such a crime nor would it be the last. In fact, Petawawa's military crime rate was, at the time, no higher on average than that of other large base areas. So Belzile tended to agree with Hewson's conclusion that the problems that plagued the Airborne were issues in most other army units as well. He also believed that the regiment's peculiar structure put much of the onus for its performance on the regimental commander and the unit COs. If the former was a strong, experienced, and well-respected soldier, he would usually set the tone for the entire unit. If he was not, then he might be little more than a postmaster and his unit COs would set the example, for better or worse.[24]

Col. J. M. R. Gaudreau was commander of the Airborne when the Hewson investigations were carried out and the report issued. He was given no special instructions to solve the problems that Hewson had unearthed. In fact, his immediate superior, the commander of the SSF, called him in to tell him that "the Hewson Report had created a lot of staff action and navel-gazing across the Army. And he did not expect . . . the Canadian Airborne Regiment to be the cause of further concern to the chain of command. In other words, good, old, military discipline and logic, words of wisdom . . . was the secret to sorting things out."[25] That seemed to work for a time. When Kent Foster returned to Petawawa as a brigadier-general and commander of the SSF in 1986, he experienced none of the major problems that Hewson had encountered. Perhaps that was because Foster revised and regularized the SSF's training regimen and made a special effort to protect the men's leave and rest periods and time with their families.[26]

Kent Foster's thorough professionalism and his humane, but no-nonsense, approach to soldiering undoubtedly took much of the slack out of the SSF in general and the Airborne in particular. But not all of it. In 1986, Peter G. Kenward, three years a major and former company commander with 1 PPCLI, was appointed the new CO of No. 2 Commando. He had been a junior officer with the Airborne in the mid-1970s and was glad to return. He found the majority of his men to be aggressive, keen, fit, and working hard to meet the challenges of airborne soldiering. As before, he was impressed by their spirit. "I noticed a tone, a general feeling in the unit that wasn't evident in the battalion I just came from." But he also identified "an element in the commando that had to be removed." These were the men with the "Rambo attitude," who affected American-style dress, bad attitudes, and a reverence for the Rebel flag.[27]

The PPCLI hockey team was named The Rebels, and that was harmless enough. After the Airborne began training with the U.S. 82nd Airborne Division in Fort Bragg, however, the Confederate flag began to show up on members' vehicles and in the barracks. One CO of No. 2 Commando had even jumped with the flag attached to his leg. To some Airborne officers, the Confederate flag signified nothing more than attachment to the PPCLI, even though neither the flag nor any other symbol of the Confederacy is in any way officially connected to that regiment. But others, Kenward among them, saw the flag as a challenge to the chain of command. The more unruly and rebellious members of No. 2 Commando seemed to have adopted the Confederate flag both as a symbol of their non-conformist attitude to soldiering and as a sign of their embracement of biker-gang and even skinhead values. Kenward found other serious problems as well. "A large number of my NCOs came to me and said that one of the biggest problems they had in the commando was they did not have the backing and the authority that their rank demanded," he said. "They found that in many cases there was far too much influence being exerted at the more junior levels, especially master corporal, and a lot of it was in the negative sense."[28]

Kenward acted decisively. The obvious troublemakers were removed. Members of his commando were charged if they sported anything but regulation kit and uniform. He backed the senior NCOs when they meted out strong disciplinary justice. The Confederate flag was banned. "I made it clear that I would hang anybody that brought the flag into open view and that this was unacceptable . . . in many ways that symbol represented something that was anti-military in my view because it was closely associated with people who were undisciplined, attacked authority . . . and had views [in the United States] on everything from basic discipline to race that was completely unacceptable in a Canadian military environment."[29] Kenward was not loved by all of the men, but his straight approach and his willingness to make waves, to tackle the troublemakers head on, earned him much deserved respect both inside and outside the regiment.

Kenward left No. 2 Commando in 1988 to attend a year-long French course. He was then posted to NDHQ. He had brought the unit back from the verge of rebellion. When he left, discipline began to deteriorate once again. The regimental CO from 1987 to 1990 was Col. M. J. R. Houghton. Houghton appears to have had a rather strange attitude to the maintenance of good order in the Airborne. When an officer such as Kenward took a no-nonsense approach towards the rebels in his unit, Houghton backed him up. But Houghton did not appear unduly worried by the appearance of the Confederate flag, which he thought of solely as a PPCLI regimental symbol, and did not press those of his officers who were lax towards disciplinary breaches. In the words of one former Airborne CO, Houghton was a "weak commander."[30]

On the night of June 1, 1990, one of the worst incidents of disciplinary breakdown in the history of the Airborne took place on the regimental parade square at Camp Petawawa. A private vehicle owned by Capt. Jonathan Ferraby, a platoon commander in No. 2 Commando, was deliberately burned and vandalized. The arsonist started the fire by burning a copy of the Airborne's routine orders on the floor of the car. Neither the military police nor Maj. David Pentney, CO of No. 2 Commando, discovered the culprits. When asked at the Somalia Inquiry at the end of October 1995 whether he had "come across any information which would suggest that this [the burning] was a direct challenge to command," Houghton answered, "No, I did not."[31] But it is hard to imagine a greater symbolic challenge to the chain of command, to the authority of the army, and to the entire ethos of professional soldiering. And yet not a soul was punished.

The end of Colonel Houghton's tour as Airborne CO coincided with a temporary freeze on promotions within the Canadian Forces that resulted from yet another government move to save money by cutting the defence budget. The motive was simple and direct: the freeze on promotions meant a freeze on promotional pay increases. And it came at a particularly bad time. The conclusion of the Cold War saw an increase in Canadian commitments to UN and other offshore operations. More Canadian soldiers were being sent on operational missions abroad than at any time since the Korean War. There was an increase in demand for captains and majors for these foreign postings. The result was a shortage of infantry majors at home. In the regular infantry battalions, captains were put in command of companies. That was not especially worrisome because Canadian infantry platoons are commanded by lieutenants and a captain commanding an infantry company is still higher in the chain of command than his platoon leaders. But this was not true in the Airborne, where platoon leaders were usually captains. During and after the rank freeze, therefore, the Airborne took majors from where it could, regardless of how qualified they were for the very difficult job of commanding an Airborne commando.

Some were not qualified. This was to prove downright dangerous at a time when a growing number of skinheads began to infiltrate the ranks of the army and particularly the Airborne. According to a list compiled by the Special Investigations Unit of National Defence Headquarters in 1992, there were probably not more than forty skinheads in the entire army, but "several" at least were found to be in all three of the Airborne commandos at CFB Petawawa, but especially in No. 2 Commando.[32] With their shaved heads, their spiderweb tattoos, and their viciously anti-social and racist behaviour, these men were the antithesis of all that the Canadian army is supposed to stand for. They are part of an international movement that has direct links to various extreme right-wing organizations such as the Aryan Nations of the United States and Canada, the White Aryan Resistance (WAR), and Rahowa (Racial Holy War). They have become well known to municipal police across Canada for their brutal attacks on those who oppose them politically, on homosexuals, and on immigrants of colour. In the fall of 1995, several skinhead members of the U.S. 82nd Airborne Division were charged with the premeditated murder of a black couple in Fort Bragg.

In the absence of strong leadership among some junior officers and commando COs, they began to dominate other men who were perhaps less bellicose, less threatening, than they were. When an officer comes to the cynical conclusion that not making waves is more likely to improve his chance of rising through the ranks, when an officer stops leading his unit and begins to manage it, it gives the thugs who find their way into armies everywhere the chance they need to begin running things.

A strong impression has emerged from the hearings of the Somalia Commission and from evidence printed in the press that No. 2 Commando was the most troublesome of the three commandos. Houghton said as much to the Somalia Inquiry in October 1995. It was doubtless true. Soldiers from No. 2 Commando were involved in most of the serious incidents that have come to light in the Airborne, especially those that represented a direct challenge to the chain of command. One high-ranking officer who was closely involved with the Airborne in the early 1990s is convinced that the PPCLI "let it down."[33] Herb Pitts vehemently denies that the PPCLI was unloading undesirable soldiers on the Airborne. "None of us would dump our garbage elsewhere," he declares.[34] In fact, all the infantry regiments were guilty of letting bad apples through. By the early 1990s, there was far less incentive in the army to send a fair share of the best to the Airborne because of structural changes in the army, budget cuts, and the changing nature of the Airborne itself.

In the summer of 1990, Col. W. M. Holmes was appointed regimental CO with the specific mission of "putting the [Airborne] back together." He was told that the regiment was "not operating effectively as a unit" and given the job of setting matters right.[35] Exercises were increased – there had only been a single short one in Houghton's entire tenure as CO – discipline was tightened, and training intensified. It had some impact. Offences for assault, impaired driving, drunkenness, and weapons misuse among Airborne members declined in 1991 and 1992. But compared to most other battalions and regiments in Land Force Command, they remained high. A study done by the military police of Special Service Force units based at CFB Petawawa from 1988 to 1992 shows that Airborne members outstripped soldiers of all other units in assault charges in each year of the survey and often, but not always, in weapons offences as well.[36]

In May 1993, Brig.-Gen. Ernie Beno, then CO of the SSF, assessed the problems in the Airborne that had led to the murder in Somalia. He wrote, "While the vast majority of the officers, NCOs and soldiers in the Canadian Airborne Regiment are individually very good, there have been, from time to time, certain individuals posted into the Regiment whose conduct, motivation, maturity and self-confidence have been below the acceptable standard. There is a high degree of second and third tours amongst the NCOs, and perhaps some of them should not have been returned. You hear of officers and NCOs being given subsequent tours because they have the 'reputation' of being the 'airborne type,' or because of an 'only the Airborne can handle them' attitude. I would think that this is rare, but no doubt there are cases."[37] That was just the sort of thing Jean-Victor Allard and Don Rochester had wanted to avoid.

That, then, was the state of the Airborne when the Canadian government was approached by the United Nations to send troops to a UN peacekeeping operation in Somalia in the summer of 1992. Disciplinary problems were rampant. Col. Ian Fraser's once formidable maroon beret course had long since disappeared as a combined refresher course and initiation rite. Leadership was uneven at all levels. A vicious streak of racism and anti-social behaviour ran through the regiment, particularly through No. 2 Commando. Degrading hazing rituals for new recruits, some of which involved not only verbal but also physical abuse and degradation (such as being forced to eat feces), had become the norm. On July 30, and again on August 30, some of these hazings were carried out behind the barracks of No. 2 Commando. On the second occasion, a captain from regimental HQ was present with some forty-nine master corporals and corporals. Videotape of portions of such hazings would show up later on CBC-TV. An informal and deleterious leadership had taken hold at the junior levels, especially among the master corporals, who often seemed to be running their platoons.

The Airborne contained the best and the worst of the Canadian army, including a large number – the majority no doubt – of professional, conscientious, and very tough officers and NCOs. But there was a cancer growing in its midst and no one to perform the surgery that was so vitally necessary. From NDHQ down to the platoon leaders, a dangerous "boys will be boys" attitude prevailed. Careerism, apathy, cynicism, simple gutlessness, and sheer chance had allowed the army's – and especially the Airborne's – problems, many of which can be traced back to the 1960s, to multiply and spread unchecked. The failure to address these problems would lead, finally, to the shocking murder of Shidane Abukar Arone.

9

SOMALIA

DECEMBER 28, 1992. The U.S. army Blackhawk helicopters flew low and fast over the arid countryside of central Somalia. The side doors were open, but the air blasting through the interior did little to cool the soldiers inside. In full combat gear, with helmets strapped to their heads, flak jackets closed tight around their bodies, and C-7 assault rifles between their knees, they could have been movie extras feigning a helicopter assault in some Vietnam rice paddy. But this was not Vietnam, this was Somalia, and there was no pretence about the mission.

The soldiers aboard the Blackhawks were a mixed force of Canadian paratroopers and soldiers of the U.S. army's crack 10th Mountain Division. The Canadians were from No. 2 Commando, the Canadian Airborne Regiment Battle Group. They were flying from Baledogle to Belet Huen to seize and secure the airstrip there in preparation for the arrival of the remainder of the Canadian Airborne Battle Group by Hercules transport from Baledogle and Mogadishu. These Blackhawks were designed specifically for helicopter assault missions; as Apache helicopter gunships hovered nearby to provide heavy support, the Blackhawks swooped in, landed fast, disgorged their troops, then picked up speed and left the landing zone (LZ).

The men fanned out; the Americans to one end of the airstrip, the Airborne to the other. Assault rifles were loaded and charged. The light machine gunners followed just a few steps behind the riflemen. Eyes swept the countryside in the glare of the hot sun, ears strained to hear the sound of incoming rifle or machine-gun fire against the noise of the helicopters. A Somali warlord's gang equipped with "technicals" had been spotted at the airstrip just the day before. The multiple barrel anti-aircraft machine guns they mounted were designed to destroy planes or soft-skinned vehicles. They made a terrible mess of human beings. As a Chapter VII UN authorized mission, the rules of engagement (ROEs) were clear. If the soldiers believed themselves or their mission to be menaced by others, in trucks, on foot, or hidden in bunkers or buildings, they could open fire and shoot to kill.

No one knew what to expect at Belet Huen that day. Most reports had indicated that it was one of the quieter areas, that the men ought not to expect a hot LZ. But soldiers know that men who are not keenly aware of their surroundings and ready for any possibility die fast. These men were ready. They moved to the end of the designated defensive zone and dug in as best they could in the powderlike sand. Behind them more Blackhawks landed and more Canadian paratroopers and American soldiers ran forward to fill out the defensive perimeter and to set up the radio and other equipment that would guide the Hercules aircraft that followed. The airstrip was a mess – broken-down Somali military planes and abandoned vehicles littered the area – but the runway was usable.

The Hercs started to come in before nightfall. For the rest of the night and the next few days, they landed at regular intervals. With engines running, they quickly unloaded men and supplies before returning north and east for more. In airborne assault, by parachute or by helicopter, the point is to surprise the enemy. Get down fast, secure the drop zone or the landing zone, and get the men, the communications equipment, the heavier weapons, and the food and water on the ground as fast as possible. Build up the landing forces before the enemy can react. The Canadian Airborne Regiment had trained for this sort of operation for almost a quarter-century. At Belet Huen, they pulled it off without a hitch. By nightfall, patrols from No. 2 Commando were entering Belet Huen itself.

The assault landing at Belet Huen was initiated almost six months to the day after Col. W. M. Holmes handed over command of the regiment to Lt.-Col. Paul Morneault, who had been Holmes's deputy commander. The handover took place June 24, 1992, on the large parade square at CFB

Petawawa. As with all formal handovers, it was an elaborate ceremony. The paratroopers were drawn up in perfect formation. The guests from the army high command, from other regiments, and from the town watched from the stands. A band played as Holmes inspected the troops, then reported his unit to be in good order. Morneault recited the orders that placed him in command.

In fact, Holmes was uneasy about Morneault's accession to command and so were some others in the army. Morneault had no experience in command of a battalion-sized formation. He was eligible to command now only because his take-over coincided with yet another change in the Airborne's structure and status. Earlier in the year, the commander of Land Force Command, Lt.-Gen. J. C. Gervais, had announced that the regiment would be reduced to 601 all ranks and that it would assume the organizational structure of a regular infantry battalion. The three commandos and service commando would also lose their "unit" status and become infantry companies in all but name. So Morneault took command as a lieutenant-colonel. Had he been required to be a full colonel as all his predecessors had been, he would not have been eligible.

In the past, accession to command of the Airborne Regiment had meant a step-up the promotion ladder for a lieutenant-colonel who had previously commanded a battalion, but no more. Putting the Airborne CO on the same command level as other battalion COs virtually guaranteed that future Airborne commanders would be neophytes at that level of command. That was unfortunate given the difficult nature of the command. The same principle now applied to officers leading the commandos. In the past, they would normally have had experience as company commanders in regular infantry battalions before coming to the Airborne, but that, too, had changed. Maj. Anthony Seward of No.2 Commando was a prime example. (Holmes worried about Seward's command capability as well.) But commando commanders still had to be majors because platoon commanders in the Airborne Regiment were still captains, as they ought to have been.

Although a good staff officer, Morneault had very limited command experience. Holmes thought Morneault was an excellent administrative officer but a "procrastinator" in matters of leadership, training, and discipline. Morneault had a reputation as "an office kind of guy," in the words of Lt.-Col. Carol Mathieu, who succeeded him. Brig.-Gen. Ernie Beno, commander of the SSF, had not wanted him either. Onetime CO of the Airborne battery, Beno would have preferred to have a man with a proven track record in command, and Morneault did not have that; as deputy commander, his job had been almost solely concerned with staff and administration. Beno and Maj.-Gen. Lewis MacKenzie, commander of Land Force Central Area and Beno's boss, preferred Peter Kenward. Kenward knew his name was being bandied about, and, even though commanding the Airborne would have been a sideways move for him (he had received his promotion to lieutenant-colonel some time before), he was definitely interested. But Kenward was a Patricia, and it was not the Patricias' turn to provide the Airborne CO. Gervais picked Morneault, who had been put forward by the R22eR regimental executive, which insisted it was its turn to supply the Airborne commander.[1]

The choice of who was to command the Airborne for the next few years was probably more crucial in the spring of 1992 than it had been for some time. It had only been seven years, after all, since the Hewson Report and two years since Holmes had been brought in to straighten out the regiment. With the end of the Cold War, UN peacekeeping operations had multiplied with great speed, and Canada's overseas commitments had grown apace. Never anxious to be left out of blue-helmet operations, Ottawa took on greater responsibilities without a commensurate increase in Canadian army resources. For the military, it was a familiar story. Ever since Lester B. Pearson, as Canada's minister of external affairs, won his Nobel Peace Prize for "inventing" modern peacekeeping in 1956, Canadians had come to see themselves as the world's foremost peacekeepers. For succeeding Canadian governments, therefore, more peacekeeping was always good politics. But Canadians also wanted budget cuts to come out of the military's hide first, and, therefore, more defence spending was bad politics.

In the summer of 1992, Canadian troops in various numbers could be found on UN missions on Cyprus and the Golan Heights, in Cambodia,

El Salvador, Kuwait, the Western Sahara, Nicaragua, and the former Yugoslavia (this last with two whole battalions). Canadian soldiers were also serving on a non-UN operation in the Sinai Desert. And yet when the UN sought Canadian assistance for still another peacekeeping mission, this time in Somalia, the government hardly hesitated. Everybody with a TV set knew about the ravaged African country, after all, where millions of people were starving to death. There was no problem with the supply of food aid. The problem was that local warlords were battling each other for control of a country with no government. Their gunmen either hijacked the food or took large portions of the aid as tolls, or transit fees, or to purchase a guarantee of "safe" passage. The Somalis were incapable of saving themselves, it appeared, so the UN would have to do it for them. Who else but Canada to join the worthy mission?

The Canadian government put the UN request to CDS Gen. John de Chastelaine: Could Canada squeeze out yet another contingent of troops for a UN mission? Which units should go? Through July and August, NDHQ and Land Force Command worked on the numbers. There is no evidence currently available that anyone there ever seriously considered telling the government to forget the mission. In the normal scheme of things, de Chastelaine and Deputy Minister Robert Fowler would have made the recommendation to go. Even if de Chastelaine thought the army was already overcommitted (and there is no available evidence that he did), Fowler would almost certainly have made sure that the mission was accepted. A forceful man who always did his best to protect the interests of his political masters, Fowler was the *éminence grise* of NDHQ.

In deciding which units to send, the high command had several factors to consider. Which units had been over-tasked lately? Which had not had an overseas posting for some time? Which unit was best suited to the mission? The UN mission, dubbed Operation Cordon, was projected as a traditional Chapter VI peacekeeping operation in which UN forces would patrol zones of separation between warring factions to allow international relief agencies to deliver food, medicine, and other essential supplies to the Somali hinterland. The Canadians were to be assigned to patrol Bossasso, a small port in northeast Somalia.

On August 28, 1992, the Conservative government of Prime Minister Brian Mulroney informed the United Nations that it would make available approximately 750 soldiers for UNOSOM, the UN force that was to execute Operation Cordon. The Canadian Airborne Regiment was to be the core of a larger battle group that would include engineers and other support personnel.

To accomplish its new mission, the Airborne needed to be trained to act as a light mechanized unit using vehicles such as the Grizzly, a wheeled armoured personnel carrier. The need to send a motorized unit to Somalia should have militated against the selection of the Airborne. When a soldier is taken from an infantry section and transformed into a vehicle driver, the manpower and firepower of his section is automatically weakened. But the Airborne had not been on an operational mission since 1986. The closest it had come to an overseas assignment had been its selection as part of Operation Python in the fall of 1991 (as truce observers and peacekeepers in elections in contested parts of Morocco), but that mission had been scrubbed by the UN and replaced by a much smaller operation.

The prevailing view in NDHQ and Mobile Command was that the Airborne was ready and needed an operational mission to keep its edge and to sustain unit morale. Men much closer to the scene were not so sure. Colonel Holmes thought perhaps the Airborne was indeed a suitable unit, but not at that particular time.[2] Brigadier-General Beno spoke to Lieutenant-General Gervais within two weeks of first receiving the warning order on September 4 about his "concerns relevant to the command and training preparations" of the regiment, but Gervais told him only to take care of the problem.[3] Beno specifically believed that Morneault was failing "to grasp the scope and scale of the requirement" and was not doing an adequate job of preparation. In Beno's view, Morneault was micro-managing the process and undermining his own effectiveness as a commanding officer.[4] Morneault no doubt disagreed.

Other difficulties were also becoming apparent. The burden of regimental downsizing and reorganization had fallen more heavily on No. 2 Commando than on the other two, and there was a larger turnover of junior leaders. Consequently, while most of the rest of the newly designated

Canadian Airborne Regiment Battle Group, publicly announced on September 5, trained specifically for Operation Cordon, the training in No. 2 Commando emphasized basic combat skills to achieve the required cohesion at the fire team (two people) and section level (ten people).

Just as seriously, NDHQ was having difficulty deciding on mission ROEs. The ROEs for Operation Cordon were initially to be based on the ones then in use by Canadian troops in the former Yugoslavia, but delays and confusion at NDHQ caused delays in delivering the ROEs to the battle group. It is next to impossible to give soldiers mission-specific training when they don't know what ROEs they will be subject to.

Finally, the armoured regiment tasked to train the Airborne in the use of armoured vehicles, the Royal Canadian Dragoons, reported that the process was less than smooth. Although the Airborne had much to learn about driving the Grizzlies, some Airborne members were downright apathetic about the task. They refused to work weekends, they showed up late for their courses, and, like naughty schoolboys, they failed to pay attention to their instructors.[5]

On September 22, Beno issued specific training instructions to Morneault detailing what needed to be done to get the Airborne Battle Group ready for the upcoming mission. He told Morneault there were three "basic rules" for a peacekeeping operation: "minimum use of force, maximum use of deterrence, and conflict resolution at the lowest possible level." He instructed Morneault to aim "to deploy and return from Somalia without having discharged a single weapon in anger." To that end, Beno laid out specific individual and unit goals to be accomplished before he was prepared to declare the battle group ready for the mission.[6]

As the days dragged by, Beno grew more concerned about what he considered Morneault's failure to bring the Airborne Regiment up to the required standard of operational readiness. On September 29, Beno spoke to MacKenzie over the telephone about his fears. When MacKenzie visited CFB Petawawa on October 2 to inspect 1 RCR, then about to depart for the former Yugoslavia, Beno repeated his concerns. Morneault's problems got considerably worse the night of October 2. That evening a group of paratroopers, later identified by Ontario Provincial Police as having been from No. 2 Commando, celebrated the end of a phase of especially rigorous training by getting extremely drunk at the Kyrenia Club on base. They set off two thunderflashes (designed to simulate the loud noise of a grenade), two smoke grenades, and a flare. Later that night, they took their party, along with stolen thunderflashes, personal weapons, and cases of beer, into Algonquin Provincial Park. There were more explosions and a lot of gunfire. At some point in the evening, the personal car of Sergeant Wyszynski, that night's regimental orderly sergeant, was torched in front of Building L108, as Capt. Jonathan Ferraby's car had been more than two years before. Two days later, Morneault told Beno that he was frustrated with "internal disciplinary problems" within the Airborne, and especially in No. 2 Commando, which he said was dominated by a rebel group.

Morneault did not find the perpetrators behind the incidents of October 2. There is no available evidence that he received any substantial help from the man who might have straightened matters out, the RSM, Chief Warrant Officer Bud Jardine. From time immemorial, the RSM has been responsible for the discipline and conduct of the troops. He reports directly to the battalion CO. If he is effective, if he upholds the tradition that accompanies the position, he knows what is going on in the ranks, or he soon finds out. If he does not know, it can only be because he has lost touch with the NCOs who are supposed to report to him. If he cannot find out, it is because he has lost their respect and, consequently, his ability to do his job. That appears to be the case with Jardine.

Morneault ordered No. 2 Commando into the field for five days to pressure the men to give up the miscreants – without results. At the same time, Morneault suggested to Beno that No. 2 Commando might be left behind unless the culprits were identified. Beno rejected the idea as an impractical threat. He was upset, moreover, that Morneault did not seem to be worried that a Confederate flag had been hung outside the single soldiers' barracks. Morneault had no plans to discipline either the duty officer who had allowed the flag to hang or the duty sergeant who had taken no action because he now allegedly "feared for his life."

No one was charged with either of the incidents of October 2, although one corporal did come forward later to admit that he had illegally used thunderflashes. The 1993 board of inquiry into the operations of the Canadian Airborne Battle Group, headed by Maj.-Gen. Thomas de Faye, concluded, "It seems likely that lack of evidence, lack of resolve, and perhaps, even fear of somehow lessening the operational effectiveness of 2 Commando contributed to the weakening of the initial resolve to pursue this matter with vigour."[7]

Morneault's collective field punishment seems to have had the opposite effect to what he intended: the men stayed tight-lipped, and Beno was angry that the training schedule had been disrupted to no purpose. Despite his failure to get to the bottom of the disciplinary mess in No. 2 Commando, Morneault told Beno on October 9 that the battle group was ready to undertake the mission and would prove its readiness in upcoming exercises. That same day, Beno told MacKenzie that he had "no confidence" in Morneault.[8] Three days later, Morneault left Canada for Somalia with senior officers and staff to undertake a personal reconnaissance prior to the mission.

Exercise Stalwart Providence was a four-day exercise mounted from October 14 to 18 to test the Airborne Battle Group's preparation for the UN mission and particularly its newly acquired capability as a mechanized unit. The exercise was run by the Royal Canadian Dragoons, and the results were just short of disaster. The Dragoons found that the Airborne's security procedures were lax; it was weak on intelligence gathering; its soldiers were not yet proficient in the operation of their vehicles; its chain of command did not function properly, especially in passing information about operational procedures to the lowest ranks. The three Airborne commandos did not work together as a team but as three separate entities. There was still much work to do, the Dragoons CO observed, especially in the areas of "professionalism at all times; leadership at all levels; safety; and the execution of proper battle procedure."[9]

These failings were serious. There were other findings that suggested the Canadian Airborne Regiment was too much influenced by Ramboism for a peacekeeping mission. Airborne soldiers seemed too ready to use physical force on unarmed "Somali demonstrators"; they were too quick to charge their weapons; they often lost their temper with demonstrators, they seemed confused about procedures for dealing with armed versus unarmed Somalis; they were still too aggressive for the mission. The Dragoons' assessment was that the Airborne had "missed" its CO, but with a few more weeks of training would no doubt be ready.[10]

Ernie Beno was no longer sure. He was unhappy that Morneault had left for Somalia without testing the operational effectiveness of his commandos. On the day the exercise ended, Beno told MacKenzie that the Airborne's training deficiencies and disciplinary problems had not been solved and that if the regiment "was to be adequately prepared for its mission, it was necessary to replace . . . Morneault."[11]

This was an extraordinary suggestion. Replacing a battalion CO less than six months after he has taken command, and only a few weeks before a mission, is drastic action. Nonetheless, Beno was now certain that sending the Airborne to Somalia under Morneault would be to court disaster. On October 21, after obtaining approval from MacKenzie, Beno relieved Morneault of command. He told the outraged officer that he was doing so because: the battalion was still not adequately trained; Morneault had failed to assess the commandos prior to Exercise Stalwart Providence; operational matters were still unresolved; there were still significant leadership and discipline problems in the regiment; and the regiment had major problems of internal cohesion, control, standardized operational procedures, administration, and efficiency. Morneault protested that he was being unfairly treated.

Lt.-Col. Carol Mathieu took command of the Canadian Airborne Regiment five days after Morneault was fired. Mathieu had joined the military in the mid-1960s. He had been a platoon leader in 3 R22eR in 1969, received his jump training in 1970, and joined the Airborne as a captain in 1972. He had stayed with the regiment until 1976, and served with it in Cyprus during the Turkish invasion. From there he had gone to CFB Gagetown. He had served in Germany, attended staff college, and been posted to army HQ in St-Hubert. He had been promoted to lieutenant-colonel in 1988 when he returned to the Airborne as deputy commander during Colonel Houghton's term as CO. Despite his long and varied experience, Mathieu (like Morneault) had no battalion command experience and was not Beno's, nor Lewis MacKenzie's, first choice to replace Morneault. They both wanted Kenward. But Kenward was not available at that point and the R22eR regimental executive still insisted that it was its turn to supply the Airborne CO. It wanted Mathieu, and Gervais agreed.

Mathieu was aware of the problems that had plagued his predecessor and made an effort to solve them in the limited time he had available. Training was intensified. Beno suggested that Mathieu shake up the regiment by moving approximately twenty-five people around; Mathieu instead dropped six men from the order of battle.[12] Mathieu kept the OC of No. 2 Commando, Maj. Anthony Seward, and the leader of the reconnaissance platoon of HQ Commando, Capt. Michel Rainville, even though Beno suggested that Mathieu "study closely" their suitability. While still with the R22eR, Rainville had led a near-disastrous, and totally unauthorized, raid by men of the 1er Commando on the Van Doo headquarters in Quebec City the previous year. He had also been implicated in another unauthorized commando-style exercise at CFB Gagetown in February 1992, when a number of trainees were held captive and "interrogated." Master Cpl. Clayton Matchee and Cpl. Kyle Brown were also retained despite the urgings of their platoon warrant officer and platoon commander that they be left behind. On November 19, an officer of the Special Investigation Unit briefed Beno that Cpl. Matthew McKay of No. 2 Commando was under investigation for alleged involvement in right-wing activities, but he went to Somalia too. Several months later, a photograph of McKay giving the Nazi salute in front of a Swastika flag made the front pages of newspapers in Canada.

On November 1, Beno informed NDHQ that the Airborne was ready for the mission. Mathieu would later explain, "Like everything else, you never know you're ready until you get there."[13] NDHQ accepted that advice on November 13 and declared to the government that the force was ready for deployment and that equipment and personnel were prepared for the mission. Three days later, the supply and support vessel *HMCS Preserver* left Halifax bound for the coast of Somalia to provide a floating resupply and logistical base for the upcoming operation. The Airborne continued its training and the standard operating procedures

(SOPs) for the mission; the rules that would govern virtually every activity except the use of force (covered by the ROEs) were finalized.

On December 3, only days before the Airborne was due to depart, the UN Security Council changed the nature of the Somali mission at the behest of the United States. The TV screens of the Great Republic had been filled with reports of the mass starvation in Somalia and the callousness and crassness of the warlords. It was they – according to the press – whose dirty little struggle for power was dooming a starving Somali population. U.S. President George Bush decided that something more than a Chapter VI peacekeeping mission was required, something in the nature of another Gulf War operation. The Americans promised a division or more of soldiers and Marines as well as air and naval support. The Security Council agreed. Operation Cordon was killed and Operation Deliverance, a Chapter VII peace-enforcement mission, was born. UNOSOM was downgraded and UNITAF – the United Task Force under U.S. military leadership – popped into existence. Canada was asked to send troops for UNITAF and agreed. Hadn't the Airborne been training for this mission in any case?

In fact, it had not. The basic aim of Operation Deliverance was to disarm and suppress the military forces of the Somali warlords. It does not appear much thought was given in Washington or anywhere else to the complexity of the revised mission. The Somali warlords could only be disarmed and pacified when a stable political regime had been put into place. But such an objective could be achieved only by intervening massively in Somali politics. The UN would have to become the biggest warlord in the country to do that successfully! It was not prepared to take on that role. In any event, the mission the Airborne ultimately embarked upon was very different from the one it had prepared for. The regiment would be entering a hostile environment and facing, and trying to disarm, military forces that had every reason to dispute its presence. There would be no white-painted vehicles, blue berets, or UN flags for this mission.

Ottawa's decision to go ahead with the dispatch of Canadian troops to Somalia, despite the dramatic change in the nature of the mission, was wrong on two counts. First, the Canadian Airborne Regiment Battle Group had not trained for an operation in which combat was more than likely. Secondly, no rules of engagement had been devised for the mission. The ROE situation was already a mess and now it got worse. Just as NDHQ was finally ready to distribute ROEs, the mission changed. The NDHQ bureaucracy got busy again, hurriedly trying to draw up a new set of rules and to distribute them to the troops before they embarked for Somalia. The men were never trained in applying the new ROEs. This omission undoubtedly made the mission more difficult and dangerous for the Canadian troops.

No one in the chain of command seems to have questioned the feasibility or appropriateness of sending Canadian troops on a Chapter VII peace-enforcement mission at that late juncture. No one hesitated to send a unit with obvious disciplinary problems into a possible combat environment even though disciplinary problems always undermine combat effectiveness. If Beno, or MacKenzie, or Lt.-Gen. Gordon Reay (who succeeded Gervais as army commander prior to the deployment), or de Chastelaine had any qualms at the time, they have not yet come to light. Whether or not Deputy Minister Robert Fowler or Minister of National Defence Kim Campbell or Prime Minister Brian Mulroney would have been prepared to discuss the matter, or even to cancel the deployment at that late date, is another issue.

It was one thing for Ottawa to commit troops for UNITAF, but quite another to actually send them. The Airborne Battle Group was hurriedly expanded from 750 to 845 men with the addition of A Squadron of the Dragoons, a mortar platoon from 1 RCR, and other combat troops. The Dragoons would provide fire support if necessary and would be assigned to patrol a particular area of the Canadian Humanitarian Relief Sector (HRS). Col. Serge Labbé was placed in command of the total Canadian force, which included the battle group and the *Preserver*. His HQ was to be in Mogadishu. The new initial Canadian objective was to be an airfield at Baledogle, the eventual objective was Belet Huen. The Canadians were assigned to take possession of Belet Huen, pacify it by running out the local warlord's militia, then restore civil order and authority there, and patrol and police a designated HRS surrounding it.

In a Chapter VII operation, troops are authorized to use deadly force in a much wider range of circumstances than in a Chapter VI mission. That is appropriate since peace enforcement invariably means armed conflict against the forces whose interests are being threatened. In both Chapter VI and Chapter VII operations, soldiers have a fundamental right to defend themselves, but in the latter type of mission, they get the benefit of the doubt in a potentially hostile situation. For Operation Deliverance, for example, UNITAF soldiers who spotted a "technical" and harboured a reasonable belief that it threatened them, or their mission, could open fire on it; on Cyprus, even in Bosnia, that was not allowed – soldiers could only fire back when actually fired upon.

The new version of the Canadian ROEs was drafted in accordance with overall guidelines laid down by the force commander, U.S. Marine Corps Lt.-Gen. R. B. Johnston. Such coordination between the militaries of participating countries is imperative in a Chapter VII mission. Without it, the Italians, for example, might open fire under an entirely different set of circumstances than the Canadians, which introduces an arbitrary and chaotic element into the overall chain of command. Each participating country, however, almost always adapts the ROEs to its own particular circumstances and military culture. The interpretation of the ROEs is left in the hands of the force commander (in the Canadian case, Labbé, who handed the job over to Mathieu), who then puts his own twist on them, though he is not allowed to alter them in substance. ROEs are invariably long and sometimes complex: they must be boiled down to their essence for the line soldiers who will actually enforce them. The standard practice is to distribute to the line soldiers small plasticized cards on which the reduced version of the ROEs have been printed. The soldiers are required to learn them by rote.

Mathieu was eventually brought to court martial twice for allegedly altering the Canadian ROEs in such a way as to authorize the use of deadly force in a much greater number of circumstances than was intended by NDHQ. He was acquitted both times. In fact, the courts martial seem to have been a bald attempt to pin the blame on him for the general confusion that prevailed in NDHQ with respect to the Operation Deliverance ROEs.

Labbé arrived in Somalia on December 14. The first of the Canadian troops began to arrive the day after. Back in Canada, a photograph of Captain Rainville with two large knives strapped to his body appeared in the *Journal de Montréal* at about the same time. Beno was outraged. He dashed off a message to Mathieu asking him to confirm whether Rainville had "been sporting knives strapped to his body" and whether Rainville had been "bragging to the media and embellishing his personal image and that of his soldiers." Above all, Beno wanted Mathieu to "ensure that your soldiers do not believe or advertise that, they are trained or mandated to execute assassinations, kidnappings and counter-terrorist operations." He concluded, "Neither you nor I want one 'RAMBO' to destroy your operational capability and/or the reputation of the Canadian Airborne Regiment. I have grave doubts about this particular officer . . . I ask that you either remove my doubts or rectify the situation."[14]

Beno's job was to generate a force for Operation Cordon and then for Operation Deliverance. It was not his choice to send or not send troops to Somalia. He might have recommended against sending the Airborne at the start of November, or when Operation Cordon became Operation Deliverance, but he believed Mathieu had got things under control.[15] In any case, such a recommendation was not his alone to make. He, too, had superiors who were aware of the state of the Airborne, or who ought to have been. The only conclusion that can be drawn is that neither he, nor those superiors, judged that the Airborne's problems were systemic. Within the constraints imposed by his assigned task, however, Beno seems to have done as much as he could do to ensure that the soldiers who went to Somalia were prepared to act as a professional force.

UNITAF began descending on Somalia at the end of the year. When the first American troops went ashore, the news cameras were there to greet them. This was not exactly a reprise of the Marines coming ashore at bloody Tarawa in 1943. The Canadian force was spearheaded by No. 2 Commando, which was also tasked with providing security for the Canadian base at Belet Huen and patrolling the town. In the first days, the situation at Belet Huen was chaotic. The Canadian vehicles were late arriving, and the locals seemed about evenly divided between those who welcomed the Canadians and those who wanted to get rid of them quickly and violently. One of the early Canadian patrols was momentarily menaced by a technical, but it withdrew before it came under fire.

In the first days of the new year, the Canadian buildup continued. Mathieu went into Belet Huen to meet with local leaders and explain his mission. Airborne patrols began to seize weapons, both individual arms and entire caches, including a quad-mounted 14.5-mm anti-aircraft gun. The living conditions at the temporary base on the airstrip were terrible. There was bottled water for drinking, nothing for sanitation. The troops subsisted on MREs (meals ready to eat), American field rations first issued in the Gulf War to a mixed reception. It was very hot. The men ate, slept, and worked in the ever-present dust. Digging trenches and other defensive positions was almost impossible. The fine sand seeped back into the holes almost as fast as the men dug it out. There were flies everywhere. In town, the sweet stink of rotting garbage pervaded everything.

Despite the deplorable conditions, the battle group made steady progress in meeting its mission objectives. After the vehicles arrived, the Dragoons and 1er and No. 3 Commandos began their mounted patrols of the sector. In and around Belet Huen, the warlord militia quickly went to ground. The Canadians worked with the local leadership to re-establish a civil police, rebuild and restart the school, and repair damaged or destroyed bridges and other key structures. They provided free medical services. Law and order returned. The locals dubbed the Canadians the "clan who never sleep." After the vehicles and the rest of the battle group arrived, the American troops left and the Canadians abandoned the airstrip to set up a new and more permanent base on the other side of town astride the main road from Belet Huen to Mogadishu.

As early as the first week in January, there were disquieting signs that all was not well within the Airborne. On January 7, Major Seward authorized a No. 2 Commando patrol to enter a prohibited compound (prohibited because it contained unexploded mines and other ordnance) in direct defiance of Mathieu's orders. This was only one of several signs that Seward was not in total control. In the first twelve days of the operation, there were five incidents of accidental discharge of weapons in his commando. One was his own. In the same period, there was just one such incident in the rest of the battle group. The accidental discharge of a weapon is a sure sign of a lack of fire discipline in a unit and is an obvious danger to others. Though a summary offence, it is usually cause for strong disciplinary measures. Mathieu also worried that Seward's men were being overly aggressive in dealing with the locals, even though the danger of an armed clash had virtually disappeared within days of the initial airlanding. In fact, of the thirty-one charges for summary offences laid by regimental police against members of the whole battle group between the start of Operation Deliverance and the end of March 1993, nine were laid against members of No. 2 Commando.

One of the biggest problems Mathieu and his men faced was that individual or small groups of Somalis repeatedly penetrated and looted the Canadian base. This was a major concern of other UNITAF contingents as well. The infiltrators not only stole important and necessary equipment but they were a potential security hazard. It was impossible to tell which Somali infiltrators wanted to steal water cans and which aimed to blow up a generator or kill UNITAF soldiers. By the end of January, the infiltration had become endemic; looters took food, water, personal articles, weapons, ammunition, web gear, jump smocks, parachutes, and radio antennas. To make matters worse, Somalis armed with knives or small arms began setting up roadblocks near Belet Huen after dark, robbing people and challenging the authority of the Canadian contingent. Some of the weapons they carried had previously been seized by the Canadians, then released when their owners claimed they needed them for protection.

At first the Somalis who were captured while infiltrating the compound were simply bound, kept overnight at the base, then released to their clans or, when a local police force was eventually re-established, brought into town. This seemed to provide no deterrent, and some of the

Canadian soldiers soon started to abuse some of the prisoners. Prisoners were blindfolded or gagged. Cloths or handkerchiefs were bound over their heads and doused with water. When the water dried, the cloth shrank, causing much pain. Trophy photographs were taken in which Canadian soldiers posed with their captives. In the words of one officer, "The prisoners were increasingly treated as prisoners of war might have been in a brutal campaign."[16]

Mathieu decided to tighten perimeter security. On January 28, he met with his officers and announced that the ROEs would henceforth be strictly enforced. The following day a patrol of No. 3 Commando came across what appeared to be a roadblock set up by bandits. They dismounted, began to sweep the area, and came across a man armed with an AK-47 assault rifle. The Canadians stopped, moved into a skirmish line, and ordered the man to halt. He turned, fired a burst, and began to run. The soldiers returned fire. They hit the gunman and began to trail him, but a sudden cloudburst obliterated all trace of him. He turned up wounded in an Italian field hospital several days later.

Mathieu informed local leaders of his decision to tighten up the application of the ROEs on January 30, but the number of serious incidents began to mount. On February 8, a small Canadian foot patrol operating about fifteen kilometres north of the main base was fired upon from a wooded area. The patrol was extricated by a mounted patrol. Nine days later, a riot broke out in Belet Huen that was directed at the humanitarian relief workers. Canadian soldiers fired shotguns over the heads of the crowd, but to no apparent effect. Then they fired into the crowd, killing one man and wounding several others. Tempers were now rising on both sides. Day after day, the Canadians patrolling Belet Huen spotted sacks of food distributed by the relief agencies being sold on the black market. Some of the soldiers wondered exactly what they were supposed to accomplish, and why they were in Somalia when the Somalis seemed to abuse the relief they were given and loot the Canadian camp in return. Beno noticed the growing frustration of the Canadian troops when he visited Belet Huen towards the month's end. He found the situation tense and the men increasingly "cynical about Somalia" and told Mathieu to try to lighten things up.[17]

The boredom, the cynicism, and the lack of anything to do off duty led some of the men to excessive drinking. The Airborne had long been noted for its high incidence of alcoholism, excessive drinking, and alcohol-related crimes. Some of the troopers seemed determined to live up to that reputation at Belet Huen. The official beer ration was two cans per day per man, but no thirsty soldier has ever been deterred by such limits. Beer was easily traded for, stolen, or hoarded. Drunkenness grew more common as the weeks stretched by and the mission, the country-side, the people, grew more unbearable. If Mathieu was overly concerned about the increasing disciplinary problems at Belet Huen that were quite evident by the end of February, particularly in No. 2 Commando, his actions (as opposed to his words) did not show it. From the start of the mission at the end of December until the first day of March, only eleven members of the battle group were sent back to Canada: two for medical reasons, five on compassionate leave. Of the four soldiers sent back for disciplinary problems, only one was from No. 2 Commando.

This mood formed the backdrop for a completely unauthorized operation to ambush Somalis mounted by Capt. Michael Sox and some men of his platoon one evening in late February. In preparation for the night's adventures, Sox applied black camouflage make-up to his face, donned a Somali robe and headgear, and drove out to the ambush site in a civilian vehicle. His heavily armed men hid in the back. The plan was for the troopers to jump out of the back in the event that anyone tried to stop the vehicle. Sgt. Mark Boland was one of the men in the back seat when the vehicle came up to a small group of locals. "I was sitting in the back thinking, 'I can't believe this is going to work,'" he later told the press. "I remember coming round the back of the vehicle and [Sox] was standing there straight upright with his gun pointed right at this guy's head. For some reason I thought he was going to pull the trigger, so I turned my head . . . and I thought I was either going to get hit by a bullet or a piece of the guy's head." The two men stared each other down, however, before the Somali broke and ran into the darkness. The paratroopers then began to blast away with auto-matic weapons fire, discharging between fifty and seventy-five rounds. This was less than one hundred metres from a Somali town. When the paratroopers returned to base, Sox ordered Boland to record that only three shots had been fired.[18]

By the beginning of March, shooting incidents involving UNITAF soldiers had become increasingly common. There were more than fifty such incidents involving American, Belgian, Australian, Italian, French, Pakistani, Botswani, Nigerian, Tunisian, and Canadian soldiers. Somalis were shot running roadblocks, trying to enter UNITAF compounds, mounting ambushes of, or pointing weapons at, UNITAF troops. The majority of the shootings were carried out by American troops, which was natural since they were more numerous than any other UNITAF contingent and tended to be situated in the most dangerous areas. Only three reported incidents (apparently Sox's ambush was not reported) involved Canadians. In part, the shootings reflected the growing propensity of young Somali males to challenge the authority of the UNITAF troops and "test" their willingness to open fire. One expert on Somali culture told the Somalia Inquiry in October 1995, "Even when the rules of engagement were disseminated properly and Somalis had a pretty good sense of what troops would or wouldn't fire, for instance, the Somali youth in particular were quite good at testing those rules of engagement. . . . There was this constant pressure on the forces . . . [which] put the troops in situations they didn't like, and . . . resulted in a number of instances in improper reactions."[19]

Towards the evening of March 4, Capt. Michel Rainville, acting on orders issued by Mathieu, took a small patrol of seven men to a position outside the Canadian wire. He told his men they were there to apprehend looters and were authorized to use all necessary force, including deadly force, to affect capture whether or not the Somalis had actually taken anything. The day before, an important helicopter refuelling pump had been stolen from the compound. There was another fuel pump in the helicopter compound, but if it too disappeared, the battle group's helicopter capability would have been drastically impaired until a new pump arrived. A more serious incident had occurred the same day when a joint

Canadian–American mounted patrol had run into mines in the Canadian HRS; an American vehicle had blown up, killing one soldier and wounding two others.

According to one press report, Rainville deliberately set out bait of rations and water near one of the helicopters. Then he split his small force into two groups; the men waited in the shadows as the night deepened around them, the sounds of the camp drifting through the dark behind them. For an hour or two, nothing happened. Then the paratroopers noticed two Somali males approaching the compound. One of the men crouched low and began to slither under the wire; the other watched. Rainville sprang forward and shouted, "Get them." The two Somalis turned to run. One of them, Abdi Hundebei Sabrie, was caught in the rear by a blast from a twelve-gauge shotgun and severely wounded in several places. He survived. The other, Ahmed Afraraho Aruush, was cut down by automatic rifle fire and died instantly. Rainville reported the shootings as soon as his patrol returned to HQ.

To this day, controversy surrounds those shootings. Army doctor Maj. Barry Armstrong, who performed an autopsy on Aruush, told Mathieu that he believed the Somali had been "killed by a close range, execution-style shot after being wounded," an allegation Mathieu dismissed.[20] There is no doubt the two men were shot in the back running away, that they had not actually stolen anything, and that they were unarmed. There is some doubt as to whether warning shots were fired, as they ought to have been. Both Rainville and Mathieu were court-martialled for the incident: Mathieu for changing the ROEs to permit such an encounter; and Rainville for "unlawfully causing bodily harm, assault, negligent performance of duty, possession of a prohibited weapon, and breach of disciplinary rules."[21] Both men were acquitted.

Were the shootings carried out in accordance with the mission ROEs? That can only be a matter of opinion. Like all such general guidelines, the ROEs contained no specific instructions as to how to deal with unauthorized persons trying to break into a guarded compound after dark in a potentially hostile situation. Background information is important and relevant: an American soldier had been killed in the Canadian sector the day before; six Canadian vehicles had been blown up by mines since the start of the mission; some young Somalis were becoming ever bolder in challenging the UNITAF forces in Belet Huen and elsewhere; shooting incidents involving, or directed at, UNITAF soldiers were occurring daily in the country; it had become clearer than ever that some of the warlords had no intention whatever of knuckling under to UNITAF. At the same time, Rainville had set and baited a trap, and two unarmed men had been gunned down. Had the Somali mission been a "blue beret," Chapter VI mission, Rainville and Mathieu would have far exceeded their authority, but it was not. All that can be said on the basis of available evidence is that Rainville acted within his authority. Whether he acted wisely or humanely is another question.

The Canadian compound outside Belet Huen had been on a state of high alert from the first days of the mission. Most of the Somalis seemed friendly, some were even grateful for the restoration of civil order and the resumption of normal life. Most of the locals probably stayed that way. But there had been shootings, the local warlord was down but not out, and infiltration into the compound had taken on epidemic proportions. Prisoners were being taken every night. Elsewhere in Somalia, there had been twenty-two shooting incidents involving UNITAF forces in the first two weeks of March, six when Somalis attempted to force entry into UNITAF compounds. On March 10, for example, U.S. Marines killed a Somali youth trying to enter their compound in Mogadishu when he refused to stop after warning shots were fired.

On the morning of March 16, 1993, Maj. Anthony Seward gathered his platoon leaders around him for the daily O group. Seward ordered Sox to take his platoon and set up a snatch patrol that night to catch a prisoner and then to make an example of him. After his earlier failed effort to play Hollywood commando, Sox was more than ready for the mission. It was later that night that Shidane Abukar Arone was beaten and kicked to death by Master Cpl. Clayton Matchee. He did it with the active help of Cpl. Kyle Brown.

But ultimately, Matchee and Brown killed Arone because Canada's people, government, military, and specifically its army have failed to keep real soldiers, combat effectiveness, and traditional military leadership at the centre of the Canadian army. That failure was caused by the remarkable apathy Canadians have towards their military and their failure to understand that nations that aspire to keep their independence and preserve their way of life must have armies that are prepared to fight wars.

AFTERWORD

The Canadian Airborne Regiment is gone. On January 23, 1995, Minister of National Defence David Collenette ordered it disbanded. Some seven weeks later, on March 5, the Airborne's colours were laid up and this once-proud regiment passed into history. The disbandment followed a chain of events set in motion by the revelation of Shidane Abukar Arone's murder. Although that death was reported to NDHQ almost immediately, the report contained only sparse and confusing details about how he had died. A press release was given to the media at Mogadishu on March 18, but there were no Canadian reporters around and the international media were too busy chasing down other stories. The first widely circulated public announcement about Arone's death did not come until March 31.

From the moment the news of Arone's death broke, politicians, bureaucrats, and senior officers have scurried to find the culprits, any culprits but themselves. There have been seven courts martial: Kyle Brown was convicted of manslaughter and torture and received a five-year prison sentence. Anthony Seward was convicted of negligent performance of duty but acquitted of unlawfully causing bodily harm; he received a reprimand, was demoted, and subsequently sentenced to three months' imprisonment. Mark Boland pleaded guilty to negligent performance of his duties and was dismissed from the Forces. All the rest were exonerated. Clayton Matchee attempted suicide when arrested for Arone's murder, but succeeded only in inflicting incurable brain damage on himself. Charges against him are still pending, but he will never be brought to trial.

From the spring of 1993, the Canadian press and public have been treated to the unfolding drama of the "Somalia affair." First, there was the story of the now infamous videotapes that led directly to the disband-ment of the Airborne. There were three of these tapes, two of which were played on national television. The first tape, aired in early 1994, showed No. 2 Commando troopers in Somalia drinking beer and making racist comments about Somalis. The second, aired in early 1995, depicted disgusting hazing rituals carried out by members of 1er Commando in 1992. When the existence of a third tape was revealed depicting a some-what milder form of hazing ritual conducted at Petawawa in the summer of 1994, the fate of the Airborne was sealed. There had been too many embarrassments caused by the members of this regiment, in the view of David Collenette, and the regiment had to go.

The second, and more central, Somalia story is that of the alleged cover-up of the affair mounted by the high command, the bureaucracy, and the Campbell government, which was in power at the time. Although the facts of the murder of March 16 are well known, and most of the rest of the Airborne's mission in Somalia has been gone over with a fine-tooth comb, other parts of the story are still missing. Were other prisoners mistreated? Was the Somali killed on March 4 actually executed, as army doctor Barry Anderson alleged? Did members of the high command and others systematically try to block the military police investigation of the murder, or destroy evidence?

But the most important story of the Somalia affair has been the one most ignored: How and why did the Airborne get "totally out of control"[1] in the words of Col. Peter Kenward, the regiment's last commander? Kenward was appointed after Mathieu with a specific mandate to clean things up. He did a good job in short order, and the regiment was ready to undertake a peacekeeping mission to Croatia when it was disbanded. But he is the first to admit that something had gone horribly wrong before and during Somalia.

That story is ignored because it is rooted in the larger story of the crisis that has been developing in the Canadian army for at least a decade, and nobody in the press seems to care much about that. That crisis was caused initially by the deliberate bleeding of the defence estab-lishment to near death by successive, mostly Liberal, governments. It was made a great deal worse by unification and the imposition on the

Canadian Forces of a structure designed to ease political and bureau-cratic burdens rather than promote military effectiveness. The sins of unification were compounded by the creation of National Defence Headquarters, designed to murder military initiative. With NDHQ safely ensconced at the top of the defence structure, it was not long before soldier-managers took control of the army and soldier-warriors were shunted aside. We now have an army in which war fighting is of secondary or even tertiary importance. Which is absurd.

All these processes took place against a backdrop of change. Canadian society changed. The Cold War ended. The army was downsized and its missions redefined. Prolonged peace is always a time of trial for any mili-tary, but in this country, where the Armed Forces are not held to play an important role in asserting national interests, it is particularly testing. It is difficult for Canadians to face the bare fact that an independent nation must have a well-run, effective, and efficient military capable of doing what military forces exist for – to fight wars. To do so, after all, would cost money that is apparently better spent on endless cycles of welfare. But unless Canadians begin to face this fact, they had better get used to the sort of thing they have been seeing from the military since the news of the Somalia murder first broke.

Armies can and must reflect the changes that take place in the larger society around them. At the same time, armies are for war, and the nature of war hasn't changed much since the first dawn. The requirements of good soldiering and good military leadership haven't changed much either. The solution to the crisis in the Canadian army is simple to prescribe but hard to put into effect. It entails the restoration of prepa-ration for war fighting and combat at the centre of the army's existence. Any other mission is peripheral. If that is done, the warriors – the real professional soldiers – will regain control. When that happens, the old-fashioned, but necessary, virtues of honour, integrity, professionalism, dedication to the military as a vocation, and acceptance of the unlimited liability of soldiers will once again form the core values of the Canadian army. Only then will the army of Vimy Ridge, the Scheldt Estuary, and Kap'yong be redeemed.

ACKNOWLEDGEMENTS

A great many people helped me write this book. The original idea belonged to Jonathan Webb, senior editor at McClelland & Stewart, who approached me in the late winter of 1995 to see if I was interested. My agent, friend, and sometime surrogate mother, Linda McKnight, helped me shape the idea and gave me the encouragement I needed to get through a lot of work in too little time.

My faithful and dedicated research assistants, Bruce McIntyre and Bert Reed, did more than I can possibly mention in helping dig out material and arrange and conduct interviews. Most of the time they managed to put up with my rare bouts of crankiness with good humour! Without their help, this book would have taken at least a year longer to complete than it did. I am very grateful to them.

A large number of serving and former soldiers gave generously of their time to help me make connections, obtain material, sit for interviews, and generally bring me up-to-date on developments in the modern Canadian army. My thanks to Bob Lockhart, Ian Fraser, Ike Kennedy, Don Reekie, Herb Pitts, Jim Cox, Ray Wlasichuk, Andy Christie, Doug Bland, Jack English, Dan Loomis, Ian Gray, Don Rochester, R. A. E. Williams, and Richard Gimblett.

I am grateful to Stan Cohen and the staff of the Somalia Inquiry for allowing me access to transcripts and other public documents held by them. Dr. Harriet Critchley gave me good pointers and shared valuable insights gained from her experience on the original Somalia Inquiry, headed by Maj.-Gen. Thomas de Faye. So, too, did General de Faye. I am also grateful to the Canadian Forces Personnel Applied Research Unit in

Toronto for supplying me with so many of the studies carried out by their staff over the last decade or so.

Peter G. Kenward, Jack Granatstein, Ross Wickware, Ken Nette, and several officers and NCOs of the Canadian Airborne Centre read the manuscript. Everyone who sat to be interviewed was more than generous with their time, and all the interviews helped me form a picture of the army today.

My wife and family endured weeks without my physical presence and many months of my living mentally with the Canadian army and the Airborne Regiment while the book was being written. They were, as usual, both understanding and encouraging.

My mistakes, as always, are on my head alone.

FOOTNOTES

Chapter 1

1. This quote and others comes from Carl von Clausewitz, *On War*, eds. and trans. Michael Howard and Peter Paret (Princeton: Princeton University Press, 1984).
2. Martin van Creveld, *The Transformation of War* (New York: The Free Press, 1991), p. 48.
3. J. Glenn Gray, *The Warriors* (New York: Harper and Row, 1967), p. 127.
4. Elmer Bendiner, *The Fall of Fortresses* (New York: Putnam, 1980), p. 116.
5. Gray, p. 28.
6. William Broyles, Jr., "Why Men Love War," *Esquire* (November 1984).
7. Ibid.
8. Harold G. Moore and Joseph L. Galloway, *We Were Soldiers Once . . . and Young* (New York: HarperPerennial, 1993), p. 99.
9. John Ellis, *The Sharp End* (New York: Charles Scribners, 1980), pp. 102, 104.
10. David Bercuson, *Battalion of Heroes* (Calgary: The Calgary Highlanders Regimental Funds Foundation, 1994), p. 60.
11. The term "non-commissioned officer" and its acronym, NCO, are used in virtually all military organizations the world over to distinguish a third level of responsibility between commissioned officers and "soldiers" or "other ranks." I have reverted to this usage more often than not in the following pages.
12. John English, *On Infantry* (New York: Praeger, 1984), p. 221.

Chapter 2

1. John Gardam, ed., *Korea Volunteer: An Oral History From Those Who Were There* (Burnstown, Ontario: General Store Publishing, 1994), pp. 47-48.
2. David Bercuson, *True Patriot: The Life of Brooke Claxton, 1898-1960* (Toronto: University of Toronto Press, 1993), p. 222.
3. Roy Rempel, "The Canadian Army and the Commitment-Credibility Gap: Central Europe, 1956-1961," *Canadian Defence Quarterly* (September 1995), p. 25.

4. Sean M. Maloney, "The Canadian Army and Tactical Nuclear Warfare Doctrine," *Canadian Defence Quarterly* (December 1993), p. 24.

5. Col. Ian Fraser (ret'd), "The Infantry Battalion" (unpublished paper given to the author by Fraser).

6. Ibid.

7. Pierre Coulombe, "Social and Cultural Composition of the Canadian Armed Forces" in *The Canadian Military: A Profile*, ed. H. J. Massey (Toronto: Copp Clark, 1972), pp. 138-168.

8. Ibid., p. 157.

Chapter 3

1. Douglas L. Bland, *Chiefs of Defence* (Toronto: Canadian Institute of Strategic Studies, 1995), p. 93.

2. Ibid., p. 108.

3. C. A. Cotton, "The Cultural Consequences of Defence Unification in Canada's Military" (Unpublished paper presented to the Inter-University Seminar on Armed Forces and Society Conference, Chicago, 1983). The paper summarized the original study conducted under the auspices of the Canadian Forces Personnel Applied Research Unit.

4. Ibid.

5. Bland, p. 124

6. Anthony Beevor, *Inside the British Army* (London: Corgi Books, 1993), p. 196.

7. C. A. Cotton, R. K. Crook, F. C. Pinch, "Canada's Professional Military: The Limits of Organization," *Armed Forces and Society* (May 1978) p. 371.

8. Confidential memo supplied to the author. Emphasis is in the original.

9. Gerald Porter, *In Retreat* (Ottawa: Deneau & Greenberg, 1978), p. 13.

10. D. C. Loomis & D. T. Lightburn, "Taking Into Account the Distinctiveness of the Military from the Mainstream of Society," *Canadian Defence Quarterly* (Autumn 1980) p. 20.

11. Bercuson interview with Maj. Anthony Thomas.

12. Bercuson interview with Lt.-Gen. Kent Foster (ret'd).

13. Beevor, p. 25.

14. Hugh Smith, "The Dynamics of Social Change and the Australian Defence Force," *Armed Forces and Society* (Summer 1995) p. 546.

15. Stuart A. Cohen, "The IDF: From a 'People's Army' to a 'Professional Military' – Causes and Implications," *Armed Forces and Society* (Winter 1995) p. 250.

16. Maj. Arthur E. Gans, "Vocation or Job: A Warrior's Place in a Rights-Driven Society," *Canadian Defence Quarterly* (December 1994) p. 13.

17. Nick Stethem, "No Battlefield Can Be 'Politically Correct,'" *Vanguard* (Summer 1995) p. 25.

18. Bercuson interview with Maj.-Gen. Thomas de Faye.
19. Ibid.

Chapter 4

1. Confidential memo acquired by the author.
2. Sean M. Maloney, "Missed Opportunity: Operation BROADSWORD, 4 Brigade and the Gulf War, 1990-1991," *Canadian Military History* (Spring 1995) pp. 37-46.
3. NDHQ, "The Future Land Force: Canada's Army into the 21st Century" (nd).
4. Bert Reed interview with Cpl. Tracy Meisner Coulter.
5. Bercuson interview with Lt.-Col. Jacques Painchaud (ret'd).
6. Bercuson interview with Brig.-Gen. Jim Cox.
7. Bercuson interview with Master Warrant Officer Don Thomas.
8. D. T. Reeves, "Ethnic Participation in the Canadian Forces: Demographic Trends," CFPARU, 1990.
9. Capt. R. O. Parker, "Canadian Forces Applicant Profile Project: Summary and Potential," CFPARU, 1992.
10. NDHQ, Directorate of Health Protection and Promotion, "1994 CF Health and Lifestyle Information System Survey."
11. The two studies were both done by Capt. R. O. Parker, "Age Differences in Voluntary Turnover Behaviour from the Canadian Forces," CFPARU, 1991; and "Canadian Forces Attrition Monitoring System: Implementation and Potential," CFPARU, 1992.
12. Confidential report in the possession of the author.
13. NDHQ, "Military and Civilian Employee Feedback Survey," June 1995.
14. Bercuson interview with Brig.-Gen. Roger Bazin (ret'd).
15. Chaplain Report, CFB Petawawa, April 30, 1995.
16. Chaplain Report, Land Force Command, February 14, 1995.
17. Chaplain Report, Roman Catholic Chaplain General, March 31, 1995.
18. Confidential report in the possession of the author.
19. de Faye interview.
20. Matthew Ridgeway, *The War in Korea* (London: The Cresset Press, 1967), p. 97.
21. Robert Woodward, *The Commanders* (New York: Simon & Schuster, 1991), p. 155.
22. Speech by Col. Ian Fraser (ret'd) to the Royal United Services Institute in Halifax, January 1994.
23. Bercuson interview with Maj. R. Blekaitis.
24. Maj. J. W. Gaudet, "Socialization of the Military Professional," CFPARU, 1983.
25. The Combat Arms School, Combat Training Centre, CFB Gagetown, "Fundamental Officer Training" p. 1.
26. Jacques Dextraze, "The Art of Leadership," *The Officer: A Manual of Leadership for Officers in the Canadian Forces* (Ottawa: DND, 1978), pp. 33ff.

27. He is often misquoted as having said "get there fustest with the mostest."

28. *The Officer: A Manual of Leadership for Officers in the Canadian Forces*, p. 27.

29. Bercuson interview with Warrant Officer Plantz et al., CFB Gagetown, July 6, 1995.

30. Williamson Murray, *German Military Effectiveness* (Baltimore: Nautical and Aviation Publishing, 1992), p. 30.

31. Capt. Eric T. Reynolds, "Ethical Competence and the Profession of Arms: A Contemporary Challenge to Military Institutions," *Canadian Defence Quarterly* (December 1993) p. 33.

32. Ibid., p. 35.

Chapter 5

1. James Kittfield, *Prodigal Soldiers* (New York: Simon & Schuster, 1995) pp. 39-40.

2. C. A. Cotton, "The Divided Army: Role Orientations among Canada's Peacetime Soldiers" (PhD thesis, Carleton University, 1980), p. 382.

3. These themes are explored in Anthony Kellett, *Combat Motivation: The Behaviour of Soldiers in Battle* (Boston: Kluwer-Nijhoff, 1982), pp. 98-101.

4. Beevor, p. 299.

5. Richard Holmes, *Acts of War: The Behavior of Men in Battle* (New York: The Free Press, 1985), p. 311.

6. Confidential interview.

7. Beevor, p. 309.

8. Quoted in Gerald Porter, *In Retreat* (Ottawa: Deneau & Greenberg, 1978), p. 113.

9. Confidential interview.

10. Bercuson interview of Lt.-Col. R. A. E. Williams.

11. Confidential interview.

12. Bert Reed interview of Master Cpl. Brian Roach.

13. Confidential interview.

14. See NDHQ, Directorate of Personnel, *Canadian Forces Personnel Newsletter*, Issue 12/94, pp. 1-2.

15. Bert Reed interview with Sgt. Bob Harkies.

16. Confidential interview.

17. Harkies interview.

18. Quoted in D. Harrison and L. Laliberté, *No Life Like It: Military Wives in Canada* (Toronto: Lorimer, 1994), p. 51.

19. Confidential interview.

20. Quoted in D. Collier, *Hurry Up and Wait: An Inside Look at Life as a Military Wife in Canada* (Carp, Ontario: Creative Bound, 1994), p. 135.

21. Harrison and Laliberté, p. 64.

22. Confidential interview.

23. Quoted in Harrison and Laliberté, p. 44.

Chapter 6

1. Bert Reed interview with Master Cpl. Phil Friday.
2. Confidential document.
3. Bert Reed interview with Master Cpl. Phil Ward.
4. Bert Reed interview with Cpl. James Strayer.
5. Bert Reed interview with Sgt. Bob Harkies.
6. Friday interview.
7. Bert Reed interview with Cpl. Tracy Meisner Coulter.
8. Strayer interview.
9. Ibid.
10. Ibid. The events of the night of July 3 were pieced together from interviews with Strayer and Meisner Coulter and from Scott Taylor, "Canucks hold their ground: take a casualty under heavy fire," *Esprit de Corps*, Vol. 4, No. 3, pp. 4-5. In the *Esprit de Corps* article, the position is mistakenly identified as Romeo One.
11. Meisner Coulter interview.
12. Strayer interview.
13. Lord Strathcona's Horse (Royal Canadians) Battle Group, "Post Operations Report, Phases 4 and 5, Op Cavalier 3."
14. Bert Reed interview with Cpl. Darren Magas.
15. Lord Strathcona's Horse (Royal Canadians), *War Diary*, August 1 to 5, 1994.
16. See *Maclean's* magazine, December 18, 1995.
17. Friday interview.
18. Bercuson interview with Sgt. R. D. Mackwood.
19. Bercuson interview with Master Cpl. Roger Laverdure.
20. Harkies interview.
21. Isfeld's story, "The Price of Duty," is told in a film produced by the National Film Board of Canada as part of its series "Protection Force," produced by Garth Pritchard and written and narrated by Gwynne Dyer. The Department of National Defence says that ten soldiers were killed in the former Yugoslavia. Other sources put the count at eleven.
22. CBC "Prime Time News," August 29, 1995.
23. Report of Lt.-Col. Murray Farwell, February 14, 1995, in the possession of the author.

Chapter 7

1. Floyd Low, "Canadian Airborne Forces, 1942-1978" (BA Honours Essay, University of Victoria, 1978).
2. Bercuson interview with Dan Hartigan and George Robertson.
3. Jean V. Allard (with Serge Bernier), *The Memoirs of General Jean V. Allard* (Vancouver: University of British Columbia Press, 1988), p. 237.

4. Ibid., p. 238.

5. The Special Air Service is Britain's elite commando and anti-terrorist unit. It was established as a long-range striking force in the North African Desert in the Second World War.

6. Lt.-Gen. W. A. B. Anderson memorandum, "Formation of the Canadian Airborne Regiment – Activation and Terms of Reference," May 15, 1967.

7. Ibid.

8. Dan G. Loomis, *Not Much Glory: Quelling the FLQ* (Toronto: Deneau, 1982), pp. 110ff.

9. Bercuson interview with Col. Don Rochester (ret'd).

10. "Memorandum to Commander Mobile Command for consideration at Command Council," September 13, 1967.

11. William C. Cockerham, "Attitude Toward Combat Among U.S. Army Paratroopers," *Journal of Political and Military Sociology* (Spring 1978) p. 4.

12. Beevor, pp. 343-344.

13. William C. Cockerham, "Selective Socialization: Airborne Training as Status Passage," *Journal of Political and Military Sociology* (Fall 1973) pp. 215ff.

14. Bercuson interview with Don B. Reekie.

15. Col. Don Rochester (ret'd), "Birth of a Regiment."

16. Bercuson interview with Ron Irwin.

17. Bercuson interview with Bob Burchell.

18. Bercuson interview with Dollard Rousseau.

19. This description was provided by Lt.-Col. K. A. Nette, commander, Canadian Airborne Centre, Edmonton.

20. Bercuson interview with John McNeil.

21. Ibid.

Chapter 8

1. Quoted in Fred Gaffen, *In the Eye of the Storm* (Toronto: Deneau & Wayne, 1987), p. 98.

2. Bercuson interview with Ron Irwin.

3. Bercuson interview with Ralph Goebel.

4. Ibid.

5. Irwin interview.

6. Ibid.

7. Bercuson interview with Master Warrant Officer Don Thomas.

8. Bercuson interview with Col. Ian Fraser (ret'd).

9. Bercuson interview with Brig.-Gen. Jim Cox.

10. I am grateful to Col. Ian Fraser (ret'd) for the chance to examine his diaries for

this period. They are invaluable for a grasp of the confusion that reigned in army circles over the future of the Airborne.

11. This point was made in a speech by Colonel Fraser (ret'd) to the Royal United Services Institute in Halifax in January 1994. It is undoubtedly correct.

12. Confidential interview.

13. Bercuson interview with Marty Clavette.

14. Col. Ian Fraser, "Airborne handover notes, Fraser/Painchaud," July 1977.

15. Bercuson interview with Maj.-Gen. Herb Pitts (ret'd).

16. Cox interview.

17. Bercuson interview with Admiral R. H. Falls (ret'd).

18. Bercuson interview with Lt.-Gen. Kent Foster (ret'd).

19. *Ex Coelis*, Canadian Airborne Regiment, Cyprus edition.

20. *Calgary Sun*, October 15, 1995. Pelletier was later forced out of the military for being gay.

21. Brig.-Gen. R. I. Stewart memo of May 7, 1984.

22. Ibid.

23. Summary of the Hewson Report is taken from the testimony of Maj.-Gen. Conrad Hewson (ret'd) to the second Somalia Inquiry (henceforth referred to as Somalia Inquiry #2), October 3, 1995.

24. Bercuson telephone interview with Lt.-Gen. Charles Belzile (ret'd), June 3, 1996.

25. Testimony of Major-General Gaudreau (ret'd) to Somalia Inquiry #2, October 5, 1995.

26. Testimony of Lt.-Gen. Kent Foster (ret'd) to Somalia Inquiry #2, October 5, 1995.

27. Bercuson interview with Col. Peter G. Kenward.

28. Ibid.

29. Ibid.

30. Confidential interview.

31. Testimony of Col. W. M. Holmes to Somalia Inquiry #2, October 10, 1995.

32. Testimony of Cmdr. Paul Jenkins to Somalia Inquiry #2, October 12, 1995.

33. Confidential interview.

34. Pitts interview.

35. Holmes testimony.

36. See Vol. IX of the evidence gathered by the Board of Inquiry, Canadian Airborne Battle Group (henceforth referred to as Somalia Inquiry #1).

37. Somalia Inquiry #1 document, "Service Paper . . . The Way Ahead . . .", prepared by Brig.-Gen. E. B. Beno, May 4, 1993.

Chapter 9

1. Bercuson interview with Lt.-Col. Carol Mathieu (ret'd).
2. Testimony of Col. W. M. Holmes to Somalia Inquiry #2, October 10, 1995.
3. Somalia Inquiry #2. Maj.-Gen. Lewis MacKenzie (ret'd), "Request for standing . . .", received by the inquiry May 24, 1995. Gervais's reply is not on the record at the time of publication, but since matters proceeded, it is reasonable to assume that he directed Beno to carry on.
4. Ibid.
5. Ibid.
6. Documentation obtained from Somalia Inquiry #2, Beno directive to Morneault, September 22, 1995.
7. Somalia Inquiry #1, "Board of Inquiry Report," Phase I, Volume XI, pp. 3307-3308.
8. Somalia Inquiry #1, exhibit 93.
9. Ibid., Report, Vol. VII, p. 2411.
10. Ibid., exhibits 16-1, 16-3, and 92.
11. Somalia Inquiry #2. Maj.-Gen. Lewis MacKenzie (ret'd), "Request for standing . . .", received by the Inquiry May 24, 1995.
12. There is controversy as to exactly what Beno told Mathieu. Beno denies ever giving Mathieu a list of names of troublemakers. *Globe and Mail*, January 31, 1996.
13. Mathieu interview.
14. Somalia Inquiry #1, exhibit 94-5.
15. Bercuson interview with Maj.-Gen. Ernie Beno.
16. Confidential interview.
17. *Globe and Mail*, March 30, 1994.
18. *Ottawa Sun*, November 27, 1995; in a story published in the *Calgary Sun* (October 15, 1995) Matt McKay, who was another of the men, claimed that about one hundred rounds had been fired. A third participant, Cpl. Kalim Kafka, estimated that up to four hundred shots were fired.
19. Testimony of Dr. Menkhaus to Somalia Inquiry #2, October 23, 1995.
20. *Globe and Mail*, October 6, 1995.
21. Ibid., February 27, 1996.

Afterword

1. *Maclean's* magazine, February 6, 1995.

BIBLIOGRAPHY

Books and Periodicals

Allard, Jean V. (with Serge Bernier). *The Memoirs of General Jean V. Allard*. Vancouver: University of British Columbia Press, 1988.

Beevor, Anthony. *Inside the British Army*. London: Corgi Books, 1993.

Bendiner, Elmer. *The Fall of Fortresses*. New York: Putnam, 1980.

Bercuson, David. *True Patriot: The Life of Brooke Claxton, 1898-1960*. Toronto: University of Toronto Press, 1993.

———. *Battalion of Heroes: The Calgary Highlanders in World War II*. Calgary: The Calgary Highlanders Regimental Funds Foundation, 1994.

Bland, Douglas L. *Chiefs of Defence*. Toronto: Canadian Institute of Strategic Studies, 1995.

Broyles, William, Jr. "Why Men Love War." *Esquire* (November 1984).

Cockerham, William C. "Selective Socialization: Airborne Training as Status Passage." *Journal of Political and Military Sociology* (Fall 1973).

———. "Attitude Toward Combat Among U.S. Army Paratroopers." *Journal of Political and Military Sociology* (Spring 1978).

Cohen, Stuart A. "The IDF: From a 'People's Army' to a 'Professional Military' – Causes and Implications." *Armed Forces and Society* (Winter 1995).

Collier, D. *Hurry Up and Wait: An Inside Look at Life as a Military Wife in Canada*. Carp, Ontario: Creative Bound, 1994.

Cotton, C. A., "The Divided Army: Role Orientations among Canada's Peacetime Soldiers." Unpublished Ph.D. thesis, Carleton University, 1980.

———, Crook, R. K., and Pinch, F. C. "Canada's Professional Military: The Limits of Organization." *Armed Forces and Society* (May 1978).

———. "Institutional and Occupational Values in Canada's Army." *Armed Forces and Society* (Fall 1981).

———. "The Cultural Consequences of Defence Unification in Canada's Military." Unpublished paper presented to the Inter-University Seminar on Armed Forces and Society Conference, Chicago, 1983.

Coulombe, Pierre. "Social and Cultural Composition of the Canadian Armed Forces." In *The Canadian Military: A Profile*, edited by H. J. Massey. Toronto: Copp Clark, 1972.

Dextraze, Jacques. "The Art of Leadership." In *The Officer: A Manual of Leadership for Officers in the Canadian Forces*. Ottawa: DND, 1978.

Ellis, John. *The Sharp End*. New York: Charles Scribners, 1980.

English, John. *On Infantry*. New York: Praeger, 1984.

Gaffen, Fred. *In the Eye of the Storm*. Toronto: Deneau & Wayne, 1987.

Gans, Maj. Arthur E. "Vocation or Job: A Warrior's Place in a Rights-Driven Society." *Canadian Defence Quarterly* (December 1994).

Gardam, John, ed. *Korea Volunteer: An Oral History From Those Who Were There*. Burnstown, Ontario: General Store Publishing, 1994.

Gray, J. Glenn. *The Warriors*. New York: Harper and Row, 1967.

Harrison, D., and Laliberté, L. *No Life Like It: Military Wives in Canada*. Toronto: Lorimer, 1994.

Holmes, Richard. *Acts of War: The Behavior of Men in Battle*. New York: The Free Press, 1985.

Kasurak, Peter C. "Civilianization and the military ethos: civil-military relations in Canada." *Canadian Public Administration* (Spring 1982).

Kellett, Anthony. *Combat Motivation: The Behaviour of Soldiers in Battle*. Boston: Kluwer-Nijhoff, 1982.

Kittfield, James. *Prodigal Soldiers*. New York: Simon & Schuster, 1995.

Loomis, Dan G. *Not Much Glory: Quelling the FLQ*. Toronto: Deneau, 1982.

Loomis, D. C. , and Lightburn, D. T. "Taking Into Account the Distinctiveness of the Military from the Mainstream of Society." *Canadian Defence Quarterly* (Autumn 1980).

Low, Floyd. "Canadian Airborne Forces, 1942-1978." BA Honours Essay, University of Victoria, 1978.

Maloney, Sean M. "The Canadian Army and Tactical Nuclear Warfare Doctrine." *Canadian Defence Quarterly* (December 1993).

———. "Missed Opportunity: Operation BROADSWORD, 4 Brigade and the Gulf War, 1990-1991." *Canadian Military History* (Spring 1995).

Moore, Harold G., and Galloway, Joseph L. *We Were Soldiers Once . . . and Young*. New York: HarperPerennial, 1993.

Murray, Williamson. *German Military Effectiveness*. Baltimore: Nautical and Aviation Publishing, 1992.

Porter, Gerald. *In Retreat: The Canadian Forces in the Trudeau Years*. Ottawa: Deneau & Greenberg, 1978.

Rempel, Roy. "The Canadian Army and the Commitment-Credibility Gap: Central Europe, 1956-1961." *Canadian Defence Quarterly* (September 1995).

Reynolds, Capt. Eric T. "Ethical Competence and the Profession of Arms: A Contemporary Challenge to Military Institutions." *Canadian Defence Quarterly* (December 1993).

Ridgeway, Matthew. *The War in Korea*. London: The Cresset Press, 1967.

Smith, Hugh. "The Dynamics of Social Change and the Australian Defence Force." *Armed Forces and Society* (Summer 1995).

Stethem, Nick. "No Battlefield Can Be 'Politically Correct.'" *Vanguard* (Summer 1995).

Taylor, Scott. "Canucks hold their ground: take a casualty under heavy fire." *Espirit de Corps* Vol. 4, No. 3.

van Creveld, Martin. *The Transformation of War*. New York: The Free Press, 1991.

von Clausewitz, Carl. *On War*. Edited and translated by Michael Howard and Peter Paret. Princeton: Princeton University Press, 1984.

Woodward, Robert. *The Commanders*. New York: Simon & Schuster, 1991.

Official Publications, Studies, and Documents

Board of Inquiry, Canadian Airborne Battle Group (1993), Proceedings and Documents.

Canadian Airborne Regiment. *Ex Coelis*. Cyprus edition.

The Combat Arms School, Combat Training Centre, CFB Gagetown. "Fundamental Officer Training."

Gaudet, Maj. J. W. "Socialization of the Military Professional." Canadian Forces Personnel Applied Research Unit (CFPARU), 1983.

Lord Strathcona's Horse (Royal Canadians) Battle Group. "Post Operations Report, Phases 4 and 5, Op Cavalier 3."

Lord Strathcona's Horse (Royal Canadians). *War Diary*.

National Defence Headquarters (NDHQ). "The Future Land Force: Canada's Army into the 21st Century," Nd.

——. "Military and Civilian Employee Feedback Survey." (June 1995).

——, Directorate of Health Protection and Promotion. "1994 CF Health and Lifestyle Information System Survey."

——, Directorate of Personnel. *Canadian Forces Personnel Newsletter*.

Oakes, L. J. "Personnel Attitudes and Perceptions Toward Conditions of Service in the Canadian Forces 1993 Survey." CFPARU, 1994.

Parker, Capt. R. O. "Age Differences in Voluntary Turnover Behaviour from the Canadian Forces." CFPARU, 1991.

——. "Canadian Forces Applicant Profile Project: Summary and Potential." CFPARU, 1992.

——. "Canadian Forces Attrition Monitoring System: Implementation and Potential." CFPARU, 1992.

Reeves, D. T. "Ethnic Participation in the Canadian Forces: Demographic Trends."
    CFPARU, 1990.
Somalia Inquiry (1995 ->), Proceedings and Documents.

Materials Supplied by Col. Ian Fraser (ret'd)
Fraser, Col. Ian. "The Infantry Battalion." Unpublished paper.
———. Daily Diaries, 1975-1977.
———. "Airborne handover notes, Fraser/Painchaud." July 1977.
———. Speech to the Royal United Services Institute in Halifax, January 1994.

Broadcast Material
National Film Board of Canada. "Protection Force" (produced by Garth Pritchard
    and written and narrated by Gwynne Dyer). Part III, "The Price of Duty."
Canadian Broadcasting Corporation. "Prime Time News." August 29, 1995.

INDEX